Mathematics for Economists

An Introduction

Mathematics for Economists

An Introduction

MARTIN TIMBRELL

Basil Blackwell

First published 1985
Reprinted 1989
Basil Blackwell Ltd
108 Cowley Road, Oxford OX4 1JF, UK

Basil Blackwell Inc.
432 Park Avenue South, Suite 1505,
New York, NY 10016, USA

British Library Cataloguing in Publication Data

Timbrell, Martin
  Mathematics for economists: an introduction.
  1. Economics, Mathematical
  I. Title
510'.2433   HB135
ISBN 0-631-14086-7
ISBN 0-631-14087-5 Pbk

Library of Congress Cataloging in Publication Data

Timbrell, Martin.
  Mathematics for economists.
  Includes index.
  1. Economics, Mathematical. I. Title.
HB135.T558 1985   510'.2433   84-28414
ISBN 0-631-14086-7
ISBN 0-631-14087-5 (pbk.)

Typeset by KEYTEC, Bridport, Dorset
Printed in Great Britain by Page Bros, Norwich

Contents

Preface

This book is the result of more than ten years of teaching mathematics to students of economics and related disciplines, during which time countless students have contributed as much to my understanding as I have to theirs. It is they who have convinced me that, with a little help, anyone can become familiar with and competent at the mathematical techniques of their subject. It is they too who have persuaded me to add to the already considerable number of mathematics texts that are available. I hope that the result justifies their enthusiasm.

My thanks go also to all my colleagues at Exeter for their encouragement as well as for more practical help, but I would like to make particular mention of Professor John Black, Dr Keith Howe and Bernard Pearson who have put so much effort into reading and improving my earlier drafts. If there are any remaining inadequacies, they must be my own.

Martin Timbrell
University of Exeter

Introduction

The use of mathematics in economics is not new; it dates back to Cournot at the beginning of the nineteenth century. The controversy surrounding its use dates from just about the same time. Economics has changed much in the last 150 years, but the arguments over the place of mathematics in economics have changed very little. Controversy arises from two main sources. First, there are those with a philosophical objection to the use of mathematical analysis, traditionally the tool of science, in what they see as a non-quantifiable, imprecise subject. Second, there are those who simply find mathematics difficult and argue that it will never help them to understand, but will merely confuse. The latter objection was well dealt with by A.C. Pigou (1877–1959), when he said: 'Objections from people innocent of mathematics are like objections to Chinese literature by people who cannot read Chinese'.[1]

The truth is that there are many ways of analysing problems; and as the choice of tools of analysis must depend upon the specific problem under consideration, there is no reason why different approaches to the subject should not happily co-exist. Why, then, so much controversy? Perhaps it is because tools of analysis are not the neutral concepts one might imagine them to be but have, in some sense, a life and direction of their own.

The lack of a particular technique leaves some problems insoluble, while the presence of others leads to an awareness of problems hitherto unrecognized. The latter may or may not be important, but the direction taken by the subject tends to reflect the developments in available techniques, rather than the other way round. Certainly there is a danger of this happening, and critics do well to call attention to it. One might argue that mathematical economists have given undue attention to the wrong problems, but there have also been real advances in our understanding through the use of mathematics. Furthermore, the general increase in the use of mathematics derives not so much from this attack on the frontiers of ignorance as from the developments in

[1] Quoted in Simon James, *A Dictionary of Economic Quotations*, Croom Helm, 1981.

computer technology. With the ability to handle large volumes of data quickly and easily, and the ready availability of sophisticated statistical and mathematical computer packages, there has come the need to specify economics in suitable forms. The whole process of developing, testing and refuting theories by econometric/statistical methods requires a precision that only mathematical formulation can give. Now, I do not maintain that this methodology is the only one of value, or even that it is the best for most problems: but I do maintain that it is an important tool in the economists' kit and one that is increasingly used in practice.

With the growing use of mathematics have come new concepts and new theories which can be properly understood only in the language in which they were conceived. At the same time, certain types of traditional analysis were particularly amenable to mathematical formulation, and it is not perhaps surprising that the tool has become associated with particular doctrines, particular schools of thought. Neither is it surprising that alternative approaches, less easy to specify in the currently fashionable terminology, should be pushed to one side as outmoded and unscientific. To say that it is not surprising is not to agree that it is correct. By the same token, those who do not subscribe to current conventional wisdom should not discard the tools of analysis simply because they do not like the views of those who make greatest use of them. In practice, mathematics can be, and has been, used by a wide range of economists, famous and otherwise, for a wide variety of purposes. On the other hand, Keynes, perhaps the most famous of all, largely turned his back on mathematics when writing *General Theory*[2] in order to communicate his essential insights to a predominantly non-mathematical profession. (In the light of recent interpretations of his work, it is arguable whether this did in fact aid communication.[3])

One of the criticisms levelled against mathematical analysis of economics is that it leads to over-formalized models with many untenable or implausible assumptions, and that postulated concepts do not conform to observable entities. But is this a criticism of the use of mathematics or of economics in general? All analysis requires assumptions, and there is much to be said for making them explicit – indeed, it is exactly by doing so that we may see for the first time the inconsistencies and inadequacies of our models. It is curious that people will accept analysis by numerical examples and diagrams (both rather unsophisticated forms of mathematics), even though the assumptions

[2] J.M. Keynes, *The General Theory of Employment, Interest and Money*, Macmillan, 1936.
[3] See for example A. Leijonhufvud, *On Keynes and Keynesian Economics*, Oxford University Press, 1976.

are the same as, or even more restrictive than, those of the more sophisticated mathematical analysis. They will accept nebulous and ill-defined concepts described in words, even if they have no direct analogy in 'reality', no observable counterpart; yet they will rebel at the mathematical representation of those ideas. The blinkers imposed by standard diagrams or conventional phraseology are no less dulling to the intellect than those arising from the use of mathematical notation.

I have argued that, while mathematics can have a useful role to play in economics – one that is essentially free of value judgements – the decision to accept or reject the theories so explained is independent of the tools used. In practical terms, the advantages of such concise and precise notation are considerable for the writers of textbooks, and as texts increasingly use empirical evidence, so these advantages multiply. Nowadays it is not just the reader of research articles in journals who requires a working knowledge of mathematics but anyone who wishes to study intermediate-level economics. While we have admitted that such an approach can have inherent dangers, that is no excuse for opting out of the challenge. Indeed, the greatest danger comes from accepting the methodology, the intuitive concepts and the evidence without properly understanding how the results have been obtained. Modern students of economics must be able to follow the analysis and to understand the implicit and explicit assumptions if they are to form an unbiased opinion.

The second source of objections to the use of mathematics comes from those who find the subject inherently difficult. Were we concerned with advanced theory there would be no answer to this criticism, but the average student of economics is not in that position. All that is required is the ability to understand the notation and the basic concepts and to follow the analysis step by step. Mathematics is a language, albeit a very powerful one, and like any language can be mastered at different levels. People who want to enjoy their holidays in France can gain much from learning some basic French; armed with a passable accent, some basic grammar and vocabulary and a phrase book, it is not difficult to make yourself understood, and the more you try the better you get, until you suddenly realize you are not conciously having to translate the language any more. You learn to think in French, even if your vocabulary, like mine, would not do justice to a children's comic.

The approach of this book is analogous to the evening classes in 'conversational French'. It seeks not to turn you into a mathematician, but to provide enough basic grammar and vocabulary of the mathematical language, together with enough mathematical 'slang', to enable you to read and understand modern economics textbooks and a fair percentage of journal articles. It also provides the mathematical background required by subsequent courses in statistical and econometric techniques.

As with any languge, the only real way to master mathematics is to use it, so you will find here worked examples, exercises and economic applications. Unlike many books in this field, we shall not be using economics to explain mathematics; rather, we shall be showing how mathematics can be used to simplify and explain economics. This, after all, is why we are interested in learning the mathematics in the first place. The mathematics itself is explained in terms of everyday concepts so as to provide an intuitive grasp of the principles, and formal proofs are included only if they help to clarify matters.

Using this book

The book is divided into six Parts, each introducing a set of related techniques. As far as possible Parts are independent of each other, and the reader may omit one or more or may choose to take them in a different order. In particular, Part I ('Simple mathematical concepts') is intended for readers who have forgotten much of what they once knew, while Part VI ('Matrix algebra') could be left out altogether. Part II is unusual in that it groups together techniques that are normally spread throughout a mathematics text but which, from the point of view of economic analysis, fit together very naturally. I have called this section 'Introduction to dynamics' and placed it near the front of the book to reflect the increasing importance that economists now attach to the dynamic analysis of the economy. Part III deals with single-variable differential calculus and Part V with multivariate calculus, which together form the core of mathematical economics. In between these two is an optional Part on 'Integral calculus' including an introduction to differential equations. Here more than anywhere else in the book, the formal mathematics has been pared back to reveal the essential importance of the technique to the economist.

A consequence of this approach is that some readers may feel that a little more formal exposition is desirable, or that some additional material would be helpful. Some such material is provided in optional sections, denoted in the text and on the contents pages by a *leading asterisk*. This material may be omitted without loss of continuity.

Each Part consists of one, two or three chapters devoted to the mathematics itself. The remaining chapter then considers the application of these techniques in various areas of economics. In these chapters the complexity of the problems/exercises increases as we progress through the book, the order being consistent with conventional courses in macro- or microeconomics, so that the text may be used as a companion to a course in economics or as a text for parallel courses in mathematics and economics. The examples themselves are however self-contained, and the book can be used independently of such courses.

Further reading

The material in this book has been taught over a number of years to students on a wide range of degree courses and with a wide variety of backgrounds, but it would be naive to think that any single book can ever suit all readers all of the time. Readers are recommended to supplement the material here with other books which expand the course in the direction of their particular interests. For those who wish to have more formal analysis of the mathematics, may I suggest

M. Casson, *An Introduction to Mathematical Economics*, Nelson, 1973;
A.C. Chiang, *Fundamental Methods of Mathematics for Economists* (3rd edn), McGraw-Hill, 1983.

Readers who wish to apply their new skills more systematically to the study of economics should look at

A. Smith, *A Mathematical Introduction to Economics*, Basil Blackwell, 1982.

A more comprehensive treatment of linear programming and its relation to the economics of optimization is to be found in the excellent

W.J. Baumol, *Economic Theory and Operations Analysis*, Prentice-Hall, 1972.

Finally, to those who are interested in following up the question of economic methodology and the use of economic models in general, I recommend

T.C. Koopmans, *Three Essays on the State of Economic Science*, McGraw-Hill, 1957;
F. Neal and R. Shone, *Economic Model Building*, Macmillan, 1976.

Part I

Simple mathematical concepts

This part contains a review of the fundamental tools of mathematical analysis. With a little notation (chapter 1) and the ability to manipulate equations (chapter 2), quite a lot of basic economic analysis can be accomplished. The economic applications dealt with in chapter 3 are the basic building blocks of such economic analysis: the determination of price and quantities sold in markets, and the determination of the aggregate level of output (and therefore employment). In both cases we will look at the ways in which governments can affect the equilibrium values by active policy.

1 Basic rules of algebra

1.1 Some basic definitions and operations

To the mathematician, number systems are elegant constructions defined by a set of rules telling us how they may be manipulated, but in practice we are all so familiar with these operations we rarely give them a thought – everyone knows how to add up and subtract, multiply and divide. Algebra entails no more than applying these same rules. If each letter of the alphabet were assigned a number such that $a = 1$, $b = 2$, $c = 3$ and so on, it would be a trivial operation to say that $a + b = c$. This is the sort of simple code that many of us may have used to send secret messages at school. In that case we replaced letters by numbers, but the principle was the same. Of course, if everyone used $a = 1$, etc., the code did not stay secret very long, so for each message a different code was used. In algebra, too, we do not know the actual numbers assigned to each letter, but we do have the advantage that you can never break the rules – the message survives the manipulations while you put it into a form where it can be more easily read.

Conventions and conventional notations play an important part in algebra (as in most areas of mathematics), and much apparent confusion can be simply a lack of appreciation of these conventions, so at the risk of appearing tedious they are spelt out carefully in this chapter. One would not expect to learn a foreign language without its colloquial phrases and short forms, and mathematics is no different from any other language in this respect.

1.1.1 Numbers

Since the first thing we learn about mathematics is counting, where more natural to start? Indeed, we call the counting numbers 0, 1, 2, 3, 4, ... the *natural numbers*. Adding or multiplying any of these together always gives another natural number, but this is not true for subtraction, which can produce *negative numbers* (e.g., $2 - 5 = -3$). We might say that the operation of subtraction defines the concept of negative numbers. The set of natural numbers and negative numbers are together known as *integers*. The operation of division defines a new sort of number, the *fraction*, and the combined set of integers and fractions are known as *rational numbers*. With one exception, performing any of the four standard operations of addition, subtraction, multiplication and division upon rational numbers will always produce another rational number. (The exception is that we cannot divide by zero, and to this important exception we shall return shortly.)

As I have said, numbers obey certain rules. The first is that the operations of addition and multiplication must be *commutative* – that the order in which numbers are written does not affect the answer; thus,

$$a + b = b + a \qquad\qquad [1.1]$$

$$a \times b = b \times a. \qquad\qquad [1.2]$$

Note: In algebra it is not necessary to write the multiplication sign every time. Sometimes it is replaced by a dot, sometimes it is simply omitted, and sometimes brackets are placed around one of the numbers (letters); thus, $a \times b$, $a \cdot b$, ab, $a(b)$ and $(a)b$ all represent exactly the same information. Brackets are sometimes used when actual values for the numbers are given (e.g. 4(3) means 4×3), but the other two forms are not unambiguous and should never be so used.

The second rule says that the order in which addition and multiplication are performed does not affect the answer – the so-called *associative* property. Thus,

$$(a + b) + c = a + (b + c) \qquad\qquad [1.3]$$

$$(a \times b) \times c = a \times (b \times c). \qquad\qquad [1.4]$$

Note: By convention, any operation contained inside the bracket is performed before any operation outside the brackets. This is important. In the absence of brackets, multiplication and division are always done *before* addition and subtraction. Hence the expression

$$1 + 3 \times 2 = 1 + 6 = 7$$

whereas

$$(1 + 3) \times 2 = 4 \times 2 = 8.$$

Finally we have the *distributive* law of numbers, which says that

$$a \times (b + c) = (a \times b) + (a \times c) \qquad\qquad [1.5]$$

$$a \times (b - c) = (a \times b) - (a \times c). \qquad\qquad [1.6]$$

(Notice how brackets are included in [1.5] so as to make the expression more easily readable. Alternatively, we might write $a(b + c) = ab + ac$. The reader should substitute some values for a, b and c to check this property.)

1.1.2 'Two minuses make a plus'

Negative numbers can lead to some confusion, but if you remember the simple rule, 'two minuses make a plus', you should not have any problems. It applies to both addition and multiplication, and we can illustrate it with two simple examples. First, consider the expression $4 - (x - 2)$. We must perform the operation inside the bracket first and then subtract the answer from 4, so if x represents the number 3 we have

$$4 - (3 - 2) = 4 - 1 = 3.$$

But if x represented the number 1 we would have

$$4 - (1 - 2) = 4 - (-1) = 4 + 1 = 5.$$

It is trivial to show that multiplying a positive number by a negative number gives a negative result. Thus using [1.6],

$$(1)(1 - 2) = (1)(1) - (1)(2)$$
$$(1)(-1) = 1 - 2 = -1$$

and hence, using this result and [1.6] again,

$$(-1)(1 - 2) = (-1)(1) - (-1)(2)$$
$$(-1)(-1) = -1 - (-2) = 1$$

Again we may use the mnemonic aid, 'two minuses make a plus'.

1.1.3 Division by zero

The basic arithmetic operations are so familiar to us that we rarely stop to consider their implications. Suppose we want to give 3p to each of four children; then we need $4 \times 3p = 12p$; if we give them nothing then we need $4 \times 0 = 0$, i.e. nothing. The number zero behaves just like another number in that example, but now consider the physical analogy to division. We have 12p and each platform ticket costs 3p, so how many can go on to the platform? Dividing 12p by 3p gives the answer: 4. Now, what happens if it costs nothing to go on to the platform? $12 \div 0 = ?$ There is no sensible answer to the question since any number can go on (providing there is enough room!) and the same would be true if we had nothing to start with. Mathematics does not allow for such imprecision, and we have to exclude this possibility by excluding the idea of division by zero. This is not always as simple as it sounds in algebra since it depends upon the actual numbers that the letters represent; e.g., $2 \div (x - 1)$ is perfectly all right if x is the number 2 but if x is the number 1 then we have $2 \div (1 - 1) = 2 \div 0$, which is not all right.

It follows from this that all numbers *except* zero have a *reciprocal*; e.g., the reciprocal of x is the number $1/x$. When any number is multiplied by its reciprocal the answer is 1; i.e.,

$$x.\frac{1}{x} = 1.$$ [1.7]

1.1.4 Decimal numbers

By definition, all rational numbers may be expressed as the ratio of two integers, but the representation is not unique. Thus

$$\frac{8}{25} = \frac{32}{100} = \frac{3200}{10,000} \text{ and } \frac{5}{16} = \frac{3125}{10,000}.$$

This is obviously a clumsy notation, so we write instead

$$\frac{8}{25} = 0.32 = 0.3200 \text{ and } \frac{5}{16} = 0.3125.$$

Written in this way we talk about *decimal numbers*. Apart from economy of notation, representation in this form has other advantages. It is, for example, much easier to see that 0.3200 is a larger number than 0.3125 than it is to see that 8/25 is larger than 5/16.

There are also disadvantages. For example, there is no exact representation of the fraction 1/3 in this system but a reasonable approximation is 33/100 or 0.33. A better one is 333/1000 or 0.333, and so on. We say that 1/3 is given by the *infinite decimal* 0.33333... or $0.\dot{3}$ (0.3 recurring). The fraction 1/11 may be written 0.090909.... Then there are numbers where the patterns do not repeat – examples of infinite decimals abound in mathematics. Some of them cannot be represented as *any* fraction and are said to be *irrational numbers*. Examples of these will arise in section 1.2.

The numbers so far described all have a physical analogy. If we ignore the sign they could be said to measure distance. Indeed, if we measure positive numbers as distance to the right of some fixed point called zero and negative numbers as the distance to the left, then we can arrange all these *real* numbers in a 'real line'. (There are in mathematics other sorts of numbers called 'imaginary' and 'complex' numbers (see section 1.2.3), but for the most part we shall be concerned only with real numbers.)

1.1.5 Equalities and inequalities

Having arranged all our numbers on the 'real line', there are a few things we can do with them. If a number x lies to the right of a number y

on this real line, we say that x is *greater than* y $(x > y)$, whereas if it lies to the left then x is *less than* y $(x < y)$. By contrast to these *inequalities*, if the two numbers are exactly the same then x is *equal* to y $(x = y)$. We can use these symbols singly or in combinations to describe *intervals*, so for example $0 \leqslant b < 1$ means that the letter b can take any value from 0 up to, but not including, 1.

Note: Equalities and inequalities are expressions that may or may not be true depending upon the actual values that the letters represent. If an expression is true by definition then it is said to be an *identity*, and we may represent this by a special symbol, $\equiv$. For example, $5 - 5 \equiv 0$. In practice, mathematicians often omit this distinction, but it is of some importance to the economist.

It follows from the definitions of inequalities that $-3 < 2$ since on the real line -3 lies to the left of 2. If, however, we were to measure the distance of each from the centre of the line – the point zero – then 3 is actually further away. Ignoring the minus sign, it has a greater *magnitude*. In mathematics we define the *modulus* or *absolute value* of a number as its magnitude ignoring the sign; it is written $|x|$. In the example above,

$$|-3| > |2|.$$

This convention is particularly useful in specifying intervals. Thus, $-1 < b < 1$ can also be written $|b| < 1$.

1.2 The arithmetic of powers

Mathematics is a language, and like any language it has slang. Sometimes it has alternative ways of saying the same thing and sometimes one expression can mean different things. What makes mathematics such a useful language is the variety of its short forms and the extreme rarity of ambiguities. The most common of the short forms is the power, and its use is explained in this section. In doing so we shall also learn something about numbers that are not rational numbers; but first, a definition of a *power*.

We represent the multiplication of two numbers by an expression such as $a \times b$. If the two numbers are the same, we would have $a \times a$. Another way of expressing this is to write a^2. The superscript 2 is a power denoting that two a's are to be multiplied together. In fact, it makes no difference if we multiply a number by 1 (unity), so let us think of a^2 as a 1 multiplied by a twice:

$$a^2 \equiv 1 \times a \times a.$$

By analogy we can define

$$a^3 \equiv 1 \times a \times a \times a$$

$$a^1 \equiv 1 \times a \qquad\qquad [1.8]$$

$$a^0 \equiv 1. \qquad\qquad [1.9]$$

Equations [1.8] and [1.9] are worthy of note. The former reminds us that a is really a^1 with the superscript omitted for simplicity. The latter tells us that, whatever the value of a, we find that $a^0 = 1$, which fact will be of considerable use shortly.

A simple extension of the idea is to ask what happens when we *divide* by a? We shall discover shortly that consistent terminology would suggest that

$$\frac{1}{a} \equiv a^{-1} \qquad\qquad [1.10]$$

$$\frac{1}{a^2} \equiv a^{-2}$$

and so on.

1.2.1 The basic rule

There is really only one basic rule:

$$a^m \cdot a^n = a^{m+n}. \qquad\qquad [1.11]$$

All the others follow directly from this one statement. Since it is so important, let us look at a specific example: $a^2 \cdot a^3$. By definition,

$$a^2 \equiv a \cdot a \text{ and } a^3 \equiv a \cdot a \cdot a.$$

Hence

$$a^2 \cdot a^3 \equiv a \cdot a \cdot a \cdot a \cdot a \cdot \equiv a^5.$$

We argued above that a number multiplied by its reciprocal is unity; i.e.,

$$a \cdot \frac{1}{a} = 1. \qquad\qquad [1.12]$$

Using the definitions of a^1, a^0 and a^{-1} given in [1.8], [1.9] and [1.10], we can rewrite [1.12] as

$$a^1 \cdot a^{-1} = a^0 \qquad\qquad [1.13]$$

which is consistent with the basic rule [1.11], so we find that [1.10] is indeed consistent notation. Furthermore, since $1/a$ is $1 \div a$ we could also write [1.13] as

$$a^1 \div a^1 = a^0. \qquad [1.14]$$

This is a special case of the more general statement that [1.11] implies:

$$a^m \cdot a^{-n} = a^{m+(-n)} = a^{m-n}$$

and therefore

$$a^m \div a^n = a^{m-n}. \qquad [1.15]$$

Suppose now that $b = a^2$. What is b^3? Again, this question may be answered by using the definitions directly; thus,

$$(a^2)^3 = a^2 \cdot a^2 \cdot a^2 = a^{2+2+2} = a^{2 \times 3} = a^6.$$

This is but a special case of the more general

$$(a^m)^n = a^{mn}. \qquad [1.16]$$

1.2.2 Non-integer powers

So far, we have assumed that m and n in equations [1.11], [1.15] and [1.16] are integers, but is this necessarily so? Consider the following example:

$$8^2 = 64 \text{ and } 4^3 = 64.$$

So letting b represent the number 8 and a represent the number 4, we have $b^2 = a^3$. Noting that $\frac{3}{2} \times 2 = 3$, we may write

$$b^2 = a^3 = a^{(3/2) \times 2}.$$

Using the rule given in [1.16], we can write this as

$$b^2 = (a^{(3/2)})^2$$

$$b = a^{(3/2)}$$

and we have thus demonstrated that non-integer powers must exist, though their physical analogy may be rather obscure. Indeed, one particular case is of particular interest. If $b^n = a$ it follows immediately that

$$b^n = a^{(1/n) \times n} = (a^{(1/n)})^n$$

$$b = a^{(1/n)}$$

and we say that b is the nth root of a.

Note: An alternative notation for the nth root of a is to write

$$b = \sqrt[n]{a} \equiv a^{(1/n)}.$$

There are two 'special cases'. When $n = 3$ we talk not of the third root, but the *cube root*. This follows naturally from the convention that b^3 is called 'b-cubed'. Similarly, since b^2 is 'b-squared', then $a^{(1/2)}$ is the *square root* of a, but in this case the alternative notation is simply

$$b = \sqrt{a} \equiv a^{(1/2)}$$

(i.e., the 2 in $\sqrt[2]{a}$ is assumed).

The introduction of non-integer powers brings with it two problems. First, the number so defined may not be unique. For example, we showed above that $b = a^{(1/2)}$ contained the same information as $b^2 = a$, but we can readily see that

$$(-2) \cdot (-2) = 4 \ and \ (2) \cdot (2) = 4$$

so the statement that $b = 4^{(1/2)}$ could mean *either* that $b = -2$ *or* that $b = 2$. In general, we would write $b = \pm 2$. Second, the number so defined may not be 'real'. For example, it is not possible, with the sort of numbers we have considered so far, to find a number (b) such that $b^2 = -9$. For most purposes it is sufficient to say at this point that such a number does not exist, but a mathematician is not so easily diverted – he would 'imagine' that one does. Such *imaginary* numbers are the subject of the following optional section.

Worked examples

Q. Simplify the following expressions:
  (i) $3x^2 + 2x^2$;   (ii) $3x^2 \cdot 2x^2$;   (iii) $(3x^2)^2$.

A. (i) $3x^2 + 2x^2 = (3 + 2)x^2 = 5x^2$.
  (ii) $3x^2 \cdot 2x^2 = (3 \times 2)x^2 \cdot x^2 = 6x^4$.
  (iii) $(3x^2)^2 = 3x^2 \cdot 3x^2 = (3 \times 3)x^2 \cdot x^2 = 9x^4$.

Q. Evaluate the expression $\dfrac{x^{(2/3)} \cdot x^{(1/6)}}{\sqrt{x}}$ where $x = 8$.

A. One method is to substitute $x = 8$ into the expression, but finding the sixth root of 8 is not easy. Using the basic rule of indices we can rewrite the expression as

$$\frac{x^{(2/3) + (1/6)}}{x^{(1/2)}} = \frac{x^{(5/6)}}{x^{(1/2)}} = x^{(5/6) - (1/2)} = x^{(1/3)}$$

and the cube root of 8 is easily verifiable as 2 (i.e., $2^3 = 8$).

*1.2.3 Imaginary and complex numbers

In one sense there is nothing less real about the number represented by

$\sqrt{-9}$ than there is about that represented by $\sqrt{9}$, but convention stipulates that we consider as 'real' only those numbers that have a physical analogy. Consider the statement

$$(ab)^2 = a^2b^2. \qquad [1.17]$$

If a is the number -1 and b is the number 3, then [1.17] says that

$$(-1 \times 3)^2 = (-1)^2 \cdot 3^2 = 1 \times 9 = 9. \qquad [1.18]$$

But suppose the object is to produce an answer of -9. Postulate that there exists a number i such that $i^2 = -1$, and we could write

$$(i \times 3)^2 = i^2 \cdot 3^2 = (-1) \times 9 = -9$$

The square root of -9 is seen to be (i × 3) or, since the order of multiplication is unimportant, 3i. More generally, we have established that

$$(ib)^2 = i^2 b^2 = -b^2. \qquad [1.19]$$

The procedure is of course perfectly general and can be used for any negative number; and, having established that such a number is conceptually possible, there is no reason why we should not use it in exactly the same way as all the other numbers. For example, we might wish to add one of these new 'imaginary' numbers to a 'real' number, the resulting combination being known as a *complex number*. Examples would be

$2 + 3i$; $a + ib$; $7 - i$.

Although no precise physical analogy exists, it is possible to represent such numbers diagrammatically. The real part can be measured along the horizontal axis (along what we have previously called 'the real line'). The imaginary part can be measured in a similar way along the vertical axis. Thus, a complex number represents a single point in the two-dimensional space we have defined (see figure 1.1(a)). Alternatively, we can think of it as the line joining the point (a, b) to the origin as in figure 1.1(b). The length of the line may be calculated from Pythagoras' theorem as

$$r = (a^2 + b^2)^{(1/2)} \qquad [1.20]$$

while a little basic trigonometry tells us that, by definition,

$$\cos\theta = \frac{a}{r} \text{ and } \sin\theta = \frac{b}{r} \qquad [1.21]$$

$a = r\cos\theta$; $b = r\sin\theta$.

If a complex number was represented as $(a + ib)$ as in figure 1.1, it could

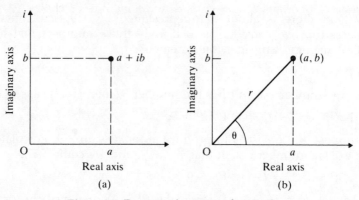

Figure 1.1 Representing a complex number

also be represented in terms of r and θ. Substituting from [1.21] gives

$$a + ib = r\cos\theta + ir\sin\theta$$

$$= r(\cos\theta + i\sin\theta). \qquad [1.22]$$

Similarly,

$$a - ib = r(\cos\theta - i\sin\theta). \qquad [1.23]$$

(The advantages of this alternative representation will become clear in section 6.3.)

1.2.4 Factorization

The introduction of indices has allowed considerable simplification of mathematical expressions, particularly when used in conjunction with the distributive law of numbers. For example, it is possible to write

$$6a^3 - 9a^2 = 3a^2(2a - 3).$$

Less obvious is

$$6a^3 - 9a^2 + 3a = 3a(2a - 1)(a - 1) \qquad [1.24]$$

but it may be easily verified. Using [1.6], we can show that

$$(2a - 1)(a - 1) = 2a(a - 1) - 1(a - 1)$$
$$= 2a^2 - 2a - a + 1$$
$$= 2a^2 - 3a + 1. \qquad [1.25]$$

Then, multiplying each side of [1.25] by $3a$ gives [1.24].

This process of reducing a *polynomial* expression, i.e., an expression involving the addition of a number of terms, each having an unknown number raised to a different power, to a product of two or more simpler expressions, or *factors*, is known as *factorization*. It is a technique that can be acquired mainly by practice and, once mastered, can often save considerable time and effort.

Two tips should help in acquiring this skill:

1   *Always* check your factorization by multiplying out the factors as we did above.

2   If it is observed that a particular value for a (say $a*$) reduces the expression to zero, then one of the factors *must* be $(a - a*)$.

The reason for this last tip is considered in the next section, but we can give an example immediately. Consider the expression on the left-hand side of [1.24]. When $a = 1$ we have

$$6(1)^3 - 9(1)^2 + 3(1) = 6 - 9 + 3 = 0$$

and so we know immediately that $(a - 1)$ is a factor, and this is confirmed by looking at the right-hand side of [1.24]. Faced with an awkward-looking expression, it is often possible to find one of the factors by trying a few simple numbers $(1, -1, 2$ or -2, for example) and then removing this factor, thus simplifying the expression one stage at a time.

Worked example

Q. Factorize $2a^3 - 5a^2 + 4a - 1$.

A. Notice first that setting $a = 1$ gives $2(1)^3 - 5(1)^2 + 4(1) - 1 = 0$ and hence that $(a - 1)$ is a factor. To remove it requires a long division thus:

$$
\begin{array}{r}
2a^2 - 3a + 1 \\
(a - 1) \,)\, \overline{\, 2a^3 - 5a^2 + 4a - 1} \\
\underline{2a^3 - 2a^2} \\
-3a^2 + 4a - 1 \\
\underline{-3a^2 + 3a} \\
a - 1 \\
\underline{a - 1} \\
0
\end{array}
$$

Therefore we can rewrite $(2a^3 - 5a^2 + 4a - 1)$ as $(a - 1)(2a^2 - 3a + 1)$. A similar process would reveal the factors of $(2a^2 - 3a + 1)$, but we have already done this in equation [1.25]. Thus our complete answer is

$$2a^3 - 5a^2 + 4a - 1 = (a - 1)(a - 1)(2a - 1). \qquad [1.26]$$

Study the technique of long division – it is extremely useful. In the worked example, you look first at the highest powers in the divisor and dividend to ascertain that dividing a into $2a^3$ gives $2a^2$ as the first term in the quotient. We now subtract $2a^2(a - 1) = 2a^3 - 2a^2$ from the dividend to leave $-3a^2 + 4a - 1$. Repeating the procedure gives the second term as $-3a$, so we subtract $-3a(a - 1) = -3a^2 + 3a$, and this leaves $a - 1$, so the last term is 1.

One major use of factorization is discussed in the next chapter, but first let us see how it may be used to simplify complex expressions. Consider the following:

$$\frac{6a^3 - 9a^2 + 3a}{2a^3 - 5a^2 + 4a - 1}. \qquad [1.27]$$

Using equations [1.24] and [1.26] we can rewrite [1.27] as

$$\frac{3a(2a - 1)(a - 1)}{(a - 1)(a - 1)(2a - 1)} = \frac{3a}{a - 1}$$

1.3 Functions

A variable y is said to be a function of another variable x if there is a rule that associates with each possible value of x a value y. Suppose x represents the temperature in degrees centigrade; then we can calculate the temperature y in degrees fahrenheit from the following rule:

$$y = \tfrac{9}{5}x + 32. \qquad [1.28]$$

Intuitively this is a very simple idea. (Notice in particular that no causality is implied; i.e., centigrade does not *determine* fahrenheit: the function simply explains the relationship between the two.)

A mathematician would wish to add two things to this definition of a function. (1) There should be only one value of y associated with each value of x (but it must be admitted that even mathematicians have been observed referring to $y = x^{(1/2)}$ as a function, so perhaps we need not worry too much about that). (2) It must be defined for a particular set of values for x. The example given above is true only of $x > -273$ since that is absolute zero. So far as we know, it is not possible to achieve a lower temperature. This set of values for x is called the *domain* and forms part of the definition of the function. If no such domain is specified, we conventionally assume it to be true for all real numbers.

Unfortunately, people are not always so careful in their definitions. For example, $y = 1/x$ is a function, but it cannot be defined for all real numbers – it is not defined when $x = 0$. Very often this is considered to be obvious and the information omitted, but we should strictly write

$$y = \frac{1}{x} \quad x \neq 0.$$

1.3.1   Implicit and inverse functions

In [1.28] we used as an example of a function the conversion from degrees centigrade to degrees fahrenheit. We could equally well write the rule in a different way, viz.:

$$x = \tfrac{5}{9}(y - 32). \qquad\qquad [1.29]$$

If we were to denote the former relationship by the mathematical statement $y = f(x)$, then the latter relationship, the *inverse function*, can be written as $x = f^{-1}(y)$.

Take care with this terminology. The letter f denotes the functional relationship between the argument x and the value of the function y, and f^{-1} refers to the reverse procedure necessary to return us to the value of x. It must *not* be confused with y^{-1}, which refers to the number $1/y$.

In this particular case the inverse function exists and is easy to calculate. In some cases it may not exist, while in others it is difficult to find.

There is a third way in which a particular relationship may be written in which neither of the variables is explicitly stated to be a function of the other, although it is implicit in the statement. Not surprisingly, this is known as an *implicit function*. For the relationship between centigrade and fahrenheit expressed in [1.28] and [1.29] we could write

$$5y - 9x - 160 = 0. \qquad\qquad [1.30]$$

1.3.2   Functional notation

The most common form of notation for functions is that used in the previous section, viz. $y = f(x)$. The function itself is $f(x)$ and y is the value that it takes for a given value of x. When a number of different functions are being considered, we distinguish between them by using different letters; e.g.,

$$u = g(x),\ t = \phi(x),\ p = p(x).$$

The last of these is the source of some confusion since the letter p had been used to denote both the value of the function *and* the function itself. It does, however, have an obvious advantage in that it is an economic use of the limited number of letters available.

When we wish to consider the value taken by a function such as $y = f(x)$ when x takes a particular value a, then this may be specified by writing $f(x = a)$ or, more usually, $f(a)$. When we are concerned with the function in general it is usually sufficient to refer to the function by its letter, in this case f. So long as we remember what is a function of what, none of this should cause any real problem, and mathematicians have a habit of switching from one notation to the other depending upon the problem in hand. If you are ever in doubt, then stick to the most general notation: $y = f(x)$, $u = g(x)$, etc.

Worked example

Q. If $f(x) = (x - 1)^2$, show that $f(x + 1) \cdot f(3) = f(2x + 1) \cdot f(0)$.

A. $f(0) = (0 - 1)^2 = 1$; $f(3) = (3 - 1)^2 = 4$
$f(x + 1) = [(x + 1) - 1]^2 = x^2$
$f(2x + 1) = [(2x + 1) - 1]^2 = 4x^2$
and therefore, by substituting these values into the expression, we have
$f(x + 1) \cdot f(3) = x^2 \cdot 4 = 4x^2 \cdot 1 = f(2x + 1) \cdot f(0)$.

1.3.3   Decomposition of functions

If we start with two functions,

$u = g(x)$ and $v = h(x)$

we can easily calculate the sum of these two as

$y = u + v = g(x) + h(x)$

and, clearly, y is also a function of x – say, $f(x)$. We could likewise calculate the product or ratio of two functions, or we could do the reverse operation – indeed, that is exactly what we did in section 1.2.4 when we factorized polynomials. There is one decomposition, however, that is extremely useful and worthy of some detailed discussion.

We have already noted that the value of a function $y = f(x)$ consequent upon a particular value of the argument $x = u$ is written as $f(u)$. Now, suppose that x itself is a function of another variable t (i.e., $x = g(t)$). The value of y now depends upon the value of t, and using the same notation we have $y = f(g(t))$.

If functions can be constructed in this way, it must also be possible to decompose them in a similar fashion. Consider the function $y = 9x^2$. In order to facilitate the decomposition we introduce an intermediate variable, say u. We can now write

$u = g(x) = 3x$ [1.31]

$y = f(u) = u^2$ [1.32]

and substituting [1.31] into [1.32],

$y = f(g(x)) = (3x)^2 = 9x^2$.   [1.33]

This decomposition is unlikely to be unique. Even in the case of a simple function like $y = 9x^2$ we can find alternative representations. Thus, if

$$v = q(x) = x^2 \qquad\qquad [1.34]$$

and

$$y = p(v) = 9v \qquad\qquad [1.35]$$

we can substitute [1.34] into [1.35] to give

$$y = p(q(x)) = 9(x^2) = 9x^2. \qquad\qquad [1.36]$$

By introducing the intermediate variables u and v the process is easy to follow, but they are not strictly necessary. Thus we could have written [1.31] and [1.32] as

$$g(x) = 3x; \ f(x) = x^2 \qquad\qquad [1.37]$$

and it is still true that

$$f(g(x)) = (3x)^2 = 9x^2 \qquad\qquad [1.33']$$

Now, however, we have to be particularly careful about the order of the substitution, for we can define an alternative function:

$$g(f(x)) = 3(x^2) = 3x^2. \qquad\qquad [1.38]$$

Both of the functions defined in [1.33'] and [1.38] are called a 'function of a function'. It is a concept that will come into its own in chapter 8.

1.3.4   Functions of more than one variable

No new principles are introduced by allowing the value of a function to be determined by the value(s) of two variables rather than one. Consider this simple illustration.

The average speed (V) at which a journey is completed depends upon the total distance travelled (S) and the time taken (T), thus:

$$V = \alpha\frac{S}{T} \qquad \alpha > 0 \qquad\qquad [1.39]$$

where the value of α reflects the particular units used in measuring V, S and T. In functional notation we would write

$$V = f(S, T). \qquad\qquad [1.40]$$

Notice, however, that we could have expressed the relationship in two other ways:

$$S = g(T, V) = \frac{1}{\alpha}V{\cdot}T \qquad\qquad [1.41]$$

$$T = h(V, S) = \alpha\frac{S}{V}. \tag{1.42}$$

The functions g and h are in some sense 'inverses' of f although not in quite the same way as with the single-variate function. The rules for manipulating all of them are no different from those governing single-variate functions, but notice that in order to define particular values for $V = f(S, T)$ one has to specify values for both S and T. Strictly speaking, then, the definition should include the domains for both S and T.

Finally, let us note that there is no reason to stop at two arguments. In general, we may postulate $y = f(x_1, x_2, \ldots)$, By introducing more than one argument, however, we raise the possibility of either changing one variable at a time or, alternatively, changing the whole scale of the function by changing all the variables at once. This is the subject matter of the following section, which may be considered optional on a first reading.

*1.3.5 Homogeneous functions

A homogeneous function is one that exhibits the special property that, if each of the arguments of the function is multiplied by the same non-negative constant, the value of the function will itself also be multiplied by a constant. Thus in the two-variable case the function $f(u, v)$ is homogeneous of degree k if and only if (iff)

$$f(\lambda u, \lambda v) = \lambda^k f(u, v) \qquad \lambda \geq 0 \tag{1.43}$$

whatever values of u, v and λ are chosen. The concept can be applied to single-variable functions thus:

$$f(x) = x^2 \tag{1.44}$$

$$f(\lambda x) = \lambda^2 x^2 = \lambda^2 f(x)$$

and [1.44] is homogeneous of degree 2 whereas the following is not:

$$f(x) = x^2 + 4 \tag{1.45}$$

$$f(\lambda x) = (\lambda x)^2 + 4 = \lambda^2 x^2 + 4.$$

Equation [1.45] actually demonstrates that no function which contains an additive constant can be homogeneous, but in practice we are more interested in homogeneity of multivariate functions and two examples are given below. They are in fact the functions defined in [1.41] and [1.42] above, so the physical analogies are very simple.

Worked example

Q. If $g(T, V) = \dfrac{1}{\alpha} \cdot V \cdot T$ and $h(V, S) = \alpha \dfrac{S}{V}$, are they both homogeneous

of the same degree?

A. (i) $g(\lambda T, \lambda V) = \dfrac{1}{\alpha}(\lambda V)(\lambda T) = \lambda^2\left[\dfrac{1}{\alpha} V \cdot T\right] = \lambda^2 g(T, V)$

and therefore g is homogeneous of degree 2.

(ii) $h(\lambda V, \lambda S) = \alpha\dfrac{(\lambda S)}{(\lambda V)} = \dfrac{\alpha S}{V} = h(V, S)$.

In this case the value of the function has not changed. We might say that it has been multiplied by 1. But any number raised to the power 0 is 1 (i.e., $\lambda^0 = 1$); hence we may write

$$h(\lambda V, \lambda S) = \lambda^0 h(V, S)$$

and conclude that h *is* homogeneous, but of degree 0.

1.4   Exercises

Section 1.2.2

Simplify where possible:

(i) $x^6 \div x^2$

(ii) $x^6 +. x^2$

(iii) $x^6 \cdot x^{-2}$

(iv) $3x^2 \div x^3$

(v) $x^{(1/2)} \cdot x^{(1/2)}$

(vi) $\dfrac{(x^2)^{(1/2)}}{x^{(2/3)}}$

(vii) $x^{-2}(x^5 + x^3)$

Section 1.2.4

Factorize the following where possible:

(i) $2x^3 + x^2 - 2x - 1$

(ii) $x^3 + x^2 - x - 1$

(iii) $x^3 - 3x - 2$

(iv) $5x - 6 - x^2$

(v) $2x^2 + x - 1$

(vi) $x^2 - 6x + 9$

(vii) $2x^3 - 3x^2 - 3x + 2$

Section 1.3 introduction

Are there any values of x for which the following do not define real values of y?

(1) $y = (4 - x^2)^{(1/2)}$

(iii) $y = x(x^2 + 4)^{-1}$

(ii) $y = (x - 2)^{-1}$

(iv) $y = x(x^2 - 4)^{-1}$

Section 1.3.1

Give, where possible, the unique inverse functions of

(i) $y = 3x - 2$

(iii) $y = 3x^3 - 2$

(ii) $y = 3x^2 - 2$

(iv) $y = x^{(1/2)}$

Section 1.3.2

If $f(x) = 2^x$, is it true that

(i) $f(x + 3) - f(x - 1) = \frac{15}{2}f(x)$?

(ii) $\dfrac{f(x + 3)}{f(x - 1)} = f(4)$?

Hint: Note that $f(a) = 2^a$ and that $2^a \cdot 2^b = 2^{a + b}$.

Section 1.3.3

If $f(x) = x^2$ and $g(x) = 1 - x$, give the simplest form of the following composite functions:

(i) $f(x) + g(x)$

(iii) $f(g(x))$

(ii) $f(x) \cdot g(x)$

(iv) $g(f(x))$

Section *1.3.5

Are the following functions homogeneous, and if so of what degree?

(i) $f(x, y) = x^2 + y^2$

(iv) $f(u, v, w) = \dfrac{uv}{w}$

(ii) $f(x, y) = x^2 + 4y^2$

(v) $f(x, y) = x^{(1/2)} \cdot y^{(1/2)}$

(iii) $f(x, y) = (x + y)^2$

(vi) $f(x, y) = ax^\alpha \cdot y^\beta$

Further exercises

1. Express the following as decimal numbers:

    (i) $\frac{7}{3}$ (iii) $\frac{1}{8}$

    (ii) $\frac{7}{30}$ (iv) $\frac{1}{12}$

2. Which of the following statements are true?

    (i) $|-2| < |3 - 2|$ (v) $27^{(1/3)} = 3$

    (ii) $x^{-1} \cdot x = 0$ (vi) $\sqrt{-49} = 7$

    (iii) $x^2 > x$ if   (vii) $\sqrt{49} = -7$

      and only if $x > 1$

    (iv) $\dfrac{x^{(1/2)}}{\sqrt{x}} = 1$ (viii) $x^4 > 0$ for any value of x

3. Is $(x + 1)$ a factor of the following expressions?
    If it is, calculate the other factors:

    (i) $x^2 - 1$ (iii) $x^3 - 6x^2 + 11x - 6$

    (ii) $x^2 - x - 2$ (iv) $x^3 - 4x^2 - 5x + 6$

2 Solving equations

An equation is an equality in which appear one or more variables with unspecified value(s). 'Solving' an equation means assigning to the unknown(s) a value or set of values that satisfies the equality, or for which the statement is true. The simplest equation is of the form $x = 3$. In fact, the solution is so obvious that we think of this as a statement rather than an equation, but it conveys the same information as $x - 3 = 0$. All equations are solved in principle by using the fact that the equality is unaffected by arithmetic operations; in other words, so long as you perform the same operations on both sides of the equality sign, the relationship between the two sides is not changed. It will make life easier, however, if we look at each sort of equation in turn.

2.1 Linear equations

Any equation that can be written as

$$ax + b = 0 \qquad\qquad [2.1]$$

is said to be linear. To solve this equation subtract b from each side

$$ax = -b$$

and then divide both sides by a to give the solution:

$$x = \frac{-b}{a}.$$

Thus, if $2x - 4 = 0$ we conclude that $x = 2$, and so on.

2.2 Higher order equations

By 'higher' order we refer to equations containing terms in x raised to some power higher than 1. Conventionally, if the highest power is 2 we call them *quadratic equations*; if the highest power is 3 they are *cubic equations* and if the highest power is 4 they are *quartic equations*. All these, and higher orders, can be solved simply if it is possible to rewrite them as the product of a number of linear equations – i.e. if they can be factorized.

In the previous chapter we saw that (equation [1.24])

$$6x^3 - 9x^2 + 3x = 3x(2x - 1)(x - 1) = 0 \qquad [2.2]$$

It follows immediately that the whole expression will be equal to zero if

$$3x = 0; 2x - 1 = 0; \text{ or } x - 1 = 0$$

and these three equations are all linear and easily solved to give

$$x = 0; x = \tfrac{1}{2} \text{ and } x = 1.$$

We see now why it was that, if substituting the value 1 into the expression reduced the value of the expression to 0, then $(x - 1)$ must be a factor. Thus the technique discussed in section 1.2.4, whereby we guess at one 'solution' and then use this to simplify the problem, will stand us in good stead here.

Factorization, however, is not always that easy. Indeed, it is not always possible, and some additional technique to help with difficult cases is desirable. For cubics and higher orders there is no generally applicable technique other than factorization, but for quadratics we can develop a simple rule.

2.2.1 Quadratic equations

The general form of the quadratic equation is

$$ax^2 + bx + c = 0. \qquad [2.3]$$

Recalling that whatever is done to one side of an equation must be done to the other, we may first divide through by a:

$$x^2 + \left(\frac{b}{a}\right)x + \left(\frac{c}{a}\right) = 0$$

and then add to each side the expression

$$\frac{b^2}{4a^2} - \frac{c}{a}$$

to give

$$x^2 + \left(\frac{b}{a}\right)x + \frac{b^2}{4a^2} = \frac{b^2}{4a^2} - \frac{c}{a} \qquad [2.4]$$

$$x^2 + 2\cdot\left(\frac{b}{2a}\right)x + \left(\frac{b}{2a}\right)^2 = \frac{b^2}{4a^2} - \frac{4ac}{4a^2}$$

$$\left(x + \frac{b}{2a}\right)^2 = \frac{b^2 - 4ac}{4a^2} \qquad\qquad [2.5]$$

Taking the square root of each side, and noting that there will in general be two answers – one positive and one negative – we have

$$\left(x + \frac{b}{2a}\right) = \frac{\pm \sqrt{(b^2 - 4ac)}}{2a}$$

and solving for x

$$x = \frac{-b \pm \sqrt{(b^2 - 4ac)}}{2a}. \qquad\qquad [2.6]$$

Equation [2.6] then represents the solution(s) of *any* quadratic equation. Notice that there are two possible values for x (say x_1 and x_2) – one when we use the positive root and the other when we use the negative root – except in the special case when $b^2 = 4ac$: in that event the expression under the square root sign is zero and we are left with $x = -b/2a$, i.e., the value of the two solutions is the same.

Note: It is common to refer to these solutions as *roots* of the equation – do *not* confuse them with square roots! If they are both the same we say that we have *repeated roots*. If $b^2 < 4ac$, the expression under the square root sign is negative. Since we cannot take the square root of a negative number it follows that there are *no real roots* (But see section 2.2.2 for a fuller discussion of this case.)

Worked examples

Q. Solve the equation $x^2 - 5x = 6$.

A. Rewrite in general form $x^2 - 5x - 6 = 0$. We can now apply the formula [2.6], noting that $a = 1$, $b = -5$ and $c = -6$; hence,

$$x_{1,2} = \frac{5 \pm \sqrt{(25 + 24)}}{2} = \frac{5 \pm 7}{2}$$

$$x = 6 \text{ or } x = -1$$

(Notice that our knowledge of factors allows us to write $x^2 - 5x - 6 = (x - 6)(x + 1)$ and hence verify the solutions obtained by the formula.)

Q. Solve the equation $x^3 - 3x^2 - 4x + 6 = 0$.

A. Note that if $x = 1$ we have $1 - 3 - 4 + 6 = 0$ so $(x - 1)$ is a factor. Dividing, we have

$$(x - 1) \overline{) \begin{array}{l} x^2 - 2x - 6 \\ x^3 - 3x^2 - 4x + 6 \end{array}}$$

$$\begin{array}{r} x^3 - x^2 \\ \hline -2x^2 - 4x + 6 \\ -2x^2 + 2x \\ \hline -6x + 6 \\ -6x + 6 \end{array}$$

We may then use the formula to find the roots of $x^2 - 2x - 6$ thus:

$$x = \frac{2 \pm \sqrt{(4 + 24)}}{2} = 1 \pm \frac{\sqrt{28}}{2} = 1 \pm \sqrt{7}$$

and the three possible solutions are $x = 1$, $x = 1 + \sqrt{7}$ and $x = 1 - \sqrt{7}$.

*2.2.2 Complex solutions

The general solution to the quadratic equation [2.3] was given in equation [2.6], but what happens if $b^2 - 4ac < 0$? If we refer back to section 1.2.3 we see that it is possible to find the square root of a negative number by introducing the imaginary i, where $i^2 = -1$. Formally, we have

$$b^2 - 4ac = (-1)(-1)(b^2 - 4ac)$$
$$b^2 - 4ac = i^2(4ac - b^2)$$

and hence

$$\sqrt{(b^2 - 4ac)} = i\sqrt{(4ac - b^2)}. \tag{2.7}$$

Substituting [2.7] into [2.6] gives

$$x = \frac{-b}{2a} \pm \frac{i\sqrt{(4ac - b^2)}}{2a} \tag{2.8}$$

Note: In general, it is always possible to find complex solutions of the form $h \pm iv$. It is of interest to note that complex solutions *always* occur in pairs (known as *complex conjugates*) since they can only arise from taking the square root of a negative number.

Worked example

Q. Solve $x^2 - 2x + 5 = 0$.

A. Using the formula,

$$x_{1,2} = \frac{2 \pm \sqrt{(4 - 20)}}{2} = 1 \pm \sqrt{-4} = 1 \pm 2i.$$

2.3 Inequalities

Solving an inequality means finding those values of the unknown variable(s) for which the inequality is true. Those values will be contained in one or more intervals. For example, the 'solution' for the inequality $2x - 6 > 0$ is $x > 3$.

There are two basic techniques that are used. The first is to manipulate the inequality as one would an equation. Arithmetic operations do not change the relative positions of points on the real line, but there is one complication. The statement $x < y$ means that x lies to the left of y on the real line and not that it has a smaller *magnitude*. This latter condition would be written as $|x| < |y|$ (see section 1.1.5), but by definition it follows that $|-x| < |-y|$. In words, we say that x (or $-x$) lies closer to the point zero than y (or $-y$). Since all negative numbers are on the left, $-y$ must lie further to the left than $-x$; that is to say, $-x > -y$.

Note: We have demonstrated that multiplying (dividing) an inequality by a negative number reverses the sign of the inequality. Hence one should never multiply (divide) by any variable unless we are sure of its sign.

Worked example

Q. Solve $x^2 < x$.

A. It is tempting to divide both sides by x to give $x < 1$ but this is *not* correct, as will be seen by letting $x = -2$. The correct procedure is to subtract x from both sides to give $x^2 - x < 0$. Factorizing, we have $x(x - 1) < 0$ which will be true only so long as one and only one of the factors is negative i.e. iff $0 < x < 1$

An alternative procedure which avoids such possible confusions is to treat the inequality as if it were an equality and solve for the roots. This will tell us *all* the values of x for which the function is zero. For example, if we are asked to solve

$$2x > 4 - 2x^2 \qquad [2.9]$$

we rewrite as

$$2x^2 + 2x - 4 > 0 \qquad [2.10]$$

and solve [2.10] as if it were an equality:

$$2(x + 2)(x - 1) = 0$$

$$x = -2 \text{ or } x = 1. \qquad [2.11]$$

If we now select a value of x that lies to the left of -2 (say, $x = -3$) we can substitute this into [2.10] to see if the inequality is satisfied:

$$2(-3)^2 + 2(-3) - 4 = 8$$

and so $x < -2$ is one possible solution. Notice that if the statement is true for one value of $x < -2$ it must be true for all. This is illustrated in figure 2.1. In the same way, we can choose a value for x that lies between the two roots of [2.11]:

$$2(0)^2 + 2(0) - 4 = -4$$

and the inequality is *not* satisfied in the range $-2 < x < 1$. Finally, we can show that it is true for $x > 1$, so the complete solution to [2.9] is

$$x < -2; \, x > 1$$

(The argument here does assume that the function is a *continuous* one; i.e. that it can be drawn without removing pen from paper. A formal definition of continuity is given in chapter 4.)

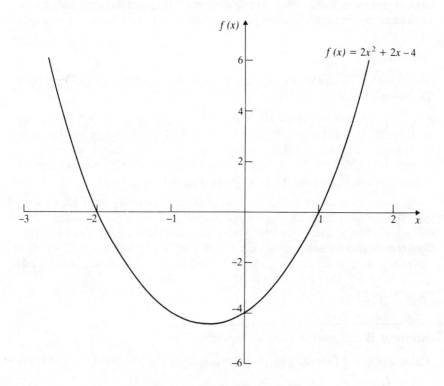

Figure 2.1 Solving an inequality

2.4 Simultaneous equations

If there are two unknowns then it is not possible to discover the values of each from one equation; for example, $x + 2y = 30$ cannot be solved as it stands. If we know the value of y then we can calculate the value of x and vice versa, but that is all. However, if we have a second equation in the same variables, e.g. $y - 2x - 5 = 0$, then it *may* be possible to solve the two equations simultaneously. There is no guarantee that a solution exists, but we can say in general that there must be at least as many equations as unknowns. If a solution does exist, there are a number of ways in which it may be found. We shall illustrate three different approaches with reference to two equations:

$$x + 2y = 30 \qquad\qquad [2.12]$$

$$y - 2x - 5 = 0. \qquad\qquad [2.13]$$

Which method one prefers may depend upon the model to be solved and/or personal taste. There is no 'best' method, and the only real advice is to get lots of practice.

Method A

Rewrite each simultaneous equation in the form $y = f_i(x)$; thus [2.12] and [2.13] become, respectively,

$$y = f_1(x) = \frac{30 - x}{2} \qquad\qquad [2.14]$$

$$y = f_2(x) = 2x + 5. \qquad\qquad [2.15]$$

Then equating [2.14] and [2.15] gives a single equation in x:

$$\frac{30 - x}{2} = 2x + 5$$

and this is solved easily to give $x = 4$. Substituting $x = 4$ into [2.14] then reveals that $y = 13$ and we should substitute both x and y values into [2.13] to check that we have made no mistakes:

$$13 - 2(4) - 5 = 0.$$

Method B

Calculate $y = f_2(x)$ as in [2.15] but substitute directly into [2.12] to give

$$x + 2(2x + 5) = 30$$

which can be solved in straightforward fashion to give $x = 4$ and hence $y = 13$ as before.

Method C

This method is rather different. The object is to derive from the original two equations a third which contains only one unknown. Multiply [2.12] by 2 and rearrange, then add [2.13] in a slightly rearranged form. The x-terms will now cancel out:

$$\begin{aligned}4y + 2x &= 60 \\ y - 2x &= 5 \\ \hline 5y \quad\quad &= 65\end{aligned}$$

[2.16]

From this it is obvious that $y = 13$, and this is substituted into either [2.12] or [2.13] to find $x = 4$.

Note: A complete solution of a simultaneous equation system consists of *one value for each of the unknowns.*

The principles used here can also be used for solving simultaneous quadratic equations, mixed systems of equations or larger sets of simultaneous systems with more unknowns.

Worked examples

Q. Solve the following simultaneous equations.

    (i) $x + 2y + 3w = 5$
    (ii) $2x + y + w = 3$
    (iii) $w + 2y - x = -1$

A. Using the most general technique, rewrite (iii) as

    (vi) $x = w + 2y + 1$

and substitute into (i) and (ii) to give

    (v) $(w + 2y + 1) + 2y + 3w = 4w + 4y + 1 = 5$

    (vi) $2(w + 2y + 1) + y + w = 3w + 5y + 2 = 3.$

Rewriting (v) gives

    $4y = 4 - 4w$ or $y = 1 - w.$

Substituting into (vi),

    $3w + 5(1 - w) = 1;\ w = 2.$

Now, $y = 1 - w = -1$, so, substituting for y and w into any of the equations, $x = 1$.

Q. Solve the following simultaneous equations:

    (i) $2x - y - w = -3$
    (ii) $x + y + w = 6$
    (iii) $x - 2y + w = 0$

A. Adding (i) and (ii) gives $3x = 3 \therefore x = 1$
Subtracting (iii) from (ii) gives $3y = 6 \therefore y = 2$
Substituting $x = 1$, $y = 2$ into any of the three equations gives $w = 3$.

Q. Solve the following simultaneous equations:

    (i) $x - 2y = 1$
    (ii) $x^2 + 4y^2 - 3x + 4y + 2 = 0$.

A. The obvious method is to rewrite (i) as $x = 1 + 2y$ and substitute into (ii):

$$(1 + 2y)^2 + 4y^2 - 3(1 + 2y) + 4y + 2 = 0$$

$$(1 + 4y + 4y^2) + 4y^2 - (3 + 6y) + 4y + 2 = 0$$

$$8y^2 + 2y = 2y(4y + 1) = 0$$

$$\therefore y = 0 \text{ or } y = \tfrac{-1}{4}$$

Substituting these values into (i) gives the corresponding values for x, and the complete solution is therefore

$$(x = 1, y = 0) \text{ and } (x = \tfrac{1}{2}, y = \tfrac{-1}{4}).$$

(A rather neater alternative is to use $x = 1 + 2y$ to deduce that

    (iii) $x^2 = 1 + 4y + 4y^2$.

Then rewrite (ii) as

$$x^2 - 3x + 1 + (4y^2 + 4y + 1) = 0$$

$$2x^2 - 3x + 1 = (2x - 1)(x - 1) = 0$$

and hence $x = \tfrac{1}{2}$ or $x = 1$, etc.)

2.5 Exercises

Section 2.2.1

Solve where possible the following equations:

    (i) $2 + x = 1 - x$ (iv) $x^2 + 3x - 3 = 0$

    (ii) $x^2 - x - 2 = 0$ (v) $x^3 - 4x^2 + 5x - 2 = 0$

    (iii) $2x^2 = 7x - 3$ (vi) $x^3 + 4x^2 = 3$

Section 2.2.2

Solve the following equations:

(i) $x^2 + 3x + 3 = 0$

(ii) $x^3 - 2x^2 + 2x - 1 = 0$

Section 2.3

Solve the following:

(i) $x^2 - 4 > 0$

(ii) $x^2 - 4 > 3x$

(iii) $x^3 - 8 < 0$

(iv) $(x - 4)^2 > 1$

(v) $x^2 - x + 1 < 0$

(vi) $|x - 2| > 0$

Section 2.4

Solve the following simultaneous equations:

(i) $y = 4x + 8$
$y = x - 1$

(iii) $y = x + w$
$2x - y = w$
$2y + 2x - 3w = 7$

(ii) $y - x = 1$
$x^2 - 2x + y - 3 = 0$

3 Economic applications I

These are applications of simultaneous equation systems. The systems and their solutions are carefully specified throughout – the actual process of solving the systems is left to the reader in the form of exercises.

3.1 Supply, demand and market equilibrium

There is a whole body of economic theory devoted to what we call the theory of demand, whose purpose is to determine the various factors that affect the demand for a product. The most important of these are considered to be:

1 the price of that product;
2 the prices of other products;
3 the incomes of the consumers;
4 tastes.

There are, of course, others that you might suggest (such as wealth, credit, interest rates and taxes), and some of these have been considered, both in theory and in practice. But for the time being we are concerned with the relationship between the quantity of a product that is demanded (Q^D) and the price of that product (P). It is this relationship that economist call the *demand function* or *demand curve*. The implicit assumption is that all other possible determinants of demand do *not* change when price changes (the so-called 'ceteris paribus' assumption). In mathematical notation we would write

$$Q^D = f(P). \tag{3.1}$$

Now, economics in fact tells us little about the shape or form of the function. In section 16.2 below we shall see how one might derive an individual's demand function from certain propositions and why we can say so little, but our mathematics is not yet up to this task. Indeed, even if it were this would not necessarily help us, since we are currently interested in the *aggregate* or *market demand curve*. Let me explain.

Suppose that a good is free (i.e., $P = 0$); it is reasonable to suppose that a consumer will use quite a lot of it. If, on the other hand, its price is high, then he or she is less likely to buy it. This relationship may be represented graphically as in figure 3.1. The simplest way to represent such a relationship algebraically is to write

$$Q^D = a - bP \quad P \geqslant 0; \; Q \geqslant 0 \tag{3.2}$$
$$a > 0; \; b > 0$$

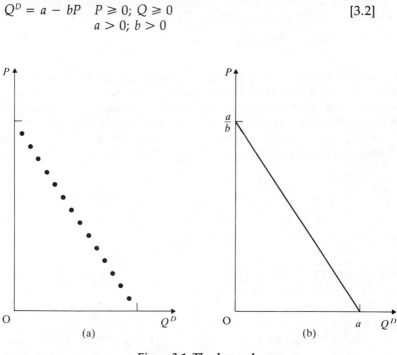

Figure 3.1 The demand curve

Note: The economic derivation implies that causality runs from prices to quantity. For reasons of historical accident rather than anything else, economists traditionally map price on the *vertical* axis, in contradiction to usual mathematical practice. Such is life!

To ascertain the points at which the function touches the axis we first set $P = 0$ and hence $Q^D = a$ in figure 3.1(b), then set $Q^D = 0$ and solve for P; i.e., $a - bP = 0 \therefore P = a/b$.

Note: We are interested only in values of P and Q that are non-negative. Unless otherwise specified, this is a generally accepted restriction and would not normally be stated explicitly. Where restrictions exist upon the values of parameters, these should be stated, but it is common to omit such specification where parameters are all positive.

3.1.1 Market demand curves

We now add a second individual with a similar, but not identical, demand curve:

$$\tilde{Q}^D = \tilde{a} - bP \quad \tilde{a} > a. \tag{3.3}$$

Given the price, total demand is the sum of the demands of the two individuals, so it is tempting to sum [3.2] and [3.3] to give

$$Q = (a - bP) + (\tilde{a} - bP)$$
$$= (a + \tilde{a}) - 2bP. \tag{3.4}$$

As it stands, however, this would be incorrect and to see this, consider figure 3.2. The first two sections represent the two individual demand curves and the final section the sum of the previous two – at each price the quantity plotted (Q) is the sum of the two demands ($Q^D + \tilde{Q}^D$). Notice the 'kink' in the function at $P = a/b$. Unlike [3.4], the 'true' demand curve is not linear.

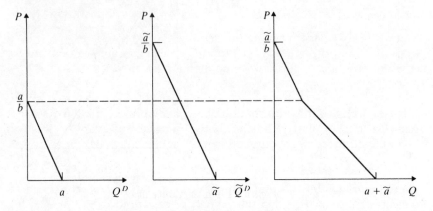

Figure 3.2 Aggregating demand curves

What did we do wrong? We forgot that our demand curve was defined only for $P, Q > 0$. When the price rose above a/b the first individual could not buy so his demand became zero. We should have defined his curve as

$$Q^D = a - bP \qquad\qquad P < a/b \tag{3.5}$$
$$= 0 \qquad\qquad\qquad P \geqslant a/b$$

and it would have immediately been obvious that we could not simply add the two mathematical functions. (Try drawing the functions if $b = 2$, $a = 20$ and $\tilde{a} = 40$ for a practical demonstration.)

There are, in fact, lots of problems with aggregation, of which this is just one, but I went over it in some detail to show two things:

1 It is very easy to make mistakes if you do not think about what you are doing. Never simply take the result of mathematical analysis of an economic problem without asking yourself if it makes sense, and always take great care in doing the analysis correctly.

2 It is in fact very difficult to *prove* anything in economics. We postulate hypotheses which we hope are subject to refutation. If we can possibly write these in mathematical formulations without doing too much injustice to the economic concept, then this has advantages – it encourages us to be precise in our definitions and enables us to infer certain consequences. If we cannot test the original propositions, then it may be possible to say something about the derived propositions. For all this we need statistical and econometric techniques, and there is no doubt that much progress has been made this way, but we have not *proved* anything. (It may of course be possible to *disprove* something. Two statements may prove to be mutually exclusive.)

3.1.2 Market equilibrium

We now move on from aggregation problems and simply assume that it is possible to find a suitable function to represent aggregate demand for a commodity. Let us write this simply as

$$Q^D = a_0 - a_1 P \qquad\qquad a_0 > 0;\ a_1 > 0. \qquad\qquad [3.6]$$

Corresponding to this information about demand, we may deduce that there exists a supply relationship between price and quantity (this will be examined more closely in section 11.2) which may be represented as

$$Q^S = b_0 + b_1 P \qquad\qquad b_1 > 0 \qquad\qquad [3.7]$$

where the model tells us that at higher prices suppliers will be prepared to supply more of the good than when prices are low.

Now we define *equilibrium* as that state in which demand and supply are equal (strictly speaking, we should say that this is the condition for markets to clear); i.e., when

$$Q^D = Q^S \qquad\qquad\qquad [3.8]$$

which gives us three equations in three unknowns, P, Q^D and Q^S. Solving [3.6], [3.7] and [3.8] gives a market equilibrium (market-clearing) price of

$$P = \frac{a_0 - b_0}{a_1 + b_1} = (\text{say})\ P^* \qquad\qquad [3.9]$$

and substituting [3.9] into either [3.6] or [3.7] gives an equlibrium quantity of

$$Q = \frac{a_0 b_1 + a_1 b_0}{a_1 + b_1} = \text{(say) } Q^*. \tag{3.10}$$

The analysis of these problems has been carried out in general terms, but it may help readers to understand the concepts better if they actually do some numerical examples. Three such are given at the end of this chapter. Notice that in the second it is assumed that the markets for two goods are related, with the price of one affecting demand for the other. Solution therefore requires simultaneous solution of both markets.

3.1.3 Comparative static analysis

We may be interested in asking what happens if some factor other than price changes. Suppose, for example, that there is a change in income or taste such that more is demanded at every price. If this change in demand is given as Δa_0 we must replace [3.6] with

$$Q^D = a_0 - a_1 P + \Delta a_0 \qquad\qquad \Delta a_0 > 0. \tag{3.11}$$

Then, solving [3.11], [3.7] and [3.8] simultaneously gives

$$P = \frac{a_0 - b_0}{a_1 + b_1} + \frac{\Delta a_0}{a_1 + b_1} = \text{(say) } P^* + \Delta P. \tag{3.12}$$

The choice of notation is, of course, purely arbitrary, but subtracting the definition of P^* in [3.9] from the new equilibrium in [3.12] gives

$$\Delta P = \frac{\Delta a_0}{a_1 + b_1} \quad \text{or} \quad \frac{\Delta P}{\Delta a_0} = \frac{1}{a_1 + b_1}. \tag{3.13}$$

The second of these two representations is known as the *comparative statics multiplier*. It shows the effect upon the equilibrium of a unit change in the intercept term a_0. Notice that, since a_1 and b_1 are both positive, this change must be positive; in other words the equilibrium price must go up. In a similar way we may calculate the new equilibrium quantity

$$Q^* + \Delta Q = \frac{a_0 b_1 + a_1 b_0}{a_1 + b_1} + \frac{b_1 \Delta a_0}{a_1 + b_1}$$

and hence the equivalent comparative static multiplier for equilibrium quantity

$$\frac{\Delta Q}{\Delta a_0} = \frac{b_1}{a_1 + b_1} \tag{3.14}$$

It follows from [3.14] that the change in equilibrium quantity is necessarily positive, but since $b_1 < (a_1 + b_1)$ the multiplier is less than 1.

Hence an arbitrary increase in demand Δa_0 is not fully translated into an increase in equilibrium quantity – part of it leads instead to an increase in price. This is shown graphically in figure 3.3.

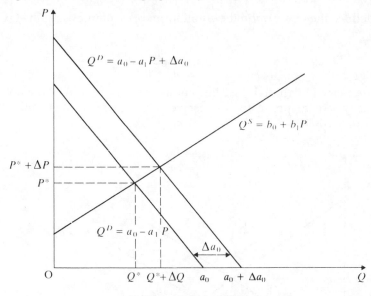

Figure 3.3 A shift in demand

Note: This sort of analysis can be very informative, but of itself does not tell us what will happen when the value of one of the parameters changes. In order to know what actually happens we need to specify the dynamic behaviour of a model. This will be the subject of chapter 5. In the meantime, we shall assume that markets are 'well behaved' and that they do settle down at equilibrium after some suitable elapse of time.

3.1.4 Imposition of an excise tax

Now let us consider a slightly more complex model in which the government has placed a tax (T) on each unit of output sold. The effect of this is to reduce the price that the supplier receives for each unit. Thus we must replace the supply function [3.7] with

$$Q^S = b_0 + b_1 P^S \qquad [3.15]$$

where the demand price (P) and the supply price (P^S) are related by

$$P^S = P - T. \qquad [3.16]$$

Together with equations [3.7] and [3.8], equations [3.15] and [3.16] give us four equations in four unknowns: Q^S, Q^D, P^S and P. Solving for P

gives

$$P = \frac{a_0 - b_0}{a_1 + b_1} + \frac{b_1 T}{a_1 + b_1} = \text{(say) } P^* + \Delta P.$$ [3.17]

We can deduce the effect upon the equilibrium price of imposing the tax as

$$\Delta P = \frac{b_1}{a_1 + b_1} \cdot T \qquad\qquad 0 < \frac{b_1}{a_1 + b_1} < 1.$$

In words, price will definitely rise but not by the full amount of the tax. Readers may like to prove for themselves that quantity must fall as shown in figure 3.4.

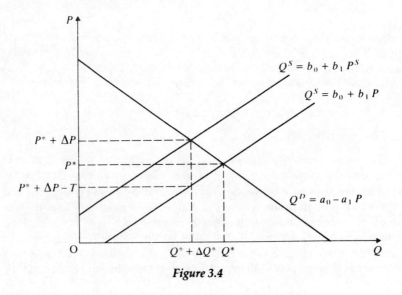

Figure 3.4

3.2 Determining the level of income

Our second example is taken from the area of macroeconomics and is a highly simplified model commonly used in textbooks to explain the determination of income.

We start from the proposition that individuals spend on consumption C a minimum amount a which may be financed from past savings, plus a proportion of their income Y, and we therefore arrive at the proposition that

$$C = a + bY \quad \text{where } a > 0$$ [3.18]

$$0 < b < 1.$$

Total expenditure E in the economy consists of consumption plus the expenditure on investment goods I, which for the time being we will assume to be determined outside the model. Thus

$$E \equiv C + I. \qquad [3.19]$$

Finally, we impose an equilibrium condition that income equals expenditure, i.e.

$$Y = E. \qquad [3.20]$$

Solving these three equations simultaneously, we can calculate the equilibrium income as

$$Y = \frac{a + I}{1 - b} = \text{(say)} \ Y^*. \qquad [3.21]$$

Note: Some texts specify the equilibrium condition as $S = I$ where S is savings. If we note that by definition $S \equiv Y - C$ (i.e., savings is what remains after consumption) and remember from [3.19] that $I \equiv E - C$, it follows immediately that $Y = E$ and hence that the two conditions are exactly the same.

3.2.1 The multiplier

One may now ask the question, 'What happens if we have a government that contributes to expenditure?' Let us call this component of expenditure G, and instead of [3.19] we have total expenditure

$$E \equiv C + I + G. \qquad [3.22]$$

Solving [3.22], [3.18] and [3.20], we have a new equilibrium:

$$Y = \frac{a + I}{1 - b} + \frac{G}{1 - b} = \text{(say)} \ Y^* + \Delta Y. \qquad [3.23]$$

Then, subtracting the old equilibrium [3.21] from [3.23], we can readily see that

$$\Delta Y = \frac{1}{1 - b} \cdot G. \qquad [3.24]$$

We have a comparative statics multiplier of $1/(1 - b)$. (This is in fact the original usage of the term 'multiplier'.) Because $0 < b < 1$, it follows that $0 < (1 - b) < 1$ and hence that $1/(1 - b) > 1$. That is to say, an additional amount of expenditure introduced by the government will increase equilibrium income by *more than the original injection*. The higher is the parameter b (which is known as the *marginal propensity to consume*), the higher will be the multiplier, and the more potent will this sort of government intervention be. (A diagramatic representation of this model is shown by figure 3.5.)

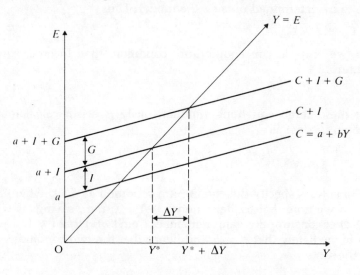

Figure 3.5 Government expenditure

3.2.2 Balanced budget

Clearly, the knowledge that government expenditure or, more correctly, *fiscal policy* can be a very potent weapon for raising the level of income is of great importance; but where, you might ask, does the money come from to finance this expenditure? If the government has to raise the revenue from increased taxation, does this not put us back where we started from? The answer to that is 'no', and to see why consider the following elaboration. This time we re-specify our consumption function to subtract out personal (i.e. income) tax before the individual gets a chance to spend his income:

$$C = a + b(Y - T) \qquad [3.25]$$

and add a new equation which imposes the requirement of a balanced budget:

$$G = T. \qquad [3.26]$$

Solving [3.25] and [3.26] simultaneously with [3.20] and [3.22], we have

$$Y = \frac{a + I}{1 - b} + G = (\text{say}) \ Y^* + \Delta Y. \qquad [3.27]$$

Subtracting [3.21] from [3.27], we can see that the total impact upon income of government expenditure is $\Delta Y = G$. In other words, equilibrium income is raised by the amount of the expenditure and the multiplier – the 'balanced budget' multiplier is 1.

3.2.3 Proportional income tax

Let us now suppose that the government does not feel obliged to balance its budget by means of taxation but that it nevertheless imposes taxes on income. These are not of the 'lump-sum' variety but rather a simple proportion (t) of income. Thus, to the model of the previous section we add

$$T = tY \qquad\qquad\qquad 0 < t < 1. \qquad\qquad\qquad [3.28]$$

Then, solving [3.20], [3.22], [3.25] and [3.28],

$$Y = \frac{a + I + G}{1 - b(1 - t)}.$$

We can see immediately that the impact of changing government expenditure will now be rather different. Instead of each unit of G leading to an increase of $1/(1 - b)$ in Y, we shall instead produce an increase of $1/[1 - b(1 - t)]$, and since $t > 0$ this must be a smaller increase. The multiplier is smaller in this case than before the introduction of income tax, though it is still greater than 1.

3.2.4 Other means of finance

If the budget is not to be balanced we shall need other means of finance. One possibility is to borrow money from the public, but this will tend to raise the rate of interest. This does not matter if the rate of interest has no other effect upon the model, but if (say) the level of investment is not in fact exogenous but is itself a function of the rate of interest, there will be an additional impact. A similar position occurs if the budget deficit (surplus), i.e. $G - T$, is financed by printing more money. To deal with such problems we must expand the model. So far we have proposed that (combining [3.20] and [3.22] into [3.29])

$$Y = C + I + G \qquad\qquad\qquad\qquad\qquad\qquad [3.29]$$

$$C = a + b(Y - T) \qquad\qquad\qquad\qquad\qquad\qquad [3.25]$$

$$T = tY \qquad\qquad\qquad\qquad\qquad\qquad\qquad\qquad [3.28]$$

$$I = d - eR \quad \text{where } d > 0, e > 0 \text{ and } R \text{ is the rate of interest.} \qquad [3.30]$$

We can no longer 'solve' this model since there are now five unknowns

(Y, C, I, T and R) but only four equations; however, we may write it more neatly, substituting [3.25], [3.28] and [3.30] into [3.29], as

$$Y = a + b(Y - T) + d - eR + G$$

and rewriting this in the form

$$Y = \frac{a + d + G}{1 - b(1 - t)} - \frac{eR}{1 - b(1 - t)}$$

[3.31]

which relates the equilibrium quantity Y to the level of R. This relationship is known as the *IS curve*, presumably since it represents all those combinations of R and Y for which $I = S$.

If we put in suitable values for the parameters we can establish the likely shape of this function. Indeed, the restrictions upon the parameters are already sufficient to establish the general shape. Readers are advised to demonstrate for themselves that it is indeed as shown in figure 3.6.

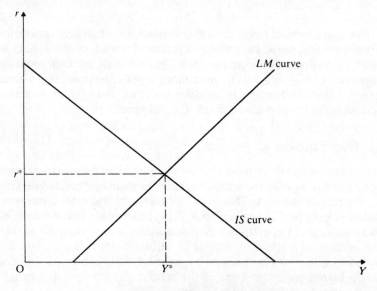

Figure 3.6 IS and LM curves

The advantages of mathematical treatment include the possibility of allowing for nonlinearities in any of the functions. To complete the solution we require another equation relating R to Y so that we can solve the two simultaneously. One way of doing this is to consider the working of the money market. Without going into the economic rationale, let us assume that the demand and supply functions for money may be written as

$$M^D = kY - lR \qquad\qquad\qquad\qquad\qquad [3.32]$$

$$M^S = \bar{M} \qquad\qquad\qquad\qquad\qquad\qquad [3.33]$$

which is a way of saying that demand is a simple linear function of income and the rate of interest, and that money supply is fixed (presumably by the authorities) at some particular level $\bar{M}$. Now, equilibrium in the money market requires demand to equal supply, so adding

$$M^D = M^S \qquad\qquad\qquad\qquad\qquad\qquad [3.34]$$

we can substitute [3.32] and [3.33] into [3.34] and then rearrange to give

$$Y = \frac{\bar{M}}{k} + \frac{l}{k}R. \qquad\qquad\qquad\qquad\qquad [3.35]$$

This is a relationship known in economics as the *LM curve*. Again, the reader should verify its shape (see figure 3.6).

Putting this together with the *IS* curve derived in section 3.2.4, we can now solve the two simultaneously. The actual solution is left to readers as an exercise, but notice that it will specify the equilibrium value Y^* as a function of the parameters (a, b, d, e, t, k and l) and of two variables (G and $\bar{M}$) determined by the authorities. Thus, it is possible to investigate the effects of changing G (fiscal policy) or of changing $\bar{M}$ (monetary policy), or indeed the effect on the model of changes in any of the parameters.

Macroeconomics texts will often take the mathematics as far as [3.31] and [3.35] and thereafter adopt a diagrammatic approach. Though this may be convenient, it may give rise to a false interpretation of the model. One must not forget that both relationships are the result of solving a set of equations which include equilibrium conditions ([3.20] and [3.33] respectively). Thus, the *IS* curve [3.31] tells us not what income (Y) *will* be for a certain value R, but rather what it *must* be if there is to be equilibrium in the market for goods.

3.3   Exercises

Section 3.1.2

1. For the following demand and supply functions, state the economically sensible ranges of P and Q for which they are defined. What are the equilibrium price and quantity?

   (i) $Q^D = 16 - 2P$ (ii) $Q^S = -4 + 3P$

2. Given the following demand and supply functions for two inter-

dependent commodities, what are the equilibrium prices and quantities?

$$Q_1^D = 8 - 2P_1 + P_2 \qquad\qquad Q_2^D = 16 + P_1 - P_2$$
$$Q_1^S = -5 + 3P_1 \qquad\qquad Q_2^S = -1 + 2P_2$$

3. Given the following nonlinear market models, find the economically meaningful solution in each case:

(i) $Q^D = Q^S$
   $Q^D = 11 - 2P^2$
   $Q^S = -5 + 2P^2$

(ii) $Q^D = Q^S$
   $Q^D = 9 - 2P^2$
   $Q^S = -5 + 3P$

Section 3.2.4

Solve the *IS/LM* model outlined in the chapter by solving equations [3.31] and [3.35] simultaneously.

Calculate the effect upon this equilibrium solution of a change in government expenditure ΔG, and hence derive the multiplier $\Delta Y/\Delta G$. Is your answer greater than or less than $1/(1 - b)$ as derived in section 3.2.1, and if so why?

Part II

Introduction to dynamics

This Part contains a number of mathematical techniques which may not, at first sight, appear to be closely related. In most mathematics books you will find them spread out in various chapters – some may even be omitted. To the economist, however, they have a coherence that may be lost on the mathematician. Much of economics is concerned with the behaviour of variables over time and each of the techniques discussed in this part is of particular use in this respect. There is one major technique that will necessarily be left until later (see chapter 12 for a discussion of differential equations), but a great deal of dynamic analysis of both discrete and continuous variables can be done with a few very simple techniques. In chapter 7 we will consider two applications. The first introduces the techniques of discounting, which is of such use in investment analysis. The second application illustrates the value of dynamic analysis in general and the technique of difference equations in particular with reference to the analysis of multipliers and the implications for government policy.

Part II

Introduction to dynamics

4 Limits and summations

4.1 Limits

For most purposes an intuitive definition will suffice. Consider the following statement:

$$\lim_{x \to a} g(x) = L.$$ [4.1]

This says that L is the limit of $g(x)$ as x tends to a, where a, L are both real numbers, and it means that if x is very close to a then the value of the function is very close to L. Similarly, the statement

$$\lim_{x \to \infty} g(x) = L$$

tells us that as the value of x becomes very large then the value of the function approaches very close to L.

Let us interpret these concepts by considering the function

$$g(x) = \frac{x^2 - 1}{x - 1} \qquad x \neq 1.$$ [4.2]

The function is not defined for $x = 1$, but we can ask what happens as x is very close to 1. To find the answer choose values of x getting progressively closer to 1:

x	3	2	1.5	1.1	1.01	1.001	....
$g(x)$	4	3	2.5	2.1	2.01	2.001	....

It is clear that the value of $g(x)$ is approaching 2. Notice two things about this function:
1 If we had started with a value for x of less than 1 we would have ended up with the same answer for $\lim g(x)$. While this is common, it does not have to be the case.
2 Provided x is never equal to 1, we can perform the division so as to simplify the function [4.2], giving

$$g(x) = x + 1 \qquad\qquad x \neq 1.$$

Notice that we can define some function $f(x) = x + 1$ which is valid for all values of x. In this case $f(1) = 2$, so we have a situation in which the limit as $x \to 1$ is identical to the value of the function when $x = 1$; i.e.,

$$\lim_{x \to 1} f(x) = f(1).$$

(A similar statement for $g(x)$ would not be true since $g(1)$ does not exist.) When it is possible to make such a statement for all values of x, then the function is said to be *continuous*.

Note: Strictly speaking, we have to assert that this is true whichever direction we come from, so we would actually define a continuous function as one in which

$$\lim_{x \to a+} f(x) = \lim_{x \to a-} f(x) = f(a) \qquad \text{for all } a \qquad [4.3]$$

where $x \to a+$ means that we are approaching a from larger numbers and $x \to a-$ means that we are approaching a from numbers less than a.

To see that left and right-hand limits need not always be the same, consider the function

$$f(x) = \frac{1}{x}. \qquad [4.4]$$

x	3	2	1	0.5	0.1	0.001	....
$f(x)$	$\frac{1}{3}$	$\frac{1}{2}$	1	2	10	1000	....

In this case we find that the function $f(x)$ increases without limit. By contrast, if we approach from the left-hand (negative) side we find that $f(x)$ *decreases* without limit:

x	-3	-2	-1	-0.5	-0.1	-0.001	....
$f(x)$	$-\frac{1}{3}$	$-\frac{1}{2}$	-1	-2	-10	-1000	....

So clearly in this case

$$\infty = \lim_{x = 0+} f(x) \neq \lim_{x = 0-} f(x) = -\infty \qquad [4.4]$$

and thus is *not* continuous at the point where $x = 0$. In general, if the $+$ or $-$ sign is omitted, it is usual to assume that the two limits are the same.

4.1.1 Limit theorems

There are a number of properties of limits which prove to be very useful. Most of them are intuitively straightforward and formal proofs are not given here. Basically, they tell is that the limits of functions behave like any other numbers, and this means that finding the limit of a complicated expression may be decomposed into a number of simpler operations. Notice in particular the 'function of a function' rule. To find the limit of, for example,

$$f(x) = (x - 1)^{17}$$

it is not necessary to expand the function out, since

$$\lim_{x \to 1} (x - 1)^{17} = [\lim_{x \to 1} (x - 1)]^{17} = 0.$$

Formally, the rules may be written as follows.

Rules: If $\lim_{x \to a} f(x) = L_1$ and $\lim_{x \to a} g(x) = L_2$, then

I $\lim_{x \to a} \{f(x) + g(x)\} = L_1 + L_2$ [4.5]

II $\lim_{x \to a} \{f(x) - g(x)\} = L_1 - L_2$ [4.6]

III $\lim_{x \to a} \{f(x) \cdot g(x)\} = L_1 \times L_2$ [4.7]

IV $\lim_{x \to a} \{f(x)/g(x)\} = L_1/L_2, \; L_2 \neq 0$ [4.8]

V $\lim_{x \to a} \{h(f(x))\} = h(L_1)$ [4.9]

where $h(x)$ is itself a continuous function at $x = a$.

Worked example

Q. Consider the simple function $f(x) = x - 3$. As x approaches the value 3 from either side, the limit is 0. Furthermore, $f(3) = 0$ and so the function is continuous at that point. Similarly, the simple function $g(x) = x^2$ is continuous at $x = 3$, the function taking the value 9. What are the limits of the following as $x \to 3$:

(i) $h(x) = \dfrac{x - 3}{x^2}$ (ii) $m(x) = \dfrac{x^2}{x - 3}$

A. (i) Using equation [4.8], we may rewrite $h(x)$ thus:
$$\lim_{x \to 3} h(x) = \lim_{x \to 3} f(x)/\lim_{x \to 3} g(x) = 0/9 = 0$$

(ii) This time we *cannot* use the same device, since it would entail dividing by zero. It is however readily apparent that, as the denominator approaches zero, the expression becomes larger in absolute value though left and right hand limits have opposite signs.

4.2 Summation

A discrete function is defined for particular values of its argument. It is common for these values to be the natural numbers 1, 2, 3, ... It is also common to want to add together the values that this function takes for a particular set of the natural numbers, (say) 1, 2, 3, ..., n. Thus, if w_t represents the wages earned in each successive period (w_1, w_2, w_3, ...), then we might wish to calculate total income over the first 12 periods. Denoting total income as y, we would have

$$y = w_1 + w_2 + w_3 + w_4 + w_5 + w_6 + w_7 + w_8 + w_9 + w_{10} + w_{11} + w_{12}$$

[4.10]

It would be easier if we could find a shorter way of representing this sum and so we introduce the idea of a *summation operator* Σ. In this notation, [4.10] would be written in a much more concise fashion:

$$y = \sum_{t=1}^{12} w_t$$

The Σ sign tells us to add together all the values of the function w_t for values of t running from 1 to 12 inclusive. The letter t is known as the *running variable*, and although t is a common letter to use one can use any symbol so long as it is clearly identified as such. The limits to the summation are given above and below the Σ. The lower limit need not be 1; it could be zero or any natural number. The upper limit can be any natural number greater than the lower limit. The following examples are all valid uses of a summation operator:

$$\sum_{i=0}^{\infty} q_i ; \quad \sum_{i=1}^{n} x_i ; \quad \sum_{i=2}^{n-1} p_i ; \quad \sum_{j=2}^{n-1} p_j$$

Notice that the third and fourth expressions represent exactly the same operation; the choice of running variable does not affect the summation in any way.

Note: Sometimes it is considered obvious which is the running variable, and/or sometimes the end-points may be considered obvious. The following variations of notation are therefore acceptable under varying circumstances:

$$\sum_{i=1}^{n} x_i ; \quad \sum_{1}^{n} x_i ; \quad \sum_{i} x_i ; \quad \sum x_i$$

4.2.1 Operations under the Σ sign

In principle, it is possible to write out in full most expressions represented by summation operators, and it is therefore possible in these cases to check that they have been manipulated correctly. It is, however, extremely tedious. In the case of infinite summations it is not even possible, although it is often possible to write out sufficient terms to deduce the appropriate solution. In every case, it is likely to be more convenient to use already established rules in order to perform these manipulations, and the basic rules are listed below. Consider the expression

$$\sum_{i=1}^{n} cx_i = cx_1 + cx_2 + \ldots + cx_n. \qquad [4.11]$$

Removing the common factor c from each expression, we can rewrite [4.11] as

$$c(x_1 + x_2 + \ldots + x_n) = c \sum_{i=1}^{n} x_i$$

and we have proved rule II below (equation [4.13]). The remaining rules may all be proved in similar fashion and this is left to readers as an exercise (answers are at the back of the book). Notice that, as ever, multiplication takes precedence over addition (rule V).

Rules:

$$\text{I} \quad \sum_{i=1}^{n} c = nc \qquad [4.12]$$

$$\text{II.} \quad \sum_{i=1}^{n} cx_i = c \sum_{i=1}^{n} x_i \qquad [4.13]$$

$$\text{III} \quad \sum_{i=1}^{n} (x_i + y_i) = \sum_{i=1}^{n} x_i + \sum_{i=1}^{n} y_i \qquad [4.14]$$

$$\text{IV} \quad \sum_{i=1}^{k} x_i + \sum_{i=k+1}^{n} x_i = \sum_{i=1}^{n} x_i \qquad [4.15]$$

$$\text{V} \quad \sum_{i=1}^{n} (x_i + y_i)^2 = \sum_{i=1}^{n} x_i^2 + 2 \sum_{i=1}^{n} x_i y_i + \sum_{i=1}^{n} y_i^2 \qquad [4.16]$$

Worked example

Q. Given that $\sum_{i=1}^{n} x_i = 15$ and $\sum_{i=1}^{n} x_i^2 = 55$, calculate $\sum_{i=1}^{n} (x_i + 1)^2$.

A. Using rule V (equation [4.16]) and substituting $y_i = c$ (i.e. the same constant value irrespective of i), we have

$$\sum_{i=1}^{n} (x_i + c)^2 = \sum_{i=1}^{n} x_i^2 + 2 \sum_{i=1}^{n} x_i c + \sum_{i=1}^{n} c^2. \qquad [4.17]$$

Substituting [4.12], [4.13] into [4.17], i.e. using rules I and II, we have

$$\sum_{i=1}^{n} (x_i + c)^2 = \sum_{i=1}^{n} x_i^2 + 2c \sum_{i=1}^{n} x_i + nc^2. \qquad [4.18]$$

If $c = 1$, then

$$\sum_{i=1}^{n} (x_i + 1)^2 = \sum_{i=1}^{n} x_i^2 + 2 \sum_{i=1}^{n} x_i + n$$

$$= 55 + 2(15) + n$$

$$= 85 + n.$$

4.2.2 Double summations

Suppose that we need to calculate y^2 where $y = \Sigma_{i=1}^{n} x_i$. Since $y^2 = y \cdot y$ we can write

$$y^2 = y \cdot \sum_{i=1}^{n} x_i. \qquad [4.19]$$

Since y is a constant, we can use rule II above and write [4.19] as

$$y^2 = \sum_{i=1}^{n} x_i y = \sum_{i=1}^{n} x_i \left(\sum_{j=1}^{n} x_j \right). \qquad [4.20]$$

Remember that the choice of running variable is arbitrary, so it is convenient to use a different letter for the second summation. If we define a new variable u_i such that

$$u_i = x_i \sum_{j=1}^{n} x_j \qquad [4.21]$$

then by rule II, x_i being constant for any value of j, we can write [4.21] as

$$u_i = \sum_{j=1}^{n} x_i x_j. \qquad [4.22]$$

Substituting [4.21] into [4.20] and then using [4.22], we have

$$y^2 = \sum_{i=1}^{n} u_i = \sum_{i=1}^{n} \left(\sum_{j=1}^{n} x_i x_j \right)$$ [4.23]

and we have an additional rule for our collection.

Rule:

$$\text{VI} \left(\sum_{i=1}^{n} x_i \right)^2 = \sum_{i=1}^{n} \sum_{j=1}^{n} x_i x_j.$$ [4.24]

There are other sorts of double summation that arise from time to time, but few are used by the economist. Two particular pieces of notation are worth commenting upon, however. It is sometimes desirable to exclude the cases where $i = j$, and this would be written as

$$\sum_{i=1}^{n} \sum_{j \neq i} x_i x_j.$$

Second, it is legitimate to use the running variable from the first summation as an end-point for the second. Thus the following is quite acceptable:

$$\sum_{i=1}^{n} \sum_{j=1}^{i} x_i x_j.$$

Using these various rules, it is possible to write all sorts of complex summations very concisely.

Worked example

Q. Write the following summation in short form:

$$y = x_0 + 2x_1 + 4x_2 + 8x_3 + 16x_4$$

A. The running variable goes from 0 to 4. Let us call this t. The coefficient on each term is itself a function of the running variable; $1 = 2^0$, $2 = 2^1$, $4 = 2^2$, $8 = 2^3$ and so on. We can write therefore

$$y = \sum_{t=0}^{4} 2^t x_t.$$

4.3 Exercises

Section 4.1.1

Find the limits of the following as x tends to (a) 2; (b) positive infinity:

(i) $(x - 2)^2$

(iv) $\dfrac{x^2 + x - 6}{x - 2}$

(ii) $(x - 2)^{-1}$

(v) $\dfrac{(x - 1)^3}{x}$

(iii) $4 - x^2$

Section 4.2.2

1 Write the following in short form:

(i) $x_0 + 2x_1 + 3x_2 + 4x_3 + 5x_4$

(ii) $5x_0 + 4x_1 + 3x_2 + 2x_3 + x_4$

(iii) $x_1^2 - x_2^2 + x_3^2 - x_4^2$

2 Write the following as a single summation:

$$\sum_{j=1}^{n} \sum_{i=1}^{j} x_i$$

5 Growth and logarithms

5.1 Progressions

A sequence is a discrete function defined on the ordered set of real numbers and in which successive values of the function are related in some way. The best-known of these are the simple and compound growth functions, though there are of course many others.

5.1.1 Simple growth function

Also known as an 'arithmetic progression', the simple growth function is one in which the value of x increases by a fixed amount each observation:

$$x_t = x_{t-1} + c. \tag{5.1}$$

Starting from a known value x_0 in time zero, we can deduce the value in each succeeding period thus:

$$x_1 = x_0 + c$$
$$x_2 = x_1 + c$$
$$\quad = (x_0 + c) + c = x_0 + 2c$$
$$x_3 = x_2 + c = (x_0 + 2c) + c = x_0 + 3c$$
$$\vdots$$
$$x_t = x_{t-1} + c = x_0 + ct. \tag{5.2}$$

A commonplace example of such a growth function would be a queue for the bus. At 7.00 pm there are 10 people waiting. From that point on people begin to arrive steadily, 2 every minute. At 7.15 pm (i.e. after 15 minutes) there will be

$$x_{15} = x_0 + 15c = 10 + 15(2) = 40.$$

5.1.2 Compound growth

In the previous section we assumed that the rate of arrivals at the bus stop was regular. Growth occurred in a simple fashion. But for many everyday examples this is not an appropriate assumption. It may be more reasonable to expect the size of the increase to be proportional to the current value of the variable.

Consider, for example, a savings account. An individual deposits a sum of £120 with a building society and at the end of one year receives interest at 10 per cent or 10/100 of the original investment. The account now contains a sum (x_1) given by the formula

$$x_1 = £120 + (\tfrac{1}{10} \times 120)$$

$$= £120(1 + \tfrac{1}{10}) = £120 \times 1.1 = £132.$$

In general, if the initial deposit is x_0 and the rate of interest is r, we may write

$$x_1 = x_0(1 + r).$$

After a further year the account will contain

$$x_2 = x_1(1 + r)$$

$$= x_0(1 + r)(1 + r) = x_0(1 + r)^2$$

$$x_3 = x_0(1 + r)^3$$

$$\vdots$$

$$x_t = x_0(1 + r)^t. \tag{5.3}$$

Equation [5.3] is known as a *compound growth function*. It can be written in a slightly different way by letting $c = (1 + r)$; i.e.,

$$x_t = x_0 c^t = c x_{t-1}. \tag{5.4}$$

Notice that in general c does not have to be greater than 1. It need not even be positive. If we know that $|c| < 1$, then the value of x_t will tend to zero as t tends to infinity; i.e.,

$$\lim_{t \to \infty} x_t = x_0 \lim_{t \to \infty} c^t = 0 \quad |c| < 1. \tag{5.5}$$

The sequence (known as a *geometric progression*) is said to converge. It follows that eventually x_t becomes so small that adding it to the previous terms in the sequence has an infinitesimal effect upon the total so far. It is to this summation we now turn.

5.1.3 Summing a geometric progression

Define S_n as the sum of the first n values of a geometric progression starting from $t = 0$; i.e.,

$$S_n = \sum_{t=0}^{n-1} x_t. \tag{5.6}$$

(Notice that S_n is defined only for $n = 0, 1, 2, \ldots$ and is itself a sequence function.)

If we substitute for x_t and write out the expression we have

$$S_n = x_0 + x_0c + x_0c^2 + \ldots + x_0c^{n-1}. \qquad [5.7]$$

Multiply both sides by c

$$cS_n = x_0c + x_0c^2 + \ldots + x_0c^{n-1} + x_0c^n. \qquad [5.8]$$

Subtracting [5.8] from [5.7], most of the terms cancel out, leaving

$$S_n - cS_n = x_0 - x_0c^n$$

$$S_n = \frac{x_0(1 - c^n)}{1 - c}. \qquad [5.9]$$

This formula is always correct irrespective of the value of c, but the interesting question concerns what happens as n tends to infinity. Using the rules on limits derived in the previous chapter,

$$\lim_{n \to \infty} S_n = \frac{x_0}{1 - c} \lim_{n \to \infty} (1 - c^n) \qquad [5.10]$$

and the answer depends upon the value of c. If $|c| < 1$ then, as in equation [5.5], the term c^n tends to zero and [5.10] becomes

$$\lim_{n \to \infty} S_n = \frac{x_0}{1 - c} \qquad |c| < 1. \qquad [5.11]$$

In other words, if a geometric progression x_t is itself convergent, then so is its sum – a result that proves very useful in economics.

Worked examples

Q. Calculate the sum to infinity of the following series:
$$1, -\tfrac{1}{2}, \tfrac{1}{4}, -\tfrac{1}{8}, \ldots$$

A. Taking any two sequential terms, $x_t = cx_{t-1}$; i.e., $x_t/x_{t-1} = c$. In this example

$$\frac{-\tfrac{1}{2}}{1} = \frac{\tfrac{1}{4}}{-\tfrac{1}{2}} = \ldots = -\frac{1}{2}$$

so we do in fact have a geometric progression the first term in which (x_0) is 1. Since $|-\tfrac{1}{2}| < 1$, we can use the formula in [5.11] to calculate

$$\lim_{n \to \infty} \sum_{t=0}^{n} (-\tfrac{1}{2})^t = \frac{1}{1 - (-\tfrac{1}{2})} = \frac{1}{1\tfrac{1}{2}} = \frac{2}{3}$$

$Q.$ Given the series
  3, 9, 27, 81, ...
  calculate (i) the sum of the first 8 terms;
            (ii) the sum to infinity.

$A.$ The starting value (x_0) is 3 and the ratio of successive terms (c) is also
  3, so the sum of the first n terms is given by

$$S_n = \frac{3(1 - 3^n)}{1 - 3} = -\tfrac{3}{2}(1 - 3^n).$$

If $n = 8$ then $3^8 = 6561$ and $S_n = -\tfrac{3}{2}(-6560) = 9840$. Since the value
of c is greater than 1, the series does not converge and the sum will
tend to infinity as $n \to \infty$.

5.2 The exponential function

The exponential growth function differs from the previous two in being
a continuous function – it is defined for all t. In another sense, it is a
straightforward development of compound growth. Suppose that x_0 is
deposited in a savings account which pays a rate of interest r as in the
previous example. In this case, however, interest is calculated and paid
twice à year. At the end of sixth months the interest paid is $rx_0/2$ so the
amount in the account for the second six months is

$$x(\tfrac{1}{2}) = (1 + \tfrac{r}{2})x_0.$$

By the same argument we may express the amount available at the end
of the second six months as

$$x(1) = (1 + \tfrac{r}{2})x(\tfrac{1}{2}) = (1 + \tfrac{r}{2})^2 x_0. \qquad [5.12]$$

(Notice the slight change in notation. Now that we are concerned with a
continuous function we use the associated notation; hence [5.12] defines
$x(1)$ rather than the x_1 which we used for the discrete function.)

This savings account paid interest twice a year. Had it paid interest
four times a year we would have

$$x(1) = (1 + \tfrac{r}{4})^4.$$

In general, we may conclude that if interest is paid n times in a year then

$$x(1) = (1 + \tfrac{r}{n})^n x_0. \qquad [5.13]$$

Strictly speaking, [5.13] defines $x(1)$ for any finite number n, but for a
truly continuous function we need to know what happens as n tends to
infinity and we have 'continuous compounding'; i.e., we need to
evaluate

$$\lim_{n \to \infty} (1 + \tfrac{r}{n})^n \qquad\qquad [5.14]$$

The solution to this exercise is called the *exponential function*. It is a function since its precise value depends upon the value of the rate of interest r and is represented as exp (r). Thus, if $r = 1$,

$$\exp(1) \equiv \lim_{n \to \infty} (1 + \tfrac{1}{n})^n.$$

We might seek to evaluate exp (1) by looking at the series for ever-increasing values of n thus:

n	1	10	100	1000	10000	...
$(1 + \tfrac{1}{n})^n$	2	2.5937	2.7048	2.7169	2.7181	

It would appear that the sequence is convergent, but unfortunately it turns out that the limit cannot be expressed as a rational number. It is convenient to have a quick way of representing the number so we call it e; i.e.,

$$e \equiv \exp(1) \equiv \lim_{n \to \infty} (1 + \tfrac{1}{n})^n = 2.718281.... \qquad\qquad [5.15]$$

This is a particularly useful convention, as we see from the following. Define a number m such that

$$m = \frac{n}{r}. \qquad\qquad [5.16]$$

It follows immediately that

$$n = mr; \quad \frac{1}{m} = \frac{r}{n}. \qquad\qquad [5.17]$$

Substituting [5.17] into [5.14] we have

$$\lim_{n \to \infty} \left[\left(1 + \frac{r}{n}\right)^n \right] = \lim_{n \to \infty} \left[\left(1 + \frac{1}{m}\right)^{mr} \right]. \qquad\qquad [5.18]$$

The rules of limits discussed in the previous chapter now come in handy. In particular, rule V (equation [4.9]) tells us that

$$\lim_{n \to \infty} \left[\left(1 + \frac{1}{m}\right)^{mr} \right] = \left[\lim_{n \to \infty} \left(1 + \frac{1}{m}\right)^{m} \right]^r. \qquad\qquad [5.19]$$

Substituting [5.19] into [5.18] and noting that from [5.16] m tends to infinity as n tends to infinity, we have

$$\lim_{n \to \infty} \left[\left(1 + \frac{r}{n}\right)^n \right] = \left[\lim_{m \to \infty} \left(+ \frac{1}{m}\right)^{m} \right]^r. \qquad\qquad [5.20]$$

By definition of e in equation [5.15],

$$\exp(r) \equiv \lim_{n \to \infty} \left[\left(1 + \frac{r}{n} \right)^n \right] = [e]^r$$

$$\exp(r) = e^r. \hspace{6cm} [5.21]$$

Armed with this newly defined exponential function, we can now return to the example of the savings account. If interest is compounded continuously then [5.13] becomes

$$x(1) = x_0 \exp(r) = x_0 e^r.$$

After two periods

$$x(2) = x(1)e^r = (x_0 e^r)e^r = x_0 e^{2r}$$

and in general

$$x(t) = x_0 e^{rt}. \hspace{6cm} [5.22]$$

The exponential growth function given by [5.22] can be evaluated for *any* value of t. While it is not common to find savings accounts that pay continuously compounded interest, there are certainly loan companies that come pretty close to charging it! More seriously, there is a wide variety `of economic variables which we must assume are growing continuously, unconfined by our arbitrary definitions of time – for example the population.

Worked example

Q. If national income grows at 2.7 per cent exponentially, by how much will it have grown after six years? Is this greater or less than a compound rate of growth of 2.7 per cent?

A. The formula for exponential growth is $Y(t) = Y_0 e^{rt}$. The rate of growth over the whole period is

$$\frac{Y(t) - Y_0}{Y_0} = \frac{Y(t)}{Y_0} - 1.$$

Substituting for $Y(t)$ from the formula therefore gives

$$\frac{Y_0 e^{rt}}{Y_0} - 1 = e^{rt} - 1$$

and with $r = 0.027$, $t = 6$ this is $(e^{0.162} - 1) = (1.1759 - 1) = 0.1759$. In percentage terms, then, there has been a 17.59 per cent increase in six years. Had the growth been compound, we would have $Y_t = (1 + r)^t Y_0$ and the rate of growth becomes $(1 + r)^t - 1$, which in this case is $(1.027)^6 - 1 = 1.1733 - 1 = 0.1733$ or 17.33 per cent. It is therefore less than the continuously compounded sum.

5.3 Logarithms

It was shown in chapter 2 that many functions have an inverse. Thus the function $y = 2x - 2$ has an inverse which may be written $x = \frac{1}{2}y + 1$; the relationship between the two variables x, y is exactly the same, but is simply expressed in different ways. Suppose now that we start from a function $y = e^x$: is it possible to rewrite this in the form $x = f^{-1}(y)$? This inverse function is not so easy to see, and we introduce a special terminology to cater for this case. We write

$$x = \log_e(y). \tag{5.23}$$

The inverse function log is called the *logarithm to the base e*. It is also referred to as the *natural* or *Napierian* logarithm and may be written as

$$x = \ln(y). \tag{5.24}$$

If we can define logarithms for the number e, then why not for any number? This is a good question, and we can in fact define the inverse of $y = a^x$ as

$$x = \log_a y \qquad\qquad a > 0, a \neq 1 \tag{5.25}$$

Logarithms are very common in mathematics for a number of reasons, some of which we shall consider briefly here. Provided that you remember that the information contained in the statement $x = \log_a(y)$ is no more and no less than that contained in the statement $y = a^x$, they need present no problem at all.

There are, in fact, two particular variations which have a special place in mathematics. One is the natural logarithm discussed above. As for the other, since we use a decimal system of numbers, it would be surprising indeed if the most common value for a were not 10. In fact, when the base is 10 we talk about *common logarithms*. We shall return to these in section 5.3.2.

5.3.1 Properties of logarithms

The essential information about logarithms is contained in the statement

$$x = \log_a y \iff y = a^x \tag{5.26}$$

where the symbol $\iff$ may be interpreted as 'implies and is implied by'. Having said that, it is convenient to remember certain properties of logarithms which follow directly from [5.26]. Analogous to [5.26], we may write

$$v = \log_a w \iff w = a^v.$$ [5.27]

Now, multiplying y by w gives

$$y \cdot w = a^x \cdot a^v = a^{x+v}.$$

But, by the definition of logarithms,

$$y \cdot w = a^{x+v} \iff x + v = \log_a(y \cdot w).$$ [5.28]

So, putting [5.26], [5.27] and [5.28] together, we discover that

$$\log_a y + \log_a w = \log_a(y \cdot w).$$

All the other rules may be proven in a similar fashion using just the basic definitions and the arithmetic of powers. The actual proofs are left to the reader as exercises but the most useful rules are listed below:

Rules:

I $\log_a(y) + \log_a(w) = \log_a(y \cdot w)$ [5.29]

II $\log_a(y) - \log_a(w) = \log_a(y/w)$ [5.30]

III $n \log_a(y) = \log_a(y^n)$ [5.31]

IV $\log_b(y) = [\log_a(y)][\log_b(a)]$ [5.32]

V $\log_b(a) = \dfrac{1}{\log_a(b)}$ [5.33]

5.3.2 Calculating with logarithms

These properties of logarithms have proved particularly useful in the past. Suppose we wish to multiply together two numbers. If we had a method of quickly ascertaining the logarithm of each number we could use rule I to ascertain their product. Such a procedure is made possible by the publication of log tables, usually common logarithms (i.e. to the base 10); so, for example, we can look up $\log_{10}(2)$ and find that the value is 0.3010. Similarly, $\log_{10}(3) = 0.4771$

$$0.3010 + 0.4771 = 0.7782$$

and from rule I we know that 0.7782 represents $\log_{10}(2 \times 3)$. A search of the table would reveal that $\log(6) = 0.7782$, and so we have established that $2 \times 3 = 6$. In practice it would be easier still to use the knowledge that if $\log_{10}(y) = 0.7782$ then $y = 10^{0.7782}$ and look up the value of $10^{0.7782}$ in another table – the anti-log table (in this case it is a table of the function 10^x). Clearly, such a procedure is unnecessarily complicated for multiplying 2×3, but it is very useful for multiplying large numbers together and even more so for dividing two large numbers.

Today, calculators have reduced the need for this usage of logarithms, but they are still useful for performing other tasks. Indeed many calculators include the facilities of $\log_{10}$, 10^x, ln and e^x. One particular use is to raise a number to a power or to find a root. Rule III stated that $n\log_a(y) = \log_a(y^n)$, so dividing both sides by n and setting $a = 10$ we have

$$\log_{10}(y) = \frac{\log_{10}(y^n)}{n}.$$

Now, y is by definition the nth root of y^n, so if we know what y^n is we can discover y. For example, let $y^n = 8$ and $n = 3$ (i.e., we wish to know what the cube root of 8 is). Looking up 8 in the tables tells us

$$\log_{10}(8) = 0.09031.$$

Dividing by 3 gives $\log_{10}(y) = 0.9031/3 = 0.30103$. But we know that $\log_{10}(2) = 0.30103$ (we could look up $y = 10^{0.30103}$ and find $y = 2$ that way), and so the cube root of 8 is 2. This is a fairly obvious example since it is easy to verify that $2 \times 2 \times 2 = 8$, but the method is quite general.

There is one additional problem when using log tables rather than a calculator. It is not feasible to list the values of $\log_{10}(y)$ for every possible value of y. The usual solution is to list values for $1 < y < 10$. If we wish to represent the number 2000 in logarithmic form we use rule I. Thus $2000 = 2.000 \times 1000$, so

$$\log_{10}(2000) = \log_{10}(2) + \log_{10}(1000).$$

Then use the relation $x = \log_{10}(1000) \Rightarrow 1000 = 10^x$ to ascertain that $x = 3$; i.e.,

$$\log_{10}(2000) = 3 + \log_{10}(2) = 3.30103.$$

Similarly, the number 0.200 can be expressed as 2.0/10, and from rule II,

$$\log_{10}(0.2) = \log_{10}(2) - \log_{10}(10)$$

$$= 0.3010 - 1.$$

It is common to write this expresion as $\bar{1}.3010$ instead of -0.699, but a calculator will use the latter form.

Note: If $a > 0$, then $a^x > 0$ whatever the value of x. Since $y = a^x$, it necessarily follows that we can only take logarithms of positive numbers; i.e., $x = \log_a(y)$ is defined only for $y > 0$.

Worked examples

Q. If national income grows at 5 per cent exponentially, how long will it take income to double?

A. After n years national income will be $Y(n) = Y_0 e^{0.05n}$ where Y_0 is the starting value. We require that $Y(n) = 2Y_0$, i.e. that $Y_0 e^{0.05n} = 2Y_0$. This will be true iff $e^{0.05n} = 2$. Using our knowledge of logs, if $2 = e^{0.05n}$, then

$$0.05n = \log_e(2) = 0.693147$$

$$\therefore n = \frac{0.693147}{0.05} = 13.8629.$$

Q. If Mr Smith wishes to double his investment in 10 years what compound annual rate of interest must he earn?

A. If he starts with w_0, then after 10 years he will have $w_{10} = w_0(1 + r)^{10}$, but he requires that $w_{10} = 2w_0$, i.e., that $(1 + r)^{10} = 2$. To find the 10th root we may use rule III above to find

$$\log(1 + r) = \frac{\log[(1 + r)^{10}]}{10} = \frac{\log(2)}{10}. \qquad [5.34]$$

This is exactly the same as 'taking the logs of both sides', i.e.

$$\log(1 + r)^{10} = \log(2),$$

and then manipulate the left-hand side to produce [5.34]. The choice of base is unimportant. Using base 10 (common logarithms) gives

$$\log(1 + r) = \frac{0.30103}{10} = 0.030103$$

$$1 + r = 1.071773$$

$$\therefore r = 7.177\%$$

* Appendix: An alternative view of the exponential function

The exponential function is of more generality in mathematics than the derivation in chapter 5 may imply. There it was shown that

$$\exp(r) \equiv \lim_{n \to \infty} \left[\left(1 + \frac{r}{n}\right)^n \right]. \qquad [5.35]$$

Consider however the expression $(1 + a)^n$. Although this is a deceptively simple expression, it is in fact a convenient representation of an nth-order polynomial. To expand this into its full form consider first the expression

$$(1 + a)^1 = 1 + a$$

$(1 + a)^2 = 1 + 2a + a^2$

$(1 + a)^3 = 1 + 3a + 3a^2 + a^3.$

There is in fact a pattern to this expansion which suggests a way of calculating the coefficients.

n	a^0	a^1	a^2	a^3	a^4	a^5	....
0	1						
1	1	1					
2	1	2	1				
3	1	3	3	1			
4	1	4	6	4	1		

The table gives the coefficients of a^0, a^1, a^2, etc., for $n = 0, 1, 2$, etc. It is known as Pascal's triangle. To calculate a coefficient in the table, add together those directly to the north and north-west. This sort of expansion is known as the *binomial expansion*. Notice that it is symmetrical and that the coefficient on a^{n-1} is always n, that on a^{n-2} is $[n(n - 1)/2$, that on a^{n-3} is $[n(n - 1)(n - 2)]/(3 \times 2)$ and so on.

If we now use this to expand $(1 + r/n)^n$, we have

$$\left(1 + \frac{r}{n}\right)^n = 1 + n\left(\frac{r}{n}\right) + \frac{n(n - 1)}{2} \cdot \frac{r^2}{n^2} + \frac{n(n - 1)(n - 2)}{3 \times 2} \cdot \frac{r^3}{n^3} + \ldots$$

[5.36]

$$= 1 + r + \frac{n - 1}{n} \cdot \frac{r^2}{2!} + \frac{(n - 1)}{n} \cdot \frac{(n - 2)}{n} \cdot \frac{r^3}{3!} + \ldots$$

where $2! = 2 \times 1$; $3! = 3 \times 2 \times 1$; $4! = 4 \times 3 \times 2 \times 1$ and so on. ($n!$ is called *n-factorial*.)

When n is very large $(n - 1)/n$ is very close to unity, so taking the limits as n tends to infinity gives

$$\exp(r) \equiv \lim_{n \to \infty} \left[\left(1 + \frac{r}{n}\right)^n\right] = 1 + r + \frac{r^2}{2!} + \frac{r^3}{3!} + \ldots$$

[5.37]

5.4 Exercises

Section 5.1.3

Calculate the sum to infinity of the following series:

(i) 1, 2, 4, 8, ...

(ii) 8, 4, 2, 1, ...

(iii) $1, \dfrac{1}{r}, \dfrac{1}{r^2}, \dfrac{1}{r^3}, \ldots \quad r > 1$

(iv) $\dfrac{1}{r}, -\dfrac{1}{r^2}, \dfrac{1}{r^3}, -\dfrac{1}{r^4}, \ldots \quad r > 1$

Section 5.2

Three towns, Ayton, Beeham and Ceaford, all had the same population – 50,000 in 1960. The population in Ayton increased in simple fashion by 5000 per year. In Beeham researchers discovered an exponential rate of growth of 7.5%. At Ceaford expansion did not start until 1965 but thereafter it grew more rapidly with an exponential growth rate of 10%. Which town had the largest population in

(i) 1965?   (ii) 1970?   (iii) 1980?

Section 5.3.2

Use logarithms to calculate the following:

(i) 326×17.5 (iv) $(17.5)^3$

(ii) $326 \div 17.5$ (v) $(17.5)^{(1/3)}$

(iii) $17.5 \div 326$ (vi) $\sqrt[3]{0.0175}$

Further exercises

1. If the index of retail prices has a value of £100 in 1963 and prices rise at an annual compound rate of 4%, what will the index be by 1983?

2. In Friedland, inflation was running at 8% per annum between 1960 and 1970. A change in policy reduced the rate to only 4% between 1970 and 1980. What was the average annual (compound) rate of inflation over the 20-year period?

3. If a bank charges a simple rate of interest of 12% per year, is this the same as charging 1% per month on the outstanding amount? If not, what is the true rate of interest in this case?

4. If population doubles in 10 years, what exponential rate of growth does this imply?

6 Difference equations

6.1 Difference operators

In section 5.1.1 we looked at the arithmetic progression, noting that it can be written as

$$x_t - x_{t-1} = c. \qquad [6.1]$$

The left-hand side represents the change or difference between successive values of the sequence. It is so common in mathematics that we have a special symbol for it, the *difference operator* Δ.

$$\Delta x_t \equiv x_t - x_{t-1}. \qquad [6.2]$$

The arithmetic progression can now be written in a slightly different form:

$$\Delta x_t = c.$$

Such an equation is called, not unreasonably, a *difference equation*. In fact, it is the simplest of all possible difference equations. Consider the slightly more general

$$\Delta x_t + a x_t = f(t). \qquad [6.3]$$

This is a linear first-order difference equation with constant coefficients since it contains no second difference, no power higher than 1 and the coefficient a is not itself a function of time. In this book we shall deal only with linear difference equations with constant coefficients, but we shall consider higher orders. Let

$$y_t = \Delta x_t$$

$$\Delta y_t = \Delta \Delta x_t \equiv \Delta^2 x_t. \qquad [6.4]$$

But since by definition $\Delta y_t \equiv y_t - y_{t-1}$, substitution from [6.4] gives

$$\Delta y_t = \Delta x_t - \Delta x_{t-1}.$$

Using the definition of Δx_t in [6.2] and noting that $\Delta x_{t-1} \equiv x_{t-1} - x_{t-2}$,

$$\Delta^2 x_t = \Delta y_t$$
$$= (x_t - x_{t-1}) - (x_{t-1} - x_{t-2})$$
$$= x_t - 2x_{t-1} + x_{t-2}.$$

The *second difference* is the difference between successive differences and is represented by the symbol Δ^2, but we have shown that it is also a relationship between three successive values of a sequence function, as the first difference was a relationship between two successive values. We can define a third difference, Δ^3, which would involve four successive values; and so on. This suggests that there is in general a more convenient way of writing all difference equations than the operator notation we introduced at the start of the section. Thus, [6.3] can be written

$$x_t - x_{t-1} + ax_t = f(t)$$

$$x_t - \left(\frac{1}{1+a}\right)x_{t-1} = \frac{f(t)}{1+a}. \qquad [6.5]$$

Let us define

$$a_1 = \frac{-1}{1+a} \quad \text{and} \quad g(t) = \frac{f(t)}{1+a}.$$

Then we can rewrite [6.5] as

$$x_t + a_1 x_{t-1} = g(t).$$

Similarly, we can derive a representation of any second-order difference equation

$$\Delta^2 x_t + a\Delta x_{t-1} + bx_t = f(t)$$

by suitable definition of a_1, a_2 and $g(t)$ as

$$x_t + a_1 x_{t-1} + a_2 x_{t-2} = g(t) \qquad [6.6]$$

and in general we can define that nth-order difference as

$$x_t + a_1 x_{t-1} + a_2 x_{t-2} + \dots + a_n x_{t-n} = g(t). \qquad [6.7]$$

In effect, this is a relationship between the current value of a series, x_t, and the past (lagged) values of the same series, since it can also be written in the form

$$x_t = -a_1 x_{t-1} - a_2 x_{t-2} \dots - a_n x_{t-n} + g(t).$$

A wide variety of economic models may be conceived of in this way since the current economic situation is more often than not the sum of past decisions. But we shall return to examples in the next chapter. First we need to know how to solve them.

6.2 Solving linear difference equations

The solution of all linear difference equations may be found by the following technique. We split the problem into two parts – the complementary solution and the particular solution – and the *general solution* is the sum of the two parts.

The *complementary solution* is the solution to the equation

$$x_t + a_1 x_{t-1} + \dots + a_n x_{t-n} = 0. \qquad [6.8]$$

We have already discussed methods for solving polynomial functions (see chapter 2), and one possible approach is to try and turn [6.8] into a polynomial. In practice this proves to be quite simple. Let us assume

$$x_t = cb^t.$$

Then

$$x_{t-1} = cb^{t-1}; \quad x_{t-2} = cb^{t-2}; \text{ (etc.)}$$

and [6.8] becomes

$$cb^t + a_1 cb^{t-1} + a_2 cb^{t-2} + \dots + a_n cb^{t-n} = 0$$

or what is known as the *auxiliary* equation:

$$cb^{t-n}(b^n + a_1 b^{n-1} + \dots + a_{n-1} b + a_n) = 0.$$

If b or c is zero the problem becomes trivial, so the real problem is to find the roots of the polynomial in the brackets. Some will be relatively easy while others may prove quite difficult depending upon the actual values of the parameters a_1, a_2, etc., and the degree of the polynomial. In order to demonstrate the solution method we shall first restrict ourselves to the simplest case. For the first-order model we have

$$x_t + a_1 x_{t-1} = 0$$
$$cb^t + a_1 cb^{t-1} = cb^{t-1}(b + a_1) = 0. \qquad [6.9]$$

Therefore $b = -a_1$ and

$$x_t = c(-a_1)^t. \qquad [6.10]$$

An example of a second-order equation is given on page 76, but before we proceed to that we must examine the second half of the solution.

The *particular solution* is any solution that solves the complete equation [6.7]. There is no one correct way of finding such a solution, but there are some general rules that can simplify the process. To illustrate these consider first the equation

$$x_t + a_1 x_{t-1} = 2. \qquad [6.11]$$

If, as in this case, the function $g(t)$ is itself a constant, then it is likely that the particular solution will itself be constant. Let

$$x_t = x_{t-1} = (\text{say})x^*.$$

Then substitution into [6.11] gives

$$x^* = \frac{2}{1 + a_1}.$$

Such a solution is common in economics, where we postulate that the value of a variable will not change unless subject to some external influence. We talk about equilibrium values, and the particular solution may often be thought of as the equilibrium value. This sort of interpretation is not limited to economics, but neither is life always so straightforward. Indeed, consider the model with which we introduced this chapter (equation [6.1]):

$$x_t - x_{t-1} = 2. \qquad\qquad [6.12]$$

Putting $x_t = x_{t-1} = x^*$ into this equation produces the obviously nonsensical result that $0 = 2$! In this case we must find an alternative procedure, and we try instead

$$x_t = kt.$$

Then

$$x_{t-1} = k(t - 1)$$

and [6.12] becomes

$$kt - k(t - 1) = 2.$$

Therefore $k = 2$ and

$$x^* = 2t.$$

We could say that the 'equilibrium' is a dynamic one rather than a static one.

Note: As a general rule, if $g(t)$ is a polynomial in t of order m, the particular solution may be found by setting x^* to be a general polynomial of the same order. If that does not work, then raise the order of the polynomial by one.

The *general solution* is obtained by adding these two component solutions together. Thus the general solution to [6.11] is

$$x_t = c(-a_1)^t + \frac{2}{1 + a_1}. \qquad\qquad [6.13]$$

Notice, however, that this solution still involves one arbitrary constant, *c*. The reason for this is not hard to find. In order to determine the value for x_t from the difference equation we need to know the value of x_{t-1}. That depends in turn upon x_{t-2}, and so on. In order to fix x_t we have to know where the series starts, and this information is contained in the *initial conditions*. These may refer to the value of x_t for any value of *t*. Suppose that we know that in the beginning ($t = 0$) the variable *x* takes a particular value; e.g.,

$$x_0 = 0. \hspace{6cm} [6.14]$$

Then we can use this piece of information to solve for *c*. Thus, substituting [6.14] into [6.13], we have

$$x_0 = c(-a_1)^0 + \frac{2}{1 + a_1} = 0$$

$$c = \frac{-2}{1 + a_1}.$$

6.2.1 Solving second-order difference equations

As we have already stated, there is no difference in technique as we move from first order to second order. To illustrate the process let us consider the equation

$$x_t + x_{t-1} - 6x_{t-2} = -4. \hspace{4cm} [6.15]$$

Setting $x_t = x_{t-1} = x_{t-2} = x^*$ (the particular solution),

$$x^* + x^* - 6x^* = -4$$

$$x^* = 1.$$

To find the complementary solution we proceed as shown on page 74 setting $x_t = cb^t$; hence

$$cb^t + cb^{t-1} - 6cb^{t-2} = 0$$

$$cb^{t-2}(b^2 + b - 6) = 0$$

$$cb^{t-2}(b + 3)(b - 2) = 0$$

Therefore

$$b = -3 \text{ or } b = 2.$$

Since either is a valid solution (i.e. will satisfy the complementary equation), any weighted sum of the two will also satisfy the equation. Noting that there is no reason why the arbitrary constant should be the same in each case, we have

$$x_t = c_1(-3)^t + c_2(2)^t + 1 \hspace{4cm} [6.16]$$

where c_1 and c_2 are arbitrary constants. Since we now have two arbitrary constants in the general solution, we will need not one but two initial conditions to eliminate them. Thus, if we know that [6.15] describes the time-path of a variable that takes the value 4 at time zero and the value 3 one period later,

$$x_0 = 4; \quad x_1 = 3$$

and we substitute these conditions into [6.16], we have

$$x_0 = c_1 + c_2 + 1 = 4$$

$$x_1 = -3c_1 + 2c_2 + 1 = 3$$

which can be solved simultaneously to give

$$c_1 = 0.8; \quad c_2 = 2.2.$$

Hence the complete solution to [6.15] is

$$x_t = 0.8(-3)^t + 2.2(2)^t + 1.$$

Note: In general, all quadratics have two solutions, but, as we showed in section 2.2.2, they need not all be real ones, nor need they be distinct. In the case where there are two distinct roots we may write the general solution as

$$x_t = c_1 b_1^t + c_2 b_2^t + x^*.$$

The case in which there are repeated roots is dealt with in section 6.2.2. The case in which there are no real solutions is dealt with in section 6.2.3, but it may be omitted without loss of continuity.

6.2.2 The case of repeated roots

Consider the general second-order equation

$$x_t + a_1 x_{t-1} + a_2 x_{t-2} = g(t). \tag{6.17}$$

This will produce the auxiliary equation

$$cb^{t-2}(b^2 + a_1 b + a_2) = 0 \tag{6.18}$$

which in turn will give us two solutions b_1 and b_2 which may be written as

$$b_{1,2} = \frac{-a_1 \pm \sqrt{(a_1^2 - 4a_2)}}{2}.$$

In the special case where $a_1^2 = 4a_2$ there will be not two but only one distinct solution. We say that we have *repeated roots*. In this event we know that

$$b = \frac{-a_1}{2} = \frac{-2a_2}{a_1} \tag{6.19}$$

and $x_t = c_1 b^t$ is a solution of [6.17]. Consider however an alternative, viz.

$$x_t = c_2 t b^t. \tag{6.20}$$

This implies that

$$x_{t-1} = c_2(t - 1)b^{t-1}; \qquad\qquad x_{t-2} = c_2(t - 2)b^{t-2}. \tag{6.21}$$

So substituting [6.20] and [6.21] into [6.17] will produce the auxiliary equation

$$c_2 b^{t-2}[b^2 t + a_1 b(t - 1) + a_2(t - 2)] = 0. \tag{6.22}$$

To confirm that it does in fact equal zero, expand [6.22] to give

$$c_2 b^{t-2}[(b^2 + a_1 b + a_2)t - (ba_1 + 2a_2)] = 0. \tag{6.23}$$

The first term in the square brackets is zero from [6.18] and the second is zero from [6.19].

For the case of repeated roots, then, the general solution may be written as

$$x_t = c_1 b^t + c_2 t b^t + x^*.$$

Worked example

Q. Solve $x_t - x_{t-1} + 0.25 x_{t-2} = 0$.

A. Setting $x_t = c b^t$ gives the auxiliary equation

$$c b^{t-2}(b^2 - b + 0.25) = 0.$$

$$\therefore b = \frac{1 \pm \sqrt{(1 - 1)}}{2} = \frac{1}{2}.$$

So the general solution is

$$x_t = c_1(\tfrac{1}{2})^t + c_2 t(\tfrac{1}{2})^t$$

(Note that the particular solution is zero since the difference equation is homogenous, $g(t) = 0$, and that with no information on the initial conditions we cannot solve for c_1 and c_2.)

*6.2.3 The case of complex roots

Consider again the general quadratic [6.17] and the roots given by [6.19]. If $a_1^2 < 4a_2$, then we have complex roots (see section 2.2.2). Specifically,

$$b_{1,2} = h \pm iv \qquad [6.24]$$

where $h = -a_1/2$ and $v = \sqrt{(4a_2 - a_1^2)}/2$. Substituting these solutions into the general solution gives us the correct but rather uninformative statement that

$$x_t = c_1(h + iv)^t + c_2(h - iv)^t + x^*. \qquad [6.25]$$

Common sense tells us that the only meaningful solutions to economic problems are real ones and it is far from clear that x_t is a real number. In section 1.2.2, however, we discovered that there is an alternative way of representing complex numbers, viz.

$$h + iv = r(\cos\theta \pm i\sin\theta) \qquad [6.26]$$

where $r = \sqrt{(h^2 + v^2)}$; $\cos\theta = h/r$. Now, there is a theorem known as De Moivre's theorem (see Chiang, pp.526–7 or similar advanced mathematics text for proof), which states that

$$(\cos\theta \pm i\sin\theta)^t = (\cos t\theta \pm i\sin t\theta). \qquad [6.27]$$

Substituting [6.26] and [6.27] into [6.25] gives

$$x_t = c_1 r^t(\cos\theta t + i\sin\theta t) + c_2 r^t(\cos\theta t - i\sin\theta t). \qquad [6.28]$$

Notice that the choice of c_1 and c_2 is entirely arbitrary, so let us assume that they are complex conjugates; i.e.,

$$c_1 = m + in; \ c_2 = m - in. \qquad [6.29]$$

Substituting [6.29] into [6.28] and collecting up terms,

$$x_t = r^t(c_1 + c_2)\cos\theta t + r^t(c_1 - c_2)i\sin\theta t$$

$$= r^t(2m)\cos\theta t + r^t(-2in)i\sin\theta t$$

$$= r^t(2m\cos\theta t + 2n\sin\theta t). \qquad [6.30]$$

Since cos and sin are both periodic functions, it follows that x_t will itself be periodic. The amplitude of the cycles will depend upon the real constants m and n and upon the value of r^t. From the definiton of r in [6.26] and the definitions of h and v in [6.24], we have

$$r^2 = \left(\frac{-a_1}{2}\right)^2 + \frac{(4a_2 - a_1^2)}{4} = a_2$$

$$r^t = a_2^{(t/2)}. \qquad [6.31]$$

Apart from being a rather neat representation of the solution which demonstrates that we can assume the solution for x_t is itself real, this formulation is of particular value when considering the nature of the time-path, and to this we now turn our attention.

Worked example

Q. Solve $x_t - 2x_{t-1} + 5x_{t-2} = 0$.

A. Setting $x_t = cb^t$ gives the auxiliary equation $cb^{t-2}(b^2 - 2b + 5) = 0$.

$$b_{1,2} = \frac{2 \pm \sqrt{(4 - 20)}}{2} = 1 \pm 2i.$$

Writing this in the alternative form, $r = a_2^{(1/2)} = \sqrt{5}$; $\cos\theta = 1/\sqrt{5}$ and

$$x_t = 5^{(t/2)}[c_1 \cos(63.43t) + c_2 \sin(63.43t)].$$

6.3 Stability

Having ascertained the solution to a difference equation, it is possible to see whether the sequence of values will converge to a limit, i.e. to find

$$\lim_{t \to \infty} \{x_t\}.$$

In economics it is more common to look at the limit of the complementary solution, since this measures the divergence of the series from the equilibrium path as given by the particular solution. In fact, the conditions for stability are exactly the same.

The solution to all linear difference equations takes the form

$$x_t = c_1 b_1^t + c_2 b_2^t + \dots$$

If $b < -1$ or if $b > 1$, then the magnitude of cb^t increases as t increases, though in the former case it alternates in sign. On the other hand,

$$\lim_{t \to \infty} \{cb^t\} = 0 \quad \text{iff} \quad |b| < 1.$$

The complementary solution is a weighted average of all possible such solutions, and so it will tend to zero only if every one of those terms does so. From this analysis we may conclude that, if a sequence x_t starts from a value that is not its equilibrium, it will tend to return to equilibrium if all the possible solutions of the auxiliary equation – the b_i – are such that $-1 < b_i < 1$. Alternative ways of stating the same thing are that all roots must lie within the 'unit circle', or that the 'dominant root' – that which is numerically greatest – must have a modulus less than one. This concept of stability is an important one in economics, and we are often more concerned with the stability of a system than with the solutions *per se*. It would be convenient, therefore, if it were possible to establish the stability or instability of a system without the need to actually solve it.

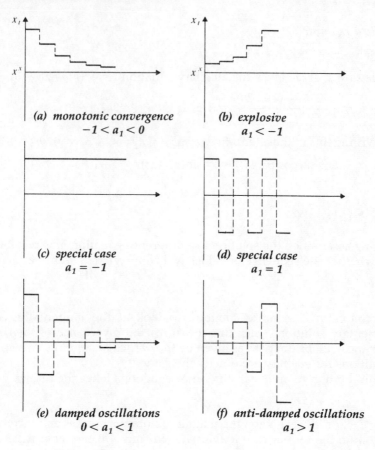

Figure 6.1 Possible time-paths for a first-order difference equation.

The term 'convergence' or 'stability' applies with respect to the deviation from equilibrium. Here this is shown as a constant, but it is quite possible that the 'equilibrium' is itself growing (declining) over time.

6.3.1 First-order equation

The solution to the first-order difference equation [6.9] was given in [6.10] as $c_1(-a_1)^t$ or $b = -a_1$. Clearly, stability in this case depends simply upon the value of a_1. It is instructive to visualize the various posible time-paths graphically, and this is done in figure 6.1.

6.3.2 Second-order equation

With second-order equations the range of possible time-paths is increased, specifically by the introduction of cycles, but all can be divided into those that are stable and those that are not. As with first-order equations, stability may be determined solely by reference to the parameters of the equation, and actual solution is not necessary.

Rule: The second-order difference equation

$x_t + a_1 x_{t-1} + a_2 x_{t-2} = g(t)$ will be stable if and only if

$$|a_2| < 1; |a_1| < 1 + a_2 \qquad [6.32]$$

and it will cycle if and only if

$$a_1^2 < 4a_2. \qquad [6.33]$$

Worked examples are given after the following optional section.

*6.3.3 Proof of the stability conditions

To demonstrate the validity of these conditions, consider the auxiliary equation $b^2 + a_1 b + a_2 = 0$. This will have two roots, b_1 and b_2. For the moment assume that they are real roots; then

$$b^2 + a_1 b + a_2 = (b - b_1)(b - b_2) = 0$$

$$b^2 - (b_1 + b_2)b + b_1 b_2 = 0$$

$$-(b_1 + b_2) = a_1 \qquad [6.34]$$

$$b_1 b_2 = a_2 \qquad [6.35]$$

and stability requires that $|b_1| < 1$ and $|b_2| < 1$. We first show that the conditions given as [6.32] are indeed sufficient. From [6.35],

$$|b_1 b_2| = |a_2| < 1. \qquad [6.36]$$

The condition that $|a_1| < 1 + a_2$ can be considered in two parts, the argument for each being essentially similar, and the two parts of the proof are given below, side by side. Substituting [6.34] and [6.35] gives

$-a_1 < 1 + a_2$	$a_1 < 1 + a_2$
$(b_1 + b_2) < 1 + b_1 b_2$	$-(b_1 + b_2) < 1 + b_1 b_2$
$(1 - b_1)(1 - b_2) > 0$	$(1 + b_1)(1 + b_2) > 0.$ [6.37]

For this inequality to be satisfied, *either* both the terms are positive *or* both the terms are negative. For the latter to be true we must have

$b_1 > 1 \ and \ b_2 > 1$	$b_1 < -1 \ and \ b_2 < -1.$

But this would imply that

$$b_1 b_2 > 1 \qquad\qquad\qquad b_1 b_2 > 1$$

which contradicts [6.36] above. Hence the only possible solution is that both terms are positive; i.e.,

$$b_1 < 1 \text{ and } b_2 < 1 \qquad\qquad b_1 > -1 \text{ and } b_2 > -1$$

and therefore that

$$-1 < b_1 < 1 \text{ and } -1 < b_2 < 1. \tag{6.38}$$

This demonstrates the sufficiency of [6.32], and to prove their necessity we simply reverse the procedure. If [6.38] is true then [6.37] must be true, while it follows directly from equation [6.35] that

$$|a_2| = |b_1| \times |b_2| < 1 \times 1.$$

For the complex case it is convenient to use the alternative form of the solution. From equations [6.30] and [6.31] we have

$$x_t = (a_2)^{(1/2)}(2m \cos t\theta + 2n \sin t\theta).$$

Both sin and cos are 'periodic functions' – their values are bounded and repeat in regular sequence, thus producing cycles in the variable x_t. Since such cycles can be produced only by these functions, the conditions for cycles and the conditions for complex roots are one and the same (viz. equation [6.33]).

Whether the cycles will die away as t tends to infinity depends upon the value of $(a_2)^{(t/2)}$. If $a_2 < 1$ then this will indeed be the case, but if $a_2 > 1$ the term $(a_2)^{(t/2)}$ will increase in magnitude without limit. (Note that if $4a_2 > a_1^2$ then $a_2 > 0$; also that

$$4a_2 + (4 + 4a_1) > a_1^2 + (4 + 4a_1) = (a_1 + 2)^2 > 0.$$

Similarly, it may be shown that $4a_2 + 4 - 4a_1 > 0$, which two results together imply that $a_2 + 1 > |a_1|$, which is [6.32].)

Worked examples

Q. Are the following stable and do they have cyclical time-paths?
   (i) $2x_t - x_{t-1} = -2 + 1.5x_{t-2}$.
   (ii) $2x_t - x_{t-1} = 10 - 1.5x_{t-2}$.

A. Rewrite in standard form as

   (i) $x_t - 0.5x_{t-1} - 0.75x_{t-2} = -1$
   (ii) $x_t - 0.5x_{t-1} + 0.75x_{t-2} = 5$.

The first condition $|a_2| < 1$ is met in each case since $|0.75| < 1$. The second condition requires that $|a_1| < 1 + a_2$. For (i) this is clearly not met since $0.5 > 0.25$, but it is true for (ii); thus (ii) is stable while (i) is not. For a second-order equation to cycle requires that $a_1^2 < 4a_2$. For (i) this is clearly impossible since $a_2 < 0$, but for (ii) $(-0.5)^2 < 4(0.75)$ and the equation does produce cycles. The time-path for (ii) is depicted in figure 6.2 for a particular set of initial conditions $(x_0 = x_1 = 0)$.

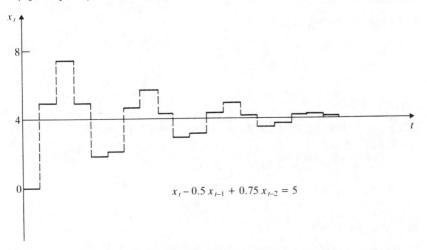

Figure 6.2 'Damped cycles'

6.3.4 Higher-order equations

It is possible to establish the stability conditions for a linear difference equation of any order, but presentation of these conditions requires the use of matrices and for these we must wait until chapter 18. In practice, it becomes difficult to interpret the conditions analytically as their complexity grows, and the more usual approach is to substitute estimated values for the parameters and to see whether the model does in fact converge for this set of estimates. A number of package programs exist that can solve the problem quickly and painlessly, and researchers can thus establish empirically the effect of changing any or all of the parameters.

6.4 Exercises

Section 6.2.2

Solve the following equations:

    (i) $x_t - 2x_{t-1} - 3x_{t-2} = 2$ $x_0 = 0,\ x_1 = 1$

    (ii) $x_t - 2x_{t-1} + x_{t-2} = 2$ $x_2 = 1,\ x_1 = 3$

    (iii) $x_{t-2} + x_{t-1} - 2x_t = 0$ $x_0 = 1,\ x_1 = 4$

*Section 6.2.3

Solve the following equations:

    (i) $x_t - x_{t-1} + x_{t-2} = 0$

    (ii) $x_{t-2} = 0.4x_{t-1} - 0.2x_t - 0.8$

Section 6.3.2

Solve the following and hence or otherwise graph their time-path for $t = 0, 1, \ldots, 6$.

    (i) $x_t + 0.5x_{t-1} + 0.5x_{t-2} = 2;\ x_0 = x_1 = 0$

    (ii) $x_t + 1.5x_{t-1} + 0.5x_{t-2} = 3;\ x_0 = x_1 = 0$

Further exercises

1 Find the complete solutions of the following and determine whether their time-paths are stable:

    (i) $y_t - \frac{1}{3}y_{t-1} = 6;$ $y_0 = 1$

    (ii) $y_t + 2y_{t-1} - 3 = 0;$ $y_0 = 2$

    (iii) $4y_t = 20 - y_{t-1};$ $y_0 = 2$

2 Do the following difference equations converge to a stable equilibrium, and if so what is it?

    (i) $2y_t - 3y_{t-1} = 6 - 1.5y_{t-2}$

    (ii) $y_t - 1.4y_{t-1} + 0.6y_{t-2} = 100$

    (iii) $y_{t-2} - 7y_{t-1} + 5y_t = -100$

3 Which, if any, of the above equations will generate cycles?

4 Find the complete solutions of the following and indicate the nature of their time-paths:

    (i) $4x_t - x_{t-2} = 3;$ $x_0 = x_1 = 0$

    (ii) $x_t = 2x_{t-1} - \frac{3}{4}x_{t-2} - 2;$ $x_0 = 4,\ x_1 = 5$

    (iii) $2x_t = 1 + 2x_{t-1};$ $x_1 = 1$

7 Economic applications II

7.1 Discounted cash flow analysis

Let us consider the problem faced by poor Mrs Jones. She wants a television set, but does not know whether to buy or rent. At the rental company she discovers that she can take out a five-year contract at a cost of £100 per year, payable on the first of January each year. She has to meet the cost from her savings account, but has she got enough money if the interest rate is 10 per cent and she has £450 in her account?

One might be tempted to say that 5 × £100 = £500 so she will be £50 short, but that would not be correct. If she pays out £100 for the first year she will have £350 left, and this will earn interest at 10 per cent until the next year, by which time it will have grown to £350 + £35 = £385. Indeed, we can soon see that at the end of the next year she will still have £(385 − 100) × 1.1 = £313.50. By the end of the third year, this has become £234.85 and by the end of the fourth, £148.34, so she can indeed pay the fifth instalment and still have £48.34 left over.

But if the answer is that £450 is more than enough, how much would actually be needed? £425? £400? To answer that we need to understand the concept of discounting.

Let us consider one instalment at a time. The first instalment (x_1) is £100. To pay the second instalment Mrs Jones must set aside x_2. After one year this will have grown to $x_2(1 + r)$. Since we know that she actually has to pay out £100, we can solve for x_2 thus:

$$x_2(1 + r) = 100$$

$$x_2 = \frac{100}{1 + r}.$$

By the same process we may deduce the sum that has to be set aside now to meet the third instalment, and so on.

$$x_3(1 + r)^2 = 100$$

$$x_3 = \frac{100}{(1 + r)^2}.$$

This process is known as *discounting*. Calculating the sum required for each instalment and then adding them up, we find the total sum required now to produce the necessary amounts in the future, and this total is known as the *present discounted value* (PDV) of the stream of payments/receipts. Thus, if we have a rate of interest of 10 per cent, Mrs Jones will need

$$PDV = 100 + \frac{100}{1.1} + \frac{100}{(1.1)^2} + \frac{100}{(1.1)^3} + \frac{100}{(1.1)^4} = £417.$$

(Notice that this sum can be calculated by the use of the formula for the sum of a geometric progression given in equation [5.9]. The starting value is 100 and the constant ratio $1/1.1 = 0.90909$.)

So if Jones has more than £417 she can afford to rent the television. Satisfied on that score, she now goes to the discount store, where she finds that she can buy a television with a five-year inclusive guarantee for only £405; so she correctly deduces that this would be a good investment – there is no more risk and the cost is less. The assistant tries to sell her a bigger model for £440 telling her that it is still cheaper than the £500 she would have to pay to rent a television, but Mrs Jones now knows better than that and puts the salesman firmly in his place.

7.1.1 Business investment

The process of discounting future payments or receipts is one much used by businessmen. Before deciding to embark upon some investment expenditure, they will study the projected stream of receipts that the new scheme will produce. In particular, they will consider how much money they would need to invest in an alternative way to produce the same stream of receipts in the future. This alternative could be anything, but it is usual to take as the reference the rate of interest that could be earned in the free market. This has the particular advantage that the investment decision will be independent of the source of finance. By definition, the market rate of interest is what the businessmen would have to pay to borrow the money for their investment project, and also the rate they can earn on any excess funds of their own. (In practice, borrowing and lending rates may differ, but that is an unnecessary complication at this point.)

If we assume that a businessman receives his income at the end of the year, then to produce £100 in the first year he would have to invest £100/$(1 + r)$ at the market rate of interest. To produce x_t in year t he needs to invest $x_t/(1 + r)^t$ now and so on. The present discounted value of the income stream is

$$\text{PDV} = \frac{x_1}{1 + r} + \frac{x_2}{(1 + r)^2} + \dots + \frac{x_n}{(1 + r)^n} = \sum_{t = 1}^{n} \frac{x_t}{(1 + r)^t}. \qquad [7.1]$$

If the PDV of the project is greater than the cost of the project, then the project is a better (cheaper) way of producing that income stream than is the free market. In fact, one could borrow this larger amount of money from the market, invest in the project and still have something left over as profit. Given a free market, then, it pays to invest in any project so long as its present discounted value is greater than its cost. Looking at equation [7.1], it is clear that the higher is the market rate of interest (r), the lower will be the calculated PDV and the less likely will it be that investment will actually take place. It is for this reason that it is often postulated that there will be an inverse relationship between the rate of interest and the level of investment; i.e.,

$$I = d - er.$$

For a good discussion of the theoretical issues involved and some of the evidence to date see R.N. Junankar, *Investment: Theories and Evidence*, Papermac, 1972. If the PDV does vary inversely with the rate of interest, then there must be some value of r for which the PDV is actually equal to the cost of the project. That value is known as the *internal rate of return*.

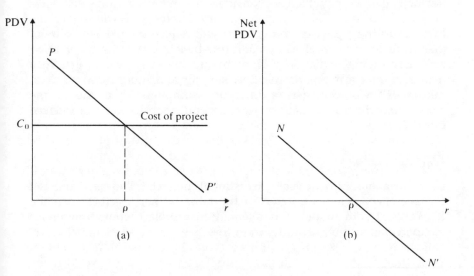

Figure 7.1 *Present discounted value and the internal rate of return.*

As we can see by reference to figure 7.1, if the market rate (r) is greater than the internal rate (ρ) the PDV is below cost and the project is not profitable. We thus have what appear to be two equivalent methods for determining business investments – PDV and internal rate of return (or, as it is often called, the marginal efficiency of investment). There are in fact subtle differences between the two which need not concern us here (for a full discussion see C.J. Hawkins and D.W. Pearce, *Capital Investment Appraisal*, Papermac, 1972), but there is also one difference of a mathematical nature. Up to now we have assumed that the full cost of the project is incurred at the outset. Defining C as the cost, our criterion was PDV > C, but an exactly equivalent criterion is PDV – C > 0. In words, we can say that *net* PDV must be positive and the internal rate of return is that value of the rate of interest that makes net PDV zero. (see figure 7.1(b)). Let $x_0 = -C$; then

$$PDV - C = PDV + x_0 = \sum_{t=0}^{n} \frac{x_t}{(1 + r)^i} \geq 0. \qquad [7.2]$$

If we allow some part of the cost of the project to be incurred at a date in the future, there will be one year in which the net income flow (x_i) will be negative. Indeed, for many real-world projects there may be a commitment to continued investment for some considerable time and net income flows may fluctuate considerably. In these circumstances it is no longer obvious that an increase in the interest rate will reduce the PDV, since the higher discount factor will reduce the present value of these future costs as well as that of future benefits. There is therefore no unique solution to equation [7.2], no unique internal rate of return. As a matter of practical economics, it is simpler and more informative to calculate PDV on the basis of different assumptions about the income stream and the appropriate rate of discount than to work in internal rates of return.

Worked example

Q. A firm has two possible investment projects. The expected net receipts for each are given in the table below, together with the PDVs at both 10 and 25 per cent. Which project would you advise the company to pursue if both projects have the same initial cost?

Year	Discount factor	PROJECT A			PROJECT B		
		Net receipts (£'000)	Discount-ed at 10% (£'000)	Discount-ed at 25% (£'000)	Net receipts (£'000)	Discount-ed at 10% (£'000)	Discount-ed at 25% (£'000)
1	$\dfrac{1}{1 + r}$	100	90.909	80	50	45.455	40
2	$\dfrac{1}{(1 + r)^2}$	100	82.645	64	75	61.983	48
3	$\dfrac{1}{(1 + r)^3}$	100	75.131	51.2	100	75.131	51.2
4	$\dfrac{1}{(1 + r)^4}$	100	68.301	40.96	150	102.452	61.44
5	$\dfrac{1}{(1 + r)^5}$	100	62.092	32.768	200	124.184	65.536
Total	PDV	–	379.079	268.928	–	409.206	266.176

A. At the lower rate of interest project B has a higher PDV and is therefore to be preferred provided the cost is less than £409.206. At the higher rate of interest the high returns for project B in later years are more heavily discounted and A becomes preferable, but notice that the cost must be considerably lower at £268.928 if either is to be profitable.

7.1.2 The value of a bond

This sort of analysis can also be used to determine the value of a bond. Suppose a bond pays a fixed return (coupon yield) of £1 per annum on the last day of each year. Using our discounting technique, we may calculate the PDV of this stream of revenue as

$$P^{B'} = \frac{1}{1 + r} + \frac{1}{(1 + r)^2} + \frac{1}{(1 + r)^3} + \dots = \sum_{t = 1}^{\infty} \frac{1}{(1 + r)^t}. \qquad [7.3]$$

This is the sum to infinity of a geometric progression whose initial value is $1/(1 + r)$ and where the (constant) ratio of successive terms is also $1/(1 + r)$. Since $0 < 1/(1 + r) < 1$, the series is convergent and its sum may be calculated from the simple formula in equation [5.11]

$$P^B = \frac{1}{1 + r} \bigg/ \left[1 - \left(\frac{1}{1 + r}\right)\right]$$

$$= \frac{1}{1 + r - 1}$$

$$= \frac{1}{r}.$$ [7.4]

The value of a bond in perpetuity (e.g. a consol) is inversely related to the rate of interest – a fact crucial to the understanding of Keynes's theory of liquidity preference and the speculative demand for money.

7.2 'Permanent' income and the analysis of multipliers

The simplest version of the income–expenditure model (discussed in section 3.2) is

$$Y_t = C_t + A$$ [7.5]

$$C_t = a + bY_t \qquad\qquad 0 < b < 1$$

where A (autonomous expenditure) is defined to include both investment (I) and government expenditure (G). In section 3.2 we discussed what would happen to the equilibrium level of income (Y^*) as a result of any change in autonomous expenditure (ΔA). Defining this change as ΔY, we established that

$$Y^* = \frac{A + a}{1 - b} \text{ and } \Delta Y = \frac{\Delta A}{1 - b}.$$ [7.6]

The approach in this section is slightly different. We shall assume that some change has already taken place such that income is not equal to the value Y^* which we know to be the static equilibrium. Our problem is to decide whether or not the economic system will settle down in due course at its equilibrium value, i.e. whether or not the economic system is stable.

To illustrate the principle, let us introduce a time lag into the consumption function so that consumption actually depends upon the *previous* period's income:

$$C_t = a + bY_{t-1} \qquad\qquad 0 < b < 1.$$ [7.7]

Substituting [7.7] into [7.5] and rearranging, we have

$$Y_t - bY_{t-1} = a + A.$$ [7.8]

To find the particular solution, set $Y_t = Y_{t-1} = Y^*$, hence

$$Y^*(1 - b) = a + A$$

and the equilibrium solution is the same as for the static model (equation [7.6]).

Note: It is common practice in economics to use lower-case letters to denote deviations from equilibrium; thus

$$y_t = Y_t - Y^* \text{ or } Y_t = Y^* + y_t.$$

Adopting the convention here, we can rewrite [7.12] as

$$y_t - by_{t-1} = 0$$

which is, of course, the complementary equation.

The complementary solution is easily determined as $y_t = cb^t$ and the general solution is

$$Y_t = Y^* + cb^t.$$

If we know that at the start of the analysis ($t = 0$) income takes the value Y_0, then

$$Y_0 = Y^* + cb^0$$

and hence

$$c = Y_0 - Y^* \equiv y_0$$

so the deviation from equilibrium at time t may be written as

$$y_t = (Y^* + y_0 b^t) - Y^* = y_0 b^t \qquad [7.9]$$

which is a monotonically decreasing function (since $0 < b < 1$) of the original disturbance (y_0).

This sort of analysis enables us to hypothesize not only about the equilibrium (comparative static) effect of a change in (say) government expenditure, but also about the speed with which the adjustment will take place. It is tempting to assume, on the basis of the comparative static multiplier, that the government would like the multiplier to be as high as possible, since any deviation from equilibrium would then require only a small change in government expenditure to correct it. In the light of our dynamic analysis, however, this is far from clear. Equation [7.9] tells us that the larger is b, and therefore the larger is the multiplier, the greater will be the deviation from equilibrium at any given time. If we associate such a deviation with unemployment, then the government faces a more awkward problem than was previously thought!

7.2.1 Expected or 'permanent' income

The model just described was a very simple one. Let us make a rather more plausible assumption about consumers' expenditure, viz. that it depends upon the income that consumers expect to receive (Y_t^e):

$$C_t = a + bY_t^e \qquad\qquad 0 < b < 1. \qquad\qquad [7.10]$$

Expectations of income are generated in some way by past expectations combined with recent or current experience. For example, we might hypotheize that

$$(Y_t^e - Y_{t-1}^e) = \lambda(Y_{t-1} - Y_{t-1}^e) \quad 0 < \lambda < 1 \qquad [7.11]$$

or, in words, that consumers revise their expectation by some proportion (λ) of the 'mistake' they made in the previous period. This is known as the *adaptive expectations hypothesis*.

Note: This hypothesis formed an integral part of a model used by Milton Friedman in 1948 to explain consumption behaviour. His model is known as the 'Permanent Income Hypothesis', and it has become common practice to refer to any income variable generated by this process as *permanent income*. This confusion is not in practice helped by a certain inconsistency in the use of the terminology by Friedman himself. We shall avoid commenting further on this controversy.

The model now consists of equations [7.5], [7.10] and [7.11]. Substituting [7.10] into [7.5], we have

$$Y_t = a + bY_t^e + A. \qquad\qquad [7.12]$$

Lag [7.12] by one period and multiply by $(1 - \lambda)$ to give

$$(1 - \lambda)Y_{t-1} = a(1 - \lambda) + b(1 - \lambda)Y_{t-1}^e + A(1 - \lambda) \qquad [7.13]$$

and subtracting [7.13] from [7.12] gives

$$Y_t - (1 - \lambda)Y_{t-1} = \lambda(a + A) + b[Y_t^e - (1 - \lambda)Y_{t-1}^e]. \qquad [7.14]$$

Now from [7.11] we can write

$$Y_t^e - (1 - \lambda)Y_{t-1}^e = \lambda Y_{t-1}. \qquad\qquad [7.15]$$

So substituting [7.15] into [7.14],

$$Y_t - (1 - \lambda)Y_{t-1} = \lambda(a + A) + b\lambda Y_{t-1}$$

$$Y_t - (1 - \lambda + \lambda b)Y_{t-1} = \lambda(a + A) \qquad\qquad [7.16]$$

which is a first-order linear difference equation with constant coefficients. The solution, which readers should verify for themselves, is

$$Y_t = Y^* + c(1 - \lambda + \lambda b)^t \qquad\qquad [7.17]$$

where $Y^* = (a + A)/(1 - b)$ and $c = Y^0 - Y^* \equiv y_0$; and hence [7.17] can be written as

$$y_t = y_0(1 - \lambda + \lambda b)^t. \qquad\qquad [7.18]$$

Again, we find that the equilibrium solution is the same as in the static model, but the interesting comparison is between [7.18] and [7.9]. Since $\lambda < 1$,

$$1 - \lambda + \lambda b = 1 - \lambda(1 - b) > 1 - (1 - b) = b$$

$$(1 - \lambda + \lambda b)^t > b^t \text{ for all } b, t.$$

And it follows that deviations from equilibrium are always greater in this more complex model than when we had a simple lagged consumption function.

7.2.2 Partial adjustment models

The dynamic behaviour of economic variables can be modelled in many different ways. One of the most common is to incorporate a *partial adjustment* process, in which expenditure plans are not achieved instantaneously. In these days when hire purchase and other forms of credit transactions are commonplace, it is easy to see how this situation may arise. Other reasons that give rise to similar models include delays in delivery and sheer inertia.

Let us assume that total expenditure (E_t) will lie somewhere between 'desired' expenditure (E_t^D) and actual expenditure last period (E_{t-1}); i.e.,

$$E_t = gE_{t-1} + (1 - g)E_t^D \qquad 0 < g < 1. \qquad [7.19]$$

We now add to this 'adaptive expectations' mechanism to determine E_t^D thus:

$$E_t^D - E_{t-1}^D = \lambda(E_{t-1} - E_{t-1}^D) \qquad 0 < \lambda < 1. \qquad [7.20]$$

To solve this model we use the same trick as in section 7.2.1, viz. lag [7.19] one period, multiply by $(1 - \lambda)$ and subtract the result from [7.19] to give

$$E_t - (1 - \lambda)E_{t-1} = gE_{t-1} - g(1 - \lambda)E_{t-2} + (1 - g)[E_t^D - (1 - \lambda)E_{t-1}^D]. \qquad [7.21]$$

Likewise, we may use [7.20] to derive

$$E_t^D - (1 - \lambda)E_{t-1}^D = \lambda E_{t-1}. \qquad [7.22]$$

Substituting [7.22] into [7.21] and collecting up terms, we have the second-order difference equation

$$E_t - (1 + g - \lambda g)E_{t-1} + g(1 - \lambda)E_{t-2} = 0. \qquad [7.23]$$

It was established in section 6.3 that the stability of the model can be derived directly from the coefficients, and the conditions for stability were stated in [6.32]. Relating these to the present model [7.23], we find that the first is met, since

$$|g(1 - \lambda)| < 1$$

but the second is *not*, since

$$|(1 + g - \lambda g)| = 1 + g(1 - \lambda).$$

The possible variations are endless, but it is interesting to note that in such a simple model as this we *cannot* assume stability. Controlling the economy is not as simple as many believe.

7.3 Exercises

Section 7.1.2

Mr Smith borrows £1200 from the bank. He pays it back in six equal instalments at the end of six months, twelve months and so on. Each instalment is £260 so the total repayment is £1560. The bank call this a 10% rate of interest since total interest paid is £360 or £120 a year for three years. What is the true annual percentage rate?

Section 7.2.2

Consider the following macroeconomic model:

(i) $C_t = 100 + 0.8Y_{t-1}$

(ii) $I_t = 0.75(C_t - C_{t-1})$

(iii) $Y_t = C_t + I_t$

Will it generate stable but cyclical movements in the level of income? Would your answer be the same if the investment function (ii) were

(ii)' $I_t = 0.25(C_t - C_{t-1})$?

Part III

Differential calculus

This is probably the single most important technique in economics. Even if the reader has studied the subject material before, I would advise careful reading of this section before progressing to the more difficult material in Parts IV and V. There is an enormous range of possible applications. Three are presented here – the concept of elasticity is actually used in areas other than economics but is most closely associated with the description of demand. The other two introduce the theory of the firm looking first at nature of a firm's costs and secondly at one theory concerning a firm's behaviour – profit maximization.

8 Differentiation

8.1 The concept of a derivative

In practice, most differentiation is the application of a set of rules. These are easily learnt , but before we proceed to look at them it is important to understand the concept – to ask what a derivative is and why we should want to calculate it. Readers already familiar with the concept, however, may like to proceed directly to the formal definition in section 8.1.2.

8.1.1 An intuitive approach

Mr Smith drives a vintage car. It is a magnificent machine capable of high speed but it does have some drawbacks. Owing to its weight, acceleration is very poor and the brakes really are not very good. Everything has to be done smoothly, and even then it is not unknown for bits to fall off! The car boasts many accessories, including a clock and a rather old-fashioned odometer (which measures the distance travelled), which works perfectly going forward but which, when the car is reversed, also runs backwards. Anxious to prove to his colleagues that his car is a sensible means of everyday travel, Mr Smith has formed the habit of recording his journeys, noting the reading on the odometer and the time on the clock at various points on his journey. His observations for one day are recorded in figure 8.1. The entire journey from his home to work takes 30 minutes (leaving at 8.30 am) and the distance to work is exactly 15 miles. His average speed therefore is $(15/30) \times 60 = 30$ mph.

Had Mr Smith driven at exactly 30 mph all the way, we could tell where he was at any particular time by reading it off the graph along the *OW* line. In fact, Mr Smith observed that he passed the 'Merry Harriers', which is exactly 3 miles from his house, at 8.42 am. Over the narrow country lanes near his home he managed to average only $(3/12) \times 60 = 15$ mph. Instead of travelling 6 miles he has travelled only 3 miles, and if we look at figure 8.1 we can see this graphically. Plotting his average speed over this section, it is clear that the slope of the line *OM* is much less than that of *OW* – indeed, it is only half as steep.

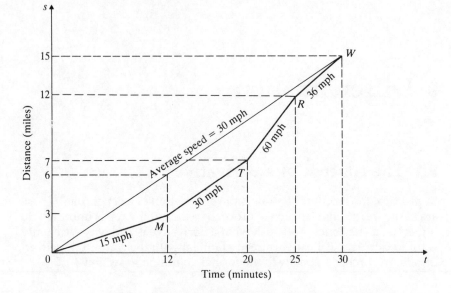

Figure 8.1 'Monday morning'

Once on the main road, progress improves and he reaches the 'Travellers' Rest' at 8.50 am. He has travelled another 4 miles in 8 minutes. From there he proceeds along the dual carriageway to the 'Red Lion', a mere 3 miles from his destination. The time is now 8.55 am, and the last 5 miles were covered in only 5 minutes (60 mph). Note that the line measuring his average speed in this section (*TR*) is much steeper than *OW*. Finally, he slows down a little as he nears his destination and the traffic becomes heavier.

By breaking the journey up in this way, we have deduced rather more about the actual speeds attained. We may think of the distances Mr Smith has travelled (*s*) as a function of the time since he left home (*t*); i.e.,

$$s = f(t)$$

and we have calculated his speed over particular parts of the journey by noting the time at which he passed particular points (t_1 and t_2) and reading from the odometer the distances (s_1 and s_2) and then dividing the change in distance ($\Delta s = s_2 - s_1$) by the change in time ($\Delta t = t_2 - t_1$). Hence average speed is

$$\frac{\Delta s}{\Delta t} = \frac{s_2 - s_1}{t_2 - t_1} = \frac{f(t_2) - f(t_1)}{t_2 - t_1}. \qquad [8.1]$$

Now, consider what happened the following morning. Driving along

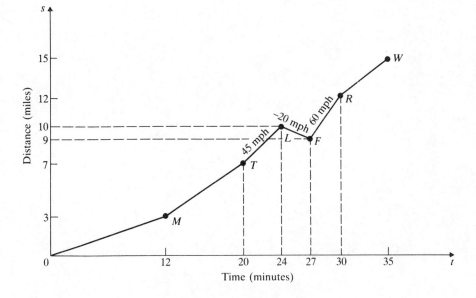

Figure 8.2 'Tuesday morning'

the dual carriageway, the radiator cap fell off. Applying the brakes, Mr Smith slowly brought the car to a stop and then reversed back up the road. Spotting the offending radiator cap, he stopped the car, replaced the cap and resumed his journey. From habit he noticed odometer readings and timings. This was just as well, for when he calculated his average speed between the 'Travellers' Rest' and the 'Red Lion' it came to only 30 mph. It had taken him 10 minutes to travel the 5 miles. Surprised, he drew out the graph shown as figure 8.2. This revealed that he should have divided this part of the journey into three distinct parts. *TL* measures the average speed up to the point he stopped the car the first time (45 mph). For the next three minutes the car was going backwards (and so was the odometer) and the average speed calculated to be negative (−20 mph). Once the cap was refitted, the rest of the journey to the 'Red Lion' was completed at 60 mph. Notice that not only does the slope tell us the speed, but the direction of the slope tells us the direction in which the car was travelling.

Of course, Mr Smith's diagrams are a little crude. Since he was driving the car he could not keep looking at the clock. Had he done so he could have produced a diagram that records the distance (odometer reading) every few *seconds* – see figure 8.3. Notice that at two points on the graph (*L* and *F*) the car was actually stationary, and at those points the graph is flat – we shall return to these 'stationary points' in the next chapter.

Mr Smith's more immediate concern was with the policeman who has

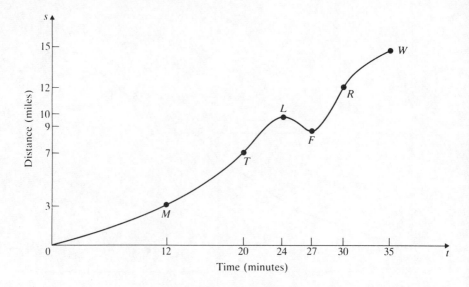

Figure 8.3 'Tuesday morning – the true picture'

just come to see him with a summons for a speeding offence. Apparently he passed through a radar trap just before the 'Red Lion' doing 80 mph. Mr Smith denies the charge and presents figure 8.2 in evidence of the fact that he was only doing 60 along that stretch of road. The policeman, however, knows his mathematics. First he shows Mr Smith that the real picture is more likely to be figure 8.3, and then he enlarges part of it. This is figure 8.4. It shows that, although the average speed from F to R was 60 mph, part of the distance was travelled at less than that speed and part of it at more than 60 mph. When Mr Smith passed the speed trap, the slope of his graph is steeper than the slope of the chord FR, and because the speed trap measures speed over a very short interval it is a much truer estimate of the actual speed at that point. Defeated by modern science, Mr Smith pays his fine and determines to learn some calculus.

The derivative of a function describes the slope of the function at each and every point on the function. (In the example given here it is the speed at which Mr Smith was travelling). It is calculated over a small, indeed, infinitesimal interval and can also be thought of as the slope of the tangent to the curve at a particular point. (Notice that, to highlight the fact that the graph is rising more steeply at X, the policeman actually drew in the line YY', which is the tangent to the slope at this point. Clearly YY' represents a faster speed than FR.)

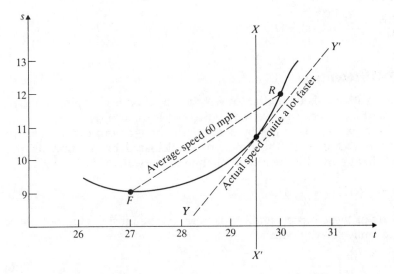

Figure 8.4 'Tuesday morning – greater detail'

8.1.2 A formal statement

Let $s = f(t)$ be a continuous function of t. The change in the value of the function (Δs) as a result of a change in its argument (Δt) is given by

$$\Delta s = f(t_2) - f(t_1) \qquad \text{where } \Delta t = t_2 - t_1. \qquad [8.2]$$

Substituting for t_2 and dividing both sides by Δt, [8.2] becomes

$$\frac{\Delta s}{\Delta t} = \frac{f(t_1 + \Delta t) - f(t_1)}{\Delta t}. \qquad [8.3]$$

This will be true for all values of t, so dropping the subscript we define the derivative with respect to t as

$$\left(\frac{ds}{dt}\right) \equiv \lim_{\Delta t \to 0} \left[\frac{f(t + \Delta t) - f(t)}{\Delta t}\right]. \qquad [8.4]$$

This expression describes the slope of the function over an infinitesimally short interval.

Note: While (ds/dt) is perhaps the most common notation, it is not the only one. The other really common one which is also used extensively in the rest of the book is $f'(t)$, but the following may also be encountered in other books:

$$\frac{df(t)}{dt}; \quad \frac{df}{dt}; \quad D(s); \quad Ds.$$

8.1.3 Differentials

The derivative tells us the *rate* at which a function is changing when its argument changes. This we may write as (ds/dt) or $f'(t)$.

If the argument changes by some very small amount (dt), then the consequent change in the function is calculated by multiplying this actual change in t by the rate of change or derivative, $f'(t)$; i.e.,

$$ds = f'(t)dt = \left(\frac{ds}{dt}\right)dt. \qquad [8.5]$$

The first of these representations is perhaps the most useful, but notice that we may rewrite both as

$$f'(t) = \left(\frac{ds}{dt}\right) = \frac{ds}{dt} \qquad [8.6]$$

and the derivative is shown to be the ratio of the *differentials* (ds, dt). While this is true for single-variate functions such as $s = f(t)$, it is *not* true for multivariate functions (e.g., $s = f(t, v)$), which will be dealt with in Part V. There *is* a meaningful distinction between derivatives and differentials, which we will have need of later.

8.2 Rules of differentiation

As indicated above, most differentiation is the systematic application of a set of rules. It may be useful, however, to note first that differentiation can be done from first principles. Thus, if

$$y = 3x^2 \qquad [8.7]$$

we may find the derivative with respect to x by using the definition [8.4]. Changing the letters to correspond with those in [8.7], we have

$$\left(\frac{dy}{dx}\right) \equiv \lim_{\Delta x \to 0}\left[\frac{f(x + \Delta x) - f(x)}{\Delta x}\right]. \qquad [8.8]$$

It is very important that readers are able to translate the rules specified in terms of particular variables into those necessary for the problem in hand. Check [8.8] carefully.

From [8.7] we know that

$$f(x + \Delta x) = 3(x + \Delta x)^2 = 3[x^2 + 2x\Delta x + (\Delta x)^2] \qquad [8.9]$$

and, therefore, substituting [8.7] and [8.9] into [8.8],

$$\frac{dy}{dx} = \lim_{\Delta x \to 0} \left[\frac{3x^2 + 6x\Delta x + 3(\Delta x)^2 - 3x^2}{\Delta x} \right]$$

$$= \lim_{\Delta x \to 0} (6x + 3\Delta x)$$

$$= 6x.$$

8.2.1 The power rule

Rule:

$$I \qquad y = ax^n \qquad \frac{dy}{dx} = nax^{n-1}. \qquad [8.10]$$

By way of an example, consider the function differentiated above, viz. $y = 3x^2$. By applying rule I we have $dy/dx = 2(3x^{2-1}) = 6x$. All of the rules can be proved from first principles, but this is beyond the scope of the book. A proof of rule I for positive integer values of n is given in the following optional section (8.2.2), but for the most part, it is sufficient to learn the rules and do plenty of examples.

*8.2.2 Proof of the power rule for $n = 1, 2, ...$

If $f(x) = ax^n$, then $f(x + \Delta x) = a(x + \Delta x)^n$ and

$$\frac{dy}{dx} \equiv \lim_{\Delta x \to 0} \left[\frac{f(x + \Delta x) - f(x)}{\Delta x} \right]$$

$$= \lim_{\Delta x \to 0} \left[\frac{a(x + \Delta x)^n - ax^n}{\Delta x} \right]. \qquad [8.11]$$

Using the binomial expansion discussed in the appendix to chapter 5, we may write

$$(x + \Delta x)^n = x^n + nx^{n-1} \cdot \Delta x + \frac{n(n-1)}{2} x^{n-2}(\Delta x)^2 + ... \qquad [8.12]$$

Substituting [8.12] into [8.11],

$$\frac{dy}{dx} = \lim_{\Delta x \to 0} \left[\frac{nx^{n-1} \cdot \Delta x + n(n-1)x^{n-2} \cdot (\Delta x)^2 + ...}{\Delta x} \right]$$

$$= \lim_{\Delta x \to 0} \left[nx^{n-1} + \frac{n(n-1)}{2} x^{n-2} \cdot \Delta x + \dots \right]$$

$$= nx^{n-1}.$$

8.2.3 The sum, product and quotient rules

Rule II below tells us that any function that consists of a number of terms added together can be dealt with one term at a time. Rule III deals with the case where a function is the product of two simpler functions. Rule IV is in fact a special case of rule III, since any quotient can be written in product form, but IV is computationally simpler.

Rules:
If $u = f(x)$ and $v = g(x)$, and if

$$\text{II } y = u + v, \qquad \frac{dy}{dx} = \frac{du}{dx} + \frac{dv}{dx} \qquad\qquad [8.13]$$

$$\text{III } y = u \cdot v, \qquad \frac{dy}{dx} = v\frac{du}{dx} + u\frac{dv}{dx} \qquad\qquad [8.14]$$

$$\text{IV } y = \frac{u}{v}, \qquad \frac{dy}{dx} = \frac{v(du/dx) - u(dv/dx)}{v^2} \qquad [8.15]$$

There now follow some worked examples, but readers who wish a more formal treatment of these rules will find it in section 8.2.5 after the discussion of rule V.

Worked examples

Q. Differentiate with respect to x the function

$$y = (1 + 2x)x^2.$$

A. There are two ways to do this.
   (i) Multiply out to give $y = x^2 + 2x^3$. Then differentiate each term in turn using rule I and add the results:

$$\therefore \frac{dy}{dx} = 2x + 6x^2.$$

   (ii) Use rule III with $u = f(x) = 1 + 2x$ and $v = g(x) = x^2$. Now, $du/dx = 2$ and $dv/dx = 2x$; therefore

$$\frac{dy}{dx} = 2x^2 + 2x(1 + 2x)$$

$$\frac{dy}{dx} = 6x^2 + 2x$$

Q. Differentiate $y = (1 + x)/x$ with respect to x.

A. Using rule IV and setting $u = 1 + x$, $v = x$, we have

$$\frac{du}{dx} = \frac{dv}{dx} = 1$$

and

$$\frac{dy}{dx} = \frac{x - (1 + x)}{x^2} = \frac{-1}{x^2}.$$

8.2.4 The chain rule

The great value of rule V is that it enables us to deal with quite complex expressions in a simple fashion. (The concept of a function of a function was discussed in chapter 2.) Using the concept of differentials introduced in section 8.1.3, we may write

$$dy = \left(\frac{dy}{du}\right)du \qquad [8.16]$$

and

$$du = \left(\frac{du}{dx}\right)dx. \qquad [8.17]$$

Substituting [8.17] into [8.16],

$$dy = \left(\frac{dy}{du}\right)\left(\frac{du}{dx}\right)dx.$$

Dividing both sides by dx, and noting that for single-variate functions the derivative is equal to the ratio of the differentials, we have rule V.

Rule:

If $y = f(u)$ and $u = g(x)$, then $y = f(g(x))$ and

$$\text{V} \quad \frac{dy}{dx} = \frac{dy}{du} \cdot \frac{du}{dx}. \qquad [8.18]$$

Note that, if x itself is a function of another variable, say $x = h(w)$, then we may extend [8.18] thus:

$$\frac{dy}{dw} = \frac{dy}{du} \cdot \frac{du}{dx} \cdot \frac{dx}{dw}$$

[8.19]

and so on.

Worked example

Q. Differentiate $(x + a)^5$ with respect to x.

A. Although we could expand $(x + a)^5$ and then differentiate, this is exceedingly tedious. Instead, define two functions $y = u^5$ and $u = x + a$; then, by rule V,

$$\frac{dy}{du} = 5u^4; \quad \frac{du}{dx} = 1 \text{ and } \frac{dy}{dx} = 5(x + a)^4.$$

*8.2.5 Proof of product and quotient rules

When x is increased by some small amount, both u and v will change, by Δu and Δv respectively. The resulting value of y may be calculated as

$$y + \Delta y = (u + \Delta u)(v + \Delta v)$$

$$= uv + v \cdot \Delta u + u \cdot \Delta v + \Delta u \cdot \Delta v.$$

[8.20]

But since $y = u \cdot v$, we may subtract this from [8.20] to give

$$\Delta y = v \cdot \Delta u + u \cdot \Delta v + \Delta u \cdot \Delta v.$$

[8.21]

Dividing both sides of [8.21] by Δx gives

$$\frac{\Delta y}{\Delta x} = v \cdot \frac{\Delta u}{\Delta x} + u \cdot \frac{\Delta v}{\Delta x} + \Delta u \cdot \frac{\Delta v}{\Delta x}.$$

[8.22]

As Δx tends to zero, so does Δu, so the final term will tend to zero but $\lim_{\Delta x \to 0} \frac{\Delta u}{\Delta x}$ is the definition of du/dx or $f'(x)$. Likewise dy/dx and dv/dx, so taking limits of [8.22] as $\Delta x \to 0$,

$$\frac{dy}{dx} = v\frac{du}{dx} + u\frac{dv}{dx}$$

which is rule III.

The proof of rule IV provides a further example of the use of the chain rule and the product rule.

$$y = \frac{u}{z}$$

[8.23]

where $u = u(x)$ and $z = z(x)$ (i.e. both are functions of x). Rewriting [8.23] we have

$$y = u \cdot z^{-1}$$

and we can use the product rule (rule III) with $v = z^{-1} = \dfrac{1}{z}$.

Now, using the chain rule (rule V),

$$\frac{dv}{dx} = \frac{dv}{dz} \cdot \frac{dz}{dx} = -z^{-2} \cdot \frac{dz}{dx}. \qquad [8.24]$$

So, substituting for [8.24] in [8.14],

$$\frac{dy}{dx} = \frac{1}{z}\frac{du}{dx} + u\left(-\frac{1}{z^2} \cdot \frac{dz}{dx}\right)$$

$$= \frac{z(du/dx) - u(dz/dx)}{z^2}.$$

8.2.5 The inverse rule

In section 8.1.3 we showed that, if $y = f(x)$,

$$f'(x) \equiv \left(\frac{dy}{dx}\right) = \frac{dy}{dx}. \qquad [8.25]$$

Inverting [8.25],

$$\frac{dx}{dy} = \frac{1}{f'(x)} = \frac{1}{(dy/dx)}. \qquad [8.26]$$

But by the same definition,

$$\frac{dx}{dy} = \left(\frac{dx}{dy}\right),$$

i.e. the derivative of x with respect to y. Thus [8.26] establishes rule VI.

Rule:

$$\text{VI} \quad \frac{dy}{dx} = \frac{1}{dx/dy}. \qquad [8.27]$$

Worked example

Q. If $x = y^3$ find $\dfrac{dy}{dx}$.

A. We could rearrange the equation to $y = x^{(1/3)}$ and hence $dy/dx = \frac{1}{3}x^{-(2/3)}$, but in many cases it is unnecessary. Rather, calculate $dx/dy = 3y^2$ and hence

$$\frac{dy}{dx} = \frac{1}{3y^2}.$$

(Check for yourself that $\dfrac{1}{3y^2} = \frac{1}{3}x^{-(2/3)}$).

8.2.6 Some standard forms

The following are stated without proof. (All can be proved by utilizing power series expansions – see for example the appendix to chapter 5 for a series expansion of e^x.) The reader is advised to learn them.

Rules:

VII $\quad y = \log_e[f(x)]$ $\qquad\qquad \dfrac{dy}{dx} = \dfrac{f'(x)}{f(x)}$ $\qquad$ [8.28]

VIII $\quad y = e^{f(x)}$ $\qquad\qquad \dfrac{dy}{dx} = f'(x)e^{f(x)}$ $\qquad$ [8.29]

IX $\quad y = a^x$ $\qquad\qquad \dfrac{dy}{dx} = a^x\log_e a$ $\qquad$ [8.30]

Notice in particular two special cases of rules VII and VIII respectively.

If $y = \log_e x$ $\qquad\qquad \dfrac{dy}{dx} = \dfrac{1}{x}$ $\qquad$ [8.31]

If $y = e^x$ $\qquad\qquad \dfrac{dy}{dx} = e^x$ $\qquad$ [8.32]

8.3 Higher-order derivatives

We have seen that when a function is differentiated the result may itself be a function. Thus when $y = 3x^2$ we found $dy/dx = 6x$. But $6x$ is itself a function that can be differentiated with respect to x:

$$\frac{d(dy/dx)}{dx} = \frac{d(6x)}{dx} = 6. \qquad [8.33]$$

The notation used in [8.33] is clumsy. To represent the *second derivative* it is usual to abbreviate this to one of the following:

$$\frac{d^2y}{dx^2}; \quad f''(x); \quad f^2(x) \text{ or } D^2(y)$$

with the first two being the most common.

There is of course no reason to stop at the second derivative. We could define the third derivative, the fourth derivative or indeed the *n*th derivative. The latter would be written in one of the following notations:

$$\frac{d^n y}{dx^n}; \quad f^n(x) \text{ or } D^n(y).$$

Note: Although interpretation may not always be obvious, there are *no new techniques* involved in calculating higher-order derivatives.

8.3.1 Interpretation of high-order derivatives

Often higher orders are difficult to interpret. If we draw a graph of some function $s = f(t)$ (as in section 8.1.1), then the first derivative can be interpreted as the slope of that graph. Plotting this new information on the graph, the second derivative is the slope of the second graph, and so on.

If for example s represents distance travelled in a certain time t, then ds/dt is the velocity (speed and direction) at which the object is travelling at any particular time. The second derivative will then tell us the rate of change of velocity – a concept we know as acceleration. Thus, physicists have shown that a body in free fall will fall a distance of

$$s = 16t^2 \text{ (feet in } t \text{ seconds).} \hspace{3cm} [8.34]$$

Differentiating [8.34] gives a velocity of

$$\frac{ds}{dt} = 32t \text{ (feet per second)} \hspace{3cm} [8.35]$$

which speed clearly increases as time passes; i.e., a falling body accelerates. Differentiating again will give us the rate of acceleration as

$$\frac{d^2 s}{dt^2} = 32 \text{ (feet per second per second).} \hspace{2cm} [8.36]$$

The most useful interpretation of second-order derivatives is in terms of the shape of a function, and this will be taken up in the next chapter.

8.4 Exercises

Section 8.2.1

Differentiate the following with respect to x:

(i) $y = 2x$

(ii) $y = 2\sqrt{x}$

(iii) $y = x^{(1/2)}$

(iv) $y = 2x^3$

(v) $y = 3x^{-2}$

(vi) $y = 1/x$

Section 8.2.3

Find dy/dx when

(i) $y = (1 + x)(1 + x)$

(ii) $y = (1 + x^2)(1 + 1/x)$

(iii) $y = (1 + x^2) - (1 - x)$

(iv) $y = \dfrac{1 - x^2}{1 - x}$; $x \neq 1$

(v) $y = \dfrac{1 + x^2}{1 - x^2}$; $x \neq \pm 1$

Section 8.2.4

Find dy/dx when

(i) $y = (1 + 2x)^2$

(ii) $y = (1 + 2x)^{17}$

(iii) $y = (1 + 2x^2)^{(1/2)}$

(iv) $y = x^2(1 + x)^3$

Section 8.2.5

Find dy/dx if

(i) $x = y^3 - y$

(ii) $x = y^{(1/2)}(1 - y)^{(1/2)}$

Section 8.3.1

Find d^2y/dx^2 where

(i) $y = 3x^3 - 6x^2 + 2x + 3$

(ii) $y = (1 - 2x)^2$

(iii) $y = \log_e x$

(iv) $y = (1 - 2x)^{-2}$

(v) $y = e^x$

(vi) $y = a^x$

Further exercises

1 Find dy/dx for each of the following:

(i) $y = \left(1 + \dfrac{x}{2}\right)^n$

(iv) $x = 2^y$

(ii) $y = e^{3x}$

(v) $y = e^x \log_e x$

(iii) $y = \log_e[(1 + x)^2]$

(vi) $x = ay^\alpha$

2 Find d^2y/dx^2 for each of the following:

(i) $y = e^{ax}$

(iii) $y = ax^2 + bx + c$

(ii) $y = xe^x$

(iv) $y = \dfrac{1}{\sqrt{x}}$

9 Maxima and minima

9.1 The shape of a function

The first derivative tells us whether a function is increasing or decreasing, but there is more to the shape of a function than that. We may wish to know whether a function has a particular curvature. If a function has a negative derivative it falls from left to right. If the derivative itself is also falling (i.e. is becoming *more* negative) the curve bends down towards the horizontal axis and we say that the function is concave (strictly, it is concave from below). A function with a positive derivative will be climbing from left to right but, again, if the derivative itself is falling (becoming less positive) the curve will bend towards the horizontal axis. The behaviour of the first derivative is of course defined by the second derivative, so we have established that

$$\frac{d^2y}{dx^2} < 0 \Longleftrightarrow \text{concavity} \tag{9.1}$$

and by similar argument

$$\frac{d^2y}{dx^2} > 0 \Longleftrightarrow \text{convexity.} \tag{9.2}$$

Notice however that it is important in [9.1] and [9.2] which variable appears on which axis. In equation [8.27] it was clear that dy/dx and dx/dy always have the same sign, but this is not true of second derivatives. Let

$$y = f(x), \ u = \frac{dy}{dx} \ \text{and} \ z = u^{-1}\left(= \frac{dx}{dy}\right).$$

Then

$$\frac{d^2x}{dy^2} \equiv \frac{dz}{dy} = \frac{dz}{du} \cdot \frac{du}{dx} \cdot \frac{dx}{dy} \tag{9.3}$$

by the chain rule (equation [8.18]). Performing the differentiations,

$$\frac{\mathrm{d}z}{\mathrm{d}u} = -u^{-2} \text{ and } \frac{\mathrm{d}u}{\mathrm{d}x} = \frac{\mathrm{d}^2 y}{\mathrm{d}x^2} \tag{9.4}$$

and substituting [9.4] into [9.3],

$$\frac{\mathrm{d}^2 x}{\mathrm{d}y^2} = -u^{-2}\frac{\mathrm{d}^2 y}{\mathrm{d}x^2}\cdot\frac{\mathrm{d}x}{\mathrm{d}y}$$

$$= -\left(\frac{\mathrm{d}y}{\mathrm{d}x}\right)^{-3}\left(\frac{\mathrm{d}^2 y}{\mathrm{d}x^2}\right) \tag{9.5}$$

and the two second-order derivatives will have the same sign if and only if $\mathrm{d}y/\mathrm{d}x < 0$.

9.2 Stationary points

In chapter 8 we introduced the concept of differentiation as a method of finding the reaction of one variable to a change in another. The intuitive explanation of section 8.1.1 used the example of a man driving his car to work. If distance travelled is a function of time, then the derivative measures the rate of change of distance (i.e. the speed of the car). In the event that the car is stationary (travelling neither forwards nor backwards), that speed is of course zero, and figure 8.3 included two occasions on which that was the case. A similar picture is reproduced as figure 9.1, but this time it is for the function:

$$s = t^3 - 9t^2 + 15t + 30.$$

Figure 9.1 also includes a graph that shows the velocity at each point in time (v), which is of course

$$v \equiv \frac{\mathrm{d}s}{\mathrm{d}t} = 3t^2 - 18t + 15. \tag{9.6}$$

To start with the distance (s) is increasing, velocity ($\mathrm{d}s/\mathrm{d}t$) is positive, but the actual velocity is falling. At A the car is stationary, moving neither forwards or backwards, and at this point velocity is of course zero. For the next four minutes the car travels backwards and the velocity has a negative sign. At B it has ceased to reverse – indeed it is again stationary and the derivative is again zero – and thereafter the car proceeds forwards at an increasing speed.

The points A and B are called a *maximum* and a *minimum*, respectively. Note that they are *not* the maximum or minimum values obtained by the function; rather, they are what we call *relative* extrema. The point A is a maximum in that it has a greater value than any other point in the immediate vicinity. To put it another way, it is like a road going over the

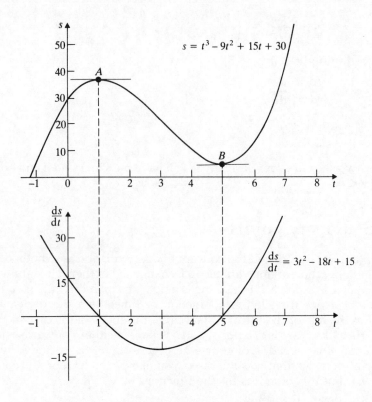

Figure 9.1 Maxima and minima

hills; A is the top of a hill, but there may be other hills that are higher. By the same token, B is a relative minimum. In terms of the road over the hills B is the worst place to break down, since whichever direction you have to push it is going to be uphill.

9.2.1 Maxima and minima

One method of locating these relative extrema is to draw a graph of the function as in figure 9.1. An alternative, and simpler, method is to notice that such points can occur only when the derivative is zero. If there is to be a maximum, then the function must first increase and then decrease – the derivative must first be positive and then negative. If the function is smooth, then the change in the slope must be a gradual one and at some point the derivative must change sign. At this point it is zero, the tangent to the curve is a horizontal line, and we have a maximum. Exactly the reverse will apply to the minimum at B.

Thus in the example above setting [9.6] equal to zero gives

$3t^2 - 18t + 15 = 0$

$3(t^2 - 6t + 5) = 0$

$3(t - 5)(t - 1) = 0$

$\therefore t = 1$ or $t = 5$.

So stationary points occur when $t = 1$ and when $t = 5$. To discover whether $t = 1$ is a maximum or minimum, we could calculate $f(1)$ and then find $f(0.9)$ and $f(1.1)$, but this is rather clumsy. Alternatively, we could look at the value of the derivative either side of $t = 1$. Calculating $f'(0)$ and $f'(2)$ is straightforward in this case, giving values of 15 and -9 respectively (see figure 9.1), but such calculations are not always easy.

If we look at the graph of ds/dt we notice that at $t = 1$ it is falling. Clearly, it must if ds/dt is to change from positive to negative, but we know that if a function is falling then it will have a negative derivative. The derivative of ds/dt is, by definition (see section 8.3), d^2s/dt^2, so we now have a simple condition for establishing the presence of a maximum, viz.:

$$\frac{d^2s}{dt^2} < 0 \text{ at } t = 1.$$

Differentiating [9.6],

$$\frac{dv}{dt} \equiv \frac{d^2s}{dt^2} = 6t - 18 \qquad\qquad < 0 \text{ if } t = 1$$

$$> 0 \text{ if } t = 5 \qquad\qquad [9.7]$$

and we can see that not only is $t = 1$ a maximum, but $t = 5$ must be a minimum, since at that point the derivative is rising (changing from negative to positive).

9.2.2 Points of inflexion

There remains one possibility, however, that has not yet been discussed. What happen if d^2s/dt^2 is itself zero?

Such a point does exist in figure 9.1. Setting [9.7] equal to zero,

$$\frac{d^2s}{dt^2} = 6t - 18 = 0 \Rightarrow t = 3.$$

When $t = 3$ the derivative of v is itself zero, and so it must be either a minimum or maximum. In this case it is a minimum, as may be established by calculating

$$\frac{d^2v}{dt^2} \equiv \frac{d^3s}{dt^3} = 6 > 0.$$

At this point the function $s = f(t)$ stops being concave (to the x-axis) and becomes convex, and we call this a *point of inflexion*.

It is possible that such a point of inflexion could coincide with a stationary point, and an example of this is given in figure 9.2.

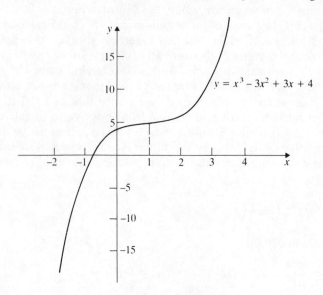

$y = x^3 - 3x^2 + 3x + 4$

Figure 9.2 Point of inflexion

Algebraically,

$$y = x^3 - 3x^2 + 3x + 4 \tag{9.8}$$

$$\frac{dy}{dx} = 3x^2 - 6x + 3 = 0$$

$$\therefore 3(x^2 - 2x + 1) = 3(x - 1)^2 = 0$$

and there is a stationary point when $x = 1$. But taking the second derivative, we find that

$$\frac{d^2y}{dx^2} = 6x - 6 = 0 \text{ if } x = 1. \tag{9.9}$$

Actually, it is neither a maximum nor a minimum but a point of inflexion, as may be seen from figure 9.2. In view of this possibility, it would seem that a more complex decision rule is needed to establish the shape of a curve when both first- and second-order derivatives are zero, and this is given in the following section.

9.3 Formal conditions for maxima and minima

In the previous section we showed that it is possible for a stationary point and a point of inflexion to coincide. One might be tempted to conclude that if the second derivative is zero then it *must* be a point of inflexion rather than a maximum or minimum. That this is not so is easily demonstrated. Consider

$$y = x^4$$

Then

$$\frac{dy}{dx} = 4x^3 = 0 \qquad\qquad \text{iff } x = 0 \qquad\qquad [9.10]$$

$$\frac{d^2y}{dx^2} = 12x^2 = 0 \qquad\qquad \text{iff } x = 0 \qquad\qquad [9.11]$$

$$\frac{d^3y}{dx^3} = 24x = 0 \qquad\qquad \text{iff } x = 0$$

$$\frac{d^4y}{dx^4} = 24 > 0 \qquad\qquad\qquad\qquad\qquad\qquad [9.12]$$

In this case [9.10] tells us that there is a stationary point at $x = 0$, Equation [9.11] might lead one to expect a point of inflexion, but that is clearly not so. Whatever non-zero value x takes, $x^4 > 0$ and so the function has a true minimum when $x = 0$. The solution is to be found by further differentiating – continuing until we find a non-zero derivative (in this case equation [9.12]). If the first non-zero derivative requires an odd number of differentiations then we do in fact have a point of inflexion, but if not, then we have a maximum or minimum as given by the sign of the derivative. In the case of equation [9.8], there was a stationary point at $x = 1$. From [9.9],

$$\frac{d^2y}{dx^2}\bigg|_{x=1} = 0 \qquad\qquad\qquad\qquad\qquad\qquad [9.13]$$

and differentiating [9.13] gives

$$\frac{d^3y}{dx^3} = 6 > 0.$$

So the first non-zero derivative required an odd number of differentiations and we did indeed have a point of inflexion.

Note the notation used in [9.13]. It tells us to evaluate the derivative
d^2y/dx^2 when $x = 1$. A simpler notation is to use the functional notation
$y = f(x)$; then [9.13] becomes

$$f''(1) = 0. \tag{9.14}$$

Using this alternative notation, we may write the formal conditions as
follows.

Rule: For any function $f(x)$ there will be a stationary point at x^* iff

$$f'(x^*) = 0.$$

This is the *first-order condition*. The *second-order conditions* state that it will
be a maximum iff

$$f''(x^*) < 0, f'(x^*) = 0 \qquad 1 \leqslant r < n \text{ and } n \text{ even.}$$

It will be a minimum iff

$$f''(x^*) > 0, f'(x^*) = 0 \qquad 1 \leqslant r < n \text{ and } n \text{ even.}$$

But it will be a point of inflexion iff

$$f''(x^*) \neq 0, f'(x^*) = 0 \qquad 1 \leqslant r < n \text{ and } n \text{ odd.}$$

9.4 Exercises

Section 9.1

Find d^2y/dx^2 where

(i) $x = y^3$ (iii) $x = \dfrac{1 + y}{1 - y}$

(ii) $x = e^y$

Section 9.2

Find any stationary points of the following. Are they maxima or
minima?

(i) $y = 2x^2 + 6x - 56$ (iv) $y = \dfrac{16x}{x^2 + 4}$

(ii) $y = 3x^2 - 7x + 2$ (v) $y = x + \dfrac{16}{x}$

(iii) $y = x^3 - 2x^2 + 2x - 1$

Section 9.3

Sketch the following functions by finding the nature of any stationary points, the curvature of the function, its limits and/or values when it cuts the axes. (Not all the information may be necessary for each function.)

(i) $y = \log_e x$

(ii) $y = \frac{1}{3}x^3 - x^2 + 12$

(iii) $y = 1 - 2x^4$

(iv) $y = xe^{-x}$

(v) $y = ay^\alpha$, $\alpha > 1$

(vi) $y = \dfrac{1}{x}$

10 Economic applications III

10.1 Demand, supply and the concept of elasticity

The demand curve gives the relationship between quantity demanded (Q^D) and the price paid (P). In demand analysis it is usual to write this as

$$Q^D = f(P) \qquad\qquad [10.1]$$

notwithstanding the usual graphical representation with P on the vertical axis. In section 10.3 we shall discuss the theory of firms' behaviour, and then it will be convenient to write the relationship the other way round:

$$P = g(Q) = f^{-1}(Q). \qquad\qquad [10.2]$$

In practice however this may not prove such a problem. From the rules for differentiating inverse functions (see equations [8.27] and [9.5]) we know that

$$\frac{dP}{dQ} = 1\Big/\frac{dQ}{dP} \qquad\qquad [10.3]$$

$$\frac{d^2P}{dQ^2} = -\left(\frac{dQ}{dP}\right)^{-3}\left(\frac{d^2Q}{dP^2}\right) \qquad\qquad [10.4]$$

which is all we shall need to determine the shape of the function.

10.1.1 The shape of the demand curve

The most commonly postulated form for [10.1] is the linear function

$$Q^D = a - bP \quad a > 0,\ b > 0. \qquad\qquad [10.5]$$

The slope of this function is given by dP/dQ (P on the vertical axis):

$$\frac{dQ}{dP} = -b; \quad \frac{dP}{dQ} = \frac{-1}{b}$$

$$\frac{d^2Q}{dP^2} = 0; \quad \frac{d^2P}{dQ^2} = 0.$$

So the demand curve slopes down from left to right and the slope is constant (i.e. independent of price and quantity). A quadratic demand curve such as

$$Q^D = a - bP^2 \qquad\qquad a > 0, \, b > 0$$

will have a slope given by

$$\frac{dP}{dQ} = -\frac{1}{2bP}.$$

Notice that in this case the slope varies with P. At high prices (low quantity) the value of dP/dQ tends to zero, whereas at low prices it tends towards negative infinity. It would seem that the demand curve is concave, and we can confirm this by calculating the second derivative. Indeed, using the relationships in [10.3] and [10.4], we know that d^2P/dQ^2 and d^2Q/dP^2 will have the same sign since $dQ/dP < 0$ and $d^2Q/dP^2 = -2b < 0$.

While this shape is possible for some products, it is generally believed that demand curves are convex to the origin, so we are forced to conclude that the quadratic form is not very satisfactory. Consider instead

$$Q = aP^{-\alpha} \quad \alpha > 0 \tag{10.6}$$

$$\frac{dQ}{dP} = -\alpha aP^{-\alpha - 1} < 0$$

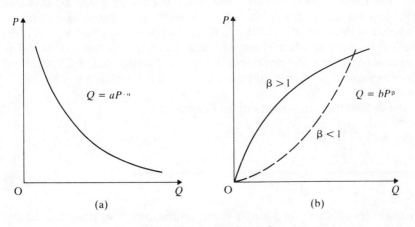

Figure 10.1 Demand and supply curves

$$\frac{d^2Q}{dP^2} = \alpha(\alpha + 1)aP^{-\alpha - 2} > 0. \tag{10.7}$$

For this function, $dP/dQ < 0$ and $d^2P/dQ^2 > 0$, and we have the desired convex shape as pictured in figure 10.1(a).

10.1.2 Shape of the supply curve

Applying a similar analysis to the supply curve, we might consider

$$Q^s = bP^\beta \qquad\qquad \beta > 0 \tag{10.8}$$

Differentiating [10.8] gives

$$\frac{dQ}{dP} = \beta bP^{\beta - 1} > 0$$

$$\frac{d^2Q}{dP^2} = \beta(\beta - 1)P^{\beta - 2} \qquad\qquad > 0 \text{ if } \beta > 1$$

$$< 0 \text{ if } \beta < 1.$$

Notice however that, since dP/dQ, $dQ/dP > 0$, equation [10.4] tells us that d^2P/dQ^2 will have the opposite sign. Thus, if we have $\beta < 1$, then $d^2P/dQ^2 > 0$ and the supply becomes steeper as output increases, which is the more plausible case. Both possibilities are shown in figure 10.1(b).

10.1.3 Elasticity

While the derivative or slope of the function tells us something about shape of the function, it has its limitations. For example, the actual value will depend upon the units of measurement, making comparisons impossible between different products. Suppose however we were to measure not the absolute change in quantity (ΔQ) as a result of a change in price (ΔP), but the *percentage change* in quantity ($\Delta Q)/(Q)$ resulting from a percentage change in price ($\Delta P)/(P)$. Such a measure is known as as *elasticity*.

We define the price elasticity of demand as

$$\varepsilon_D = -\frac{\Delta Q}{Q} \div \frac{\Delta P}{P}$$

$$= -\frac{\Delta Q}{\Delta P} \div \frac{Q}{P}. \tag{10.9}$$

To measure elasticity at a single point on the curve we need to find the limit as $\Delta P \to 0$, but by definition

$$\lim_{\Delta P \to 0} \left(\frac{\Delta Q}{\Delta P} \right) = \frac{dQ}{dP}$$

so we can rewrite [10.9] as

$$\varepsilon_D = -\frac{dQ}{dP} \div \frac{Q}{P} = -\frac{dQ}{dP} \cdot \frac{P}{Q}. \qquad [10.10]$$

It may be of interest to note that, by the chain rule of section 8.2.4,

$$\frac{d \log Q}{d \log P} = \frac{d \log Q}{dQ} \cdot \frac{dQ}{dP} \cdot \frac{dP}{d \log P} = \frac{1}{Q} \cdot \frac{dP}{dQ} \cdot P.$$

So an alternative definition of elasticity is

$$\varepsilon_D = -\frac{d \log Q}{d \log P}. \qquad [10.11]$$

Economists consider it desirable for elasticities to be positive numbers, but demand functions are negatively sloped – hence the minus sign in the definition. Now consider the linear demand function [10.5]:

$$\varepsilon_D = -\frac{dQ}{dP} \cdot \frac{P}{Q} = b\frac{P}{Q}. \qquad [10.12]$$

Its behaviour is easier to see if we substitute [10.5] into [10.12] to give

$$\varepsilon_D = \frac{a}{Q} - 1. \qquad [10.13]$$

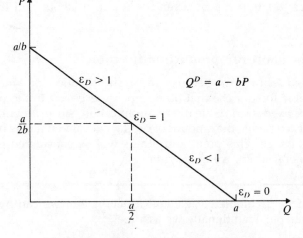

Figure 10.2 Elasticity of a linear function

At low levels of demand (high prices) elasticity will be very high, but as quantity purchased rises the elasticity will fall until eventually $Q = a$ and the elasticity is zero (see figure 10.2).

When $\varepsilon_D > 1$ we say that demand is *elastic*, and when $\varepsilon_D < 1$ we say that demand is *inelastic*. But for most demand functions it does not make sense to talk about the *function* being elastic or inelastic. In particular, the idea that because one function is more steeply sloped than another it is necessarily more inelastic is shown to be obvious nonsense. There is however one demand function for which one can make a simple statement. Equation [10.6] defined a *constant elasticity* curve, as may be seen by substituting [10.6] and [10.7] into the definition [10.10]:

$$\varepsilon_D = \alpha a P^{-\alpha - 1} \cdot \frac{P}{a P^{-\alpha}} = \alpha. \tag{10.14}$$

This goes some way to explaining its popularity among economists.

Note: The concept of elasticity is a general one – one can calculate the price elasticity of supply, the income elasticity of consumption and so on. In all cases the definition is such that the elasticity is always positive.

10.2 Cost functions

In order to determine the amount that it wishes to supply, a firm needs to know what its production actually costs. Let us start with a very simple production function in which there is only one variable input – labour. In section 10.2.2 we shall attach a cost to this labour and hence derive the cost of producing any level of output, but first we consider the physical relationship between the input of labour and the level of output.

10.1.1 The short-run production function

It is termed 'short-run' because for a short period of time it is not unreasonable to suppose that other inputs necessary to the production process are fixed. (This is clearly a simplification, since although we may not be able to change the amount of capital equipment it may be possible to vary its usage. This point and others will be considered in Chapter 16.) In general, then, we may write

$$Q = f(L) \quad L > 0. \tag{10.15}$$

This could be a completely general function, but we can hypothesize about its shape. Traditionally we assume

$$f(0) = 0. \tag{10.16}$$

In words, with no labour input there is no output. As labour increases, so output will increase. The rate of increase in output from an increase in labour is known as the *marginal product of labour* and is given by the derivative, and we require that

$$f'(L) \geq 0. \tag{10.17}$$

How it will actually vary with output levels is open to question, but it is usually assumed that it will first rise and then fall; i.e.,

$$f''(L) > 0 \quad L < L^*$$
$$< 0 \quad L > L^*. \tag{10.18}$$

We say that such a function has *diminishing returns*.

It is possible that at some stage there is so much labour that 'too many cooks spoil the broth', and we might replace [10.17] with the more general form:

$$f'(L) \geq 0 \quad L < L^{**}$$
$$< 0 \quad L > L^{**} > L^*. \tag{10.19}$$

A diagrammatic representation of such a function is given in figure 10.3. The top half of the diagram depicts $f(L)$ itself. Let us call this total product (TP); the lower half of the diagram gives $f'(L)$ or the marginal product (MP) and $f(L)/L$, which is the average product (AP) per unit of labour.

(Recall that Q/L may be represented by the slope of the line drawn from the origin to the point on the curve. The dashed line $0B$, which is tangential to the curve at B, is therefore the maximum value of average product. If the line were drawn any steeper it would not touch the curve at all. Note also that the tangent measures the slope or derivative of the curve at that point, so at B the marginal product and average product are both represented by $0B$; i.e. they are equal.)

The obvious question to ask at this point is, 'Is there a simple function that possesses these properties?' The answer is yes. Consider

$$\text{TP} = Q = aL^3 + bL^2 + cL + d. \tag{10.20}$$

To satisfy [10.16] we must set $d = 0$. Differentiating [10.20] gives

$$\text{MP} = \frac{dQ}{dL} = 3aL^2 + 2bL + c. \tag{10.21}$$

This will be a maximum at L^*, so to find L^* we differentiate [10.21] and set the result equal to zero:

$$\frac{d(\text{MP})}{dL} = \frac{d^2Q}{dL^2} = 6aL + 2b = 0 \tag{10.22}$$

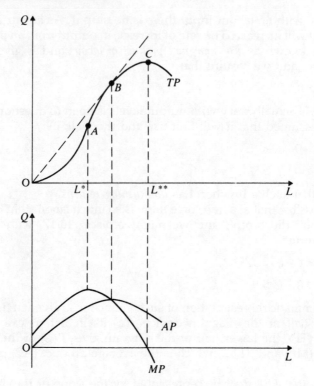

Figure 10.3 Short-run production function

$$L^* = \frac{-2b}{6a}.$$ [10.23]

For this to be a maximum requires that the second derivative be negative; hence

$$\frac{d^2(MP)}{dL^2} = \frac{d^3Q}{dL^3} = 6a < 0.$$ [10.24]

Equation [10.24] will be true only if $a < 0$, and substituting into [10.23] we see that for $L^* > 0$ it follows that $b > 0$. Finally, setting $L = 0$ in [10.21], it is clear that to satisfy [10.19] we must have $c \geq 0$.

We may conclude therefore that a satisfactory representation of the short production function is given by

$$Q = a_1L + a_2L^2 - a_3L^3 \qquad a_1 \geq 0, \, a_2 > 0, \, a_3 \geq 0.$$ [10.25]

10.2.2 Cost functions

If labour is paid a constant wage w, then total costs are given by

$$C = wL + F \qquad\qquad w, L, F > 0 \qquad\qquad [10.26]$$

where F denotes any *fixed costs* over and above the labour costs. Economists call the sum of *variable costs*, in this case the labour costs wL plus fixed costs defined in [10.26], *total costs* (TC). However, we are concerned primarily about the relationship between these costs and the level of output. From [10.15],

$$L = f^{-1}(Q) \qquad\qquad [10.27]$$

and substituting [10.27] into [10.26],

$$C = wf^{-1}(Q) + F \equiv C(Q). \qquad\qquad [10.28]$$

Provided that we assume that firms will never produce when marginal product is negative, we can invert the production function to establish the general shape of the cost function $C(Q)$.

If we define *marginal costs* (MC) as the rate of change of total costs with respect to output, then, using the chain rule and the inverse rule,

$$\text{MC} \equiv \frac{dC}{dQ} = \frac{dC}{dL} \cdot \frac{dL}{dQ} = \frac{dC}{dL} \div \frac{dQ}{dL}. \qquad\qquad [10.29]$$

Noting that dQ/dL is by definition the marginal product, and, differentiating [10.26] to give dC/dL, we have

$$\frac{dC}{dL} = w$$

$$\text{MC} = w \div \frac{dQ}{dL} = \frac{w}{\text{MP}}. \qquad\qquad [10.30]$$

So the marginal cost curve is the reciprocal of the marginal product curve. When marginal product is at a maximum marginal cost will be at a minimum, and so on. In figure 10.4 the cost functions are shown diagrammatically. Notice that the total cost curve does not start from the origin owing to the existence of fixed costs (F); also, where $f(L)$ was concave $C(Q)$ is convex and vice versa. The point Q_x is defined by $f(L^*)$.

We can again show graphically that *average costs* (AC) are at a minimum when they are equal to marginal costs (the proof being left to the reader as an exercise). We can also show that, if we exclude the fixed costs element and define *average variable costs* (AVC) as

$$\text{AVC} = \frac{C(Q) - F}{Q} \qquad\qquad [10.31]$$

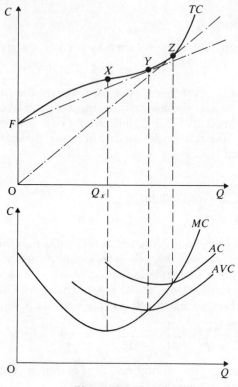

Figure 10.4 Cost function

this will also be at a minimum when AVC = MC. Furthermore, if AVC does indeed have a minimum, then AC must also have a minimum.

In order to have a sensible model we require not only that MP is positive but also that the wage rate is positive. It follows from [10.30] that marginal cost must always be positive for all values of Q (including Q_x). To illustrate these relationships consider the function

$$C = 0.5Q^3 - 6Q^2 + 30Q + 128. \qquad [10.32]$$

Marginal cost is given by

$$\frac{dC}{dQ} = 1.5Q^2 - 12Q + 30 \qquad [10.33]$$

which will be minimized when

$$\frac{d^2C}{dQ^2} = 3Q - 12 = 0$$

i.e. when $Q = 4$, at which point $dC/dQ = 6 > 0$.

Notice that when $Q = 0$, $C = 128$, so we can establish the fixed cost element (F) as 128 and hence average variable cost as

$$\text{AVC} = \frac{C - F}{Q} = 0.5Q^2 - 6Q + 30. \qquad [10.34]$$

Differentiating [10.34] and setting the result equal to zero,

$$\frac{d(\text{AVC})}{dQ} = Q - 6 = 0$$

and AVC is at a minimum when $Q = 6$. Substituting this value into [10.34], we find that minimum AVC is 12, and substituting $Q = 6$ into [10.33], we find that marginal cost is also 12. Readers are invited to prove for themselves that MC = AC at the minimum AC.

10.3 Profit maximization

Traditional economic theory of the firm characterizes the businessman (or entrepreneur) as a person seeking to maximize his profit, defining profit as the difference between total revenue and total costs. If he knows his demand function he can find the total revenue to be gained by selling any particular quantity as

$$R = P \cdot Q \qquad \text{where } P = g(Q). \qquad [10.35]$$

So R is in fact a function of Q. Let us write this *revenue function* as $R = R(Q)$; and, together with the cost function defined in [10.28], we can use it to define the *profit function*:

$$\Pi(Q) = R(Q) - C(Q). \qquad [10.36]$$

To maximize profits we differentiate [10.36] and set the derivative equal to zero:

$$\frac{d\Pi}{dQ} = \frac{dR}{dQ} - \frac{dC}{dQ} = 0 \qquad \text{or MR} = \text{MC} \qquad [10.37]$$

where we use the term *marginal revenue* (MR) to refer to the rate of change in revenue with respect to output. The first-order condition for profit maximization is therefore that marginal revenue equals marginal costs. Intuitively this is obvious. If an additional amount of output adds more to revenue than it does to costs then it should be produced; if it adds less to revenue than to costs it should be not produced. The optimum output (Q^*) is therefore defined by [10.37]; i.e.,

$$R'(Q^*) - C'(Q^*) = 0. \qquad [10.38]$$

To ensure that this is indeed a maximum (rather than a minimum or a point of inflexion) requires that

$$\Pi''(Q^*) = R''(Q^*)' - C''(Q^*) < 0 \qquad [10.39]$$

i.e. that the second derivative of the profit function, evaluated at the optimum output level Q^*, is negative. Perhaps a more instructive way of writing [10.39] is

$$\frac{d(MR)}{dQ}\bigg|_{Q = Q^*} < \frac{d(MC)}{dQ}\bigg|_{Q = Q^*} \qquad [10.40]$$

which says that, at the level of output Q^*, the marginal cost function must be rising more quickly (or falling more slowly) than the marginal revenue function. We say 'MC cuts MR from below'.

We argued in the previous section that above a certain level of output (Q_x) the cost function will be convex (i.e. $C''(Q) > 0$). If it were also true that the revenue function is concave i.e. $R''(Q) < 0$), then [10.39] is necessarily satisfied for any $Q > Q_x$. Not all revenue functions need be concave, but for the purposes of discussion here let us assume a linear demand function. Then

$$P = a - bQ \qquad\qquad a, b > 0$$

$$R \equiv P \cdot Q = aQ - bQ^2$$

$$R'(Q) = a - 2bQ$$

$$R''(Q) = -2b < 0 \qquad [10.41]$$

and [10.41] ensures that the second-order condition holds for any $Q > Q_x$. A diagrammatic representation of this model is given in figure 10.5. (Note that *average revenue* (AR) is given by $R/Q = P$ so the demand curve has been labelled AR.)

10.3.1 Elasticity again

The revenue function [10.35] may be differentiated using the product rule:

$$\frac{dR}{dQ} = P + Q\frac{dP}{dQ} = P\left(1 + \frac{Q}{P} \cdot \frac{dP}{dQ}\right). \qquad [10.42]$$

But by substituting the definition of price elasticity of demand given in [10.10] into [10.42], we have

$$\frac{dR}{dQ} = P\left(1 - \frac{1}{\varepsilon_D}\right). \qquad [10.43]$$

If the demand function is inelastic at a particular level of demand (Q^*),

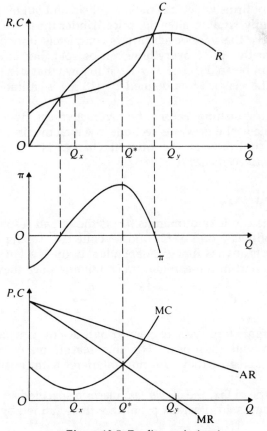

Figure 10.5 Profit maximization

then $\varepsilon_D < 1$ and $dR/dQ < 0$; i.e., revenue will fall with a rise in the quantity sold (fall in price). If on the other hand $\varepsilon_D > 1$, then $dR/dQ > 0$ and revenue will rise. Since marginal cost cannot be negative, then from [10.38]

$$R'(Q^*) \equiv \left.\frac{dR}{dQ}\right|Q = Q^* > 0$$

and it follows that at equilibrium (optimal) output demand must be elastic.

10.3.2 Perfect competition

This is not the place for a full discussion of alternative market forms; however, there is one special case that deserves mention. When there is a great number of firms which can move freely in and out of the market, none is sufficiently large to alter the price. Under these circumstances the demand curve that faces each firm is completely horizontal at the market price. At this price everything can be sold, but at any higher price nothing can be sold. Since $P = P^*$, it follows that $dP/dQ = 0$ and therefore that the elasticity as defined by [10.38] is infinite and from [10.42] that MR = P.

This is the distinguishing feature of *perfect competition*. By contrast, the assumption made in the previous sections in which the firm is assumed to have some control over the price it charges is characteristic of *monopoly* and *imperfect competition*.

10.3.3 Taxation

Taxation of firms can take numerous forms though all resolve to three basic types; profits tax, output tax and revenue tax. Taking the easiest first, a *profits tax* is any tax that is independent of the level of output. As such it plays no part in the equilibrium conditions since they are

$$\frac{d\Pi}{dQ} = 0, \ \frac{d^2\Pi}{dQ^2} < 0$$

and upon differentiating with respect to output any constants in the profits function will disappear. For this reason many economists advocate such taxes – they do not interfere with businessmen's decisions.

The second type of tax, the *output tax*, places a specified amount (t) of tax upon each unit sold. Post-tax profits are then defined by

$$\Pi^* = \Pi - tQ$$

and the equilibrium condition will have been changed by the tax.

Consider the following example. A firm has cost and demand functions given by

$$P = 90 - 2Q$$

$$C = (Q + 3)^2$$

and the government imposes a tax of t per unit sold. Then post-tax profits are

$$\Pi^* = PQ - C - tQ$$
$$= (90 - 2Q)Q - (Q + 3)^2 - tQ$$
$$= (84 - t)Q - 3Q^2 - 9.$$

To find the profit-maximizing output, we proceed as follows:

$$\frac{d\Pi^*}{dQ} = (84 - t) - 6Q = 0; \qquad \frac{d^2\Pi^*}{dQ^2} = -6$$

$$Q^* = 14 - \tfrac{1}{6}t. \hspace{8cm} [10.44]$$

From [10.44] it is clear that $dQ^*/dt < 0$, i.e. that a rise in tax leads to a fall in equilibrium quantity (and a rise in the price). A sales (output) tax is *not* neutral.

The third type of tax is a *revenue tax*, in which a certain percentage of the price paid for the good goes in tax. Let us call the rate of tax r; then, using the same cost and demand functions as in the previous example,

$$\Pi^* = \Pi - r{\cdot}PQ = (1 - r)PQ - C; \; r < 1$$

$$= (1 - r)(90 - 2Q)Q - (Q + 3)^2$$

$$= (84 - 90r)Q - (3 - 2r)Q^2 - 9$$

$$\frac{d\Pi^*}{dQ} = (84 - 90r) - 2(3 - 2r)Q = 0$$

$$Q^* = \frac{42 - 45r}{3 - 2r}$$

which is a maximum, since $d^2\Pi^*/dQ^2 = -2(3 - 2r) < 0$. So again the imposition of a revenue tax will alter the equilibrium. Since

$$\frac{dQ^*}{dr} = \frac{-51}{(3 - 2r)^2} < 0$$

the outcome will again be a higher market price and lower quantity.

10.3 Exercises

1. A firm produces two products for which the demand curves may be written as

   $$Q_1 = a_1 - b_1 P \text{ and } Q_2 = a_2 - b_2 P.$$

   If it is known that $a_1 > a_2$ and $b_1 < b_2$, what can be said of the relative elasticities
   (i) at the same price?
   (ii) at the same quantity?
   (iii) where the two curves intersect?

2. A government seeking to tax a firm may impose
   (a) a lump-sum tax on output
   (b) a unit tax on output sales

(c) a percentage tax on sales revenue

The firm has a demand function given by $P = 14 - Q/2$ and a cost function

$C = 20 + 2Q.$

The government is currently using option (b) – the unit tax – in such a way as to maximize its revenue. Would it in fact increase that revenue if it chose instead

    (i) a lump-sum tax of 24?

    (ii) a percentage sales tax of 50%?

Part IV

Integral calculus

Integration *per se* is not used a great deal in economic analysis although chapter 13 illustrates how it may be used in the analysis of consumer surplus. This Part treats integration primarily as the reverse of the differentiation process and directs us in particular to the analysis of differential equations. It is this technique that proves most valuable in economic applications, and the example presented in chapter 13 concerns the vital macroeconomic topic of stabilization policy.

11 Integration

11.1 The concept of integration

In chapter 1 we argued that if we can define a function – a rule getting from a specific value of one variable to a corresponding value of another variable – then we can conceive of an inverse function to reverse the process. In chapter 5 we introduced a special sort of function known as the exponential function and its inverse function, the natural logarithm. In each case the function and its inverse give the same information, but sometimes it is convenient to use one rather than the other, and sometimes the inverse is not unique. It would be surprising, therefore, if the process that we have defined as differentiation should not have an inverse, even if the inverse is not always unique. This reverse process is known as integration.

In section 11.3 we shall see that, like other inverse operations or functions, integration can be defined in its own right. But to start with let us consider the problem of reversing the differentiation process.

The derivative measures the rate of change of a function with respect to a particular variable. Thus, given distance travelled as a function of time, the derivative gives us velocity as a function of time. The derivative of velocity in turn gives information about the rate of acceleration (see section 8.3.1).

Now, suppose instead that we know that a body accelerates from rest at a constant rate of 32 feet per second per second: how far will it have travelled after t seconds? Denoting this distance as s and the velocity at time t as v, we may write $s = f(t)$, $v = ds/dt$ and

$$\frac{d^2s}{dt^2} = 32 \text{ or } \frac{dv}{dt} = 32. \qquad [11.1]$$

The relationships in [11.1] are called *differential equations*, and in chapter 12 we shall consider the solution to a whole range of such equations of a type common in economic analysis. This chapter is concerned with the process of getting from dv/dt to v and from ds/dt to s – the process we call *integration*.

One possible answer may be adduced by reference to equations [8.34], [8.35] and [8.36]:

$$v = 32t \Rightarrow \frac{dv}{dt} = 32 \qquad\qquad [11.2]$$

$$s = 16t^2 \Rightarrow \frac{ds}{dt} = 32t. \qquad\qquad [11.3]$$

But notice that is not the only satisfactory answer. Consider for example

$$s = 16t^2 + 9t + 8 \qquad\qquad [11.4]$$

$$\frac{ds}{dt} = 32t + 9 \qquad\qquad [11.5]$$

$$\frac{d^2s}{dt^2} = 32. \qquad\qquad [11.6]$$

Equations [11.4] – [11.6] show that each differentiation leads to the loss of one piece of information. The reverse process cannot restore that information, but it should recognize the omission by including an allowance for it – the so-called *arbitrary constant of integration*. Thus, the integral of 32 is not 32t but 32t + c. Formally,

$$\int 32 dt = 32t + c. \qquad\qquad [11.7]$$

Note: The almost universal notation for integration of a function $f(x)$ with respect to the variable x is

$$\int f(x)dx \equiv F(x) + c \qquad\qquad [11.8]$$

which implies and is implied by

$$\frac{dF(x)}{dx} = f(x). \qquad\qquad [11.9]$$

11.2 Techniques of integration

One might be forgiven for saying that the best technique for integration is guesswork – think of a function and differentiate it to see if you've got it right – but there is some scope for taking the guesswork out of it. Wherever there exists a rule for differentiation, it must be possible to reverse it. Thus the power rule (equation[8.10]) stated that

$$y = ax^n \Rightarrow \frac{dy}{dx} = nax^{n-1}. \qquad\qquad [11.10]$$

Setting $b = n \cdot a$ and $m = n - 1$, we can rewrite [11.10] as

$$y = \frac{b}{m + 1} x^{m + 1} \Rightarrow \frac{dy}{dx} = bx^{m}.$$ [11.11]

From the definitions of the integral in equations [11.8] and [11.9], it is clear that [11.11] implies rule I' below.

Rules:

$$I' \int bx^{m}dx = \frac{bx^{m + 1}}{m + 1} + c.$$ [11.12]

II' If $u = f(x)$, $v = g(x)$, then

$$\int (u + v)dx = \int udx + \int vdx + c.$$ [11.13]

Reversing rules in this way will solve many problems. Consider the following examples:

$$\frac{dy}{dx} = a^{x} \Rightarrow y = \frac{a^{x}}{\log_{e}a} + c$$

$$\frac{dy}{dx} = e^{3x} \Rightarrow y = \frac{e^{3x}}{3} + c$$

(which may be readily confirmed by reference to equations [8.30] and [8.29], respectively). The following example needs a little care. If

$$\frac{dy}{dx} = \frac{2x + 1}{x^{2}}$$

then this does not fit any of the standard rules. However, rewriting it as

$$\frac{dy}{dx} = \frac{2x}{x^{2}} + \frac{1}{x^{2}} = \frac{2x}{x^{2}} + x^{-2}$$

and the first term is in the form $f'(x)/f(x)$, so we can use the rule for differentiating logarithms (equation [8.28]) in conjunction with rules I' and II' above to deduce that

$$y = \log_{e}(x^{2}) - \frac{1}{x} + c.$$

There are however many occasions upon which standard forms cannot be used – even after manipulation of the functions, and even allowing for a rather wider range of standard forms than can be considered here. In particular, we need a technique to cope with combinations of functions. But before we proceed to this, try the first set of exercises at the end of the chapter. More than any other technique, integration is all about practice.

11.2.1 Integration by parts

When differentiating the product of two functions, we found it convenient to treat the problem in two parts. We established the product rule (equation [8.14]), which said that, if $y = u \cdot v$ where u and v are both functions of x, then

$$\frac{dy}{dx} = v\frac{du}{dx} + u\frac{dv}{dx}.$$ [11.14]

Integrating with respect to x, we may write

$$y \equiv \int \frac{dy}{dx}.dx = \int v\frac{du}{dx} \cdot dx + \int u\frac{dv}{dx} \cdot dx.$$ [11.15]

Substituting for y and rearranging [11.15] gives the *integration by parts* formula in equation [11.16]:

Rule:

$$\text{III}' \int u\frac{dv}{dx}dx = uv - \int v\frac{du}{dx}dx$$ [11.16]

to which may be added the arbitrary constant of integration, c.

Using this method, we can break down complex expressions into a series of more straightforward operations. However, the decomposition itself needs care – it is possible to make matters worse rather than better. Consider the expression

$$\int xe^x dx.$$ [11.17]

There is no standard formula allowing us to integrate [11.17], but it can be done with the use of [11.16]. Let

$$u = x; \frac{dv}{dx} = e^x$$ [11.18]

$$\frac{du}{dx} = 1; v = \int \frac{dv}{dx} = e^x$$ [11.19]

Then, substituting [11.18] and [11.19] into [11.16], we have

$$\int xe^x dx = xe^x - \int e^x dx + c$$

$$= xe^x - e^x + c$$

$$= (x - 1)e^x + c.$$ [11.20]

Notice that, had we assigned u and dv/dx the other way round, i.e. set $u = e^x$ and $dv/dx = x$, substitution in [11.16] would have given

$$\int xe^x dx = \frac{x^2 e^x}{2} - \int \frac{x^2 e^x}{2}$$

which is no help at all! This leads to the obvious conclusion that, if the first attempt makes matters worse, simply reverse the substitution. Notice also that it may be necessary to repeat the process more than once to arrive at a final answer.

Worked example

Q. Calculate $\int x^2 e^x dx$.

A. Set $u = x^2$, $dv/dx = e^x$; then $du/dx = 2x$ and $v = e^x$. Substitute into the integration by parts formula to give.

$$\int x^2 e^x dx = x^2 e^x - \int 2xe^x dx + c = x^2 e^x - 2\int xe^x dx + c. \qquad [11.21]$$

The integral $\int xe^x dx$ may itself be integrated by parts as was shown above (equation [11.20]), the answer being $(x - 1)e^x$; so substituting this into [11.21] gives

$$\int x^2 e^x dx = x^2 e^x - 2(x - 1)e^x + c = (x^2 - 2x + 2)e^x + c.$$

11.2.2 Integration by substitution

Just as we have used the product rule for differentiation to provide a rule for integration, so we can use the chain rule (see equation [8.18]) to provide another useful technique. The substitution rule stated formally in [11.22] simply seeks to replace a complex expression in one variable, x, with a rather simpler expression in another variable, u, and then to apply one of the standard integration techniques:

Rule:

$$V' \int f(u)\frac{du}{dx} dx = \int f(u)du = F(u) + c. \qquad [11.22]$$

The selection of an appropriate substitution is a matter of practice but we can illustrate the process with the following example. First of all we can calculate the answer by multiplying out the expression thus:

$$\int (x^2 + 1)2x dx = \int 2x^3 dx + \int 2x dx$$

$$= \frac{x^4}{2} + x^2 + c \qquad [11.23]$$

However, let us suppose that $u = x^2 + 1$; then $du/dx = 2x$ and we may write

$$\int (1 + x^2)2x dx = \int u \frac{du}{dx} dx = \int u du = \frac{u^2}{2} + c$$

$$= \frac{(1 + x^2)^2}{2} + c$$

$$= \frac{x^4 + 2x^2 + 1}{2} + c. \qquad [11.24]$$

In practical terms it is often easier to substitute for dx directly. In the above example du/dx = 2x; therefore dx = (1/2x)du, giving

$$\int (1 + x^2)2x dx = \int (1 + x^2)2x \frac{1}{2x} du = \int (1 + x^2) du = \int u du.$$

The result is of course the same, but the substitution itself may be easier to spot if one follows this approach. Notice also that the value of any constant remaining after integration makes no difference since it will be subsumed in the arbitrary constant of integration. Thus, [11.23] and [11.24] do indeed represent the same expression, since we can rewrite the latter as

$$\frac{x^4}{2} + x^2 + (\tfrac{1}{2} + c).$$

This technique actually enables us to tackle problems that cannot be approached in any other way. An example of such a case follows.

Worked example

Q. Integrate $\int \frac{x}{(x^2 + 4)^{(1/2)}} dx$.

A. Let $u = (x^2 + 4)$. Then

$$\frac{du}{dx} = 2x; \, dx = \frac{1}{2x} du$$

and substitution gives

$$\int \frac{x}{u^{(1/2)}} \frac{1}{2x} du = \int \tfrac{1}{2} u^{-(1/2)} du = u^{(1/2)} + c$$

and the answer is simply $(x^2 + 4)^{(1/2)} + c$.

11.3 The definite integral

So far we have discussed integration as the reverse of differentiation. The integral defined by equation [11.8] is the *indefinite integral*. We now define the *definite integral* by

$$\int_a^b f(x)dx \equiv [F(x)]_a^b \equiv F(b) - F(a).$$ [11.25]

It is the value of the integral at the upper limit (*b*) less its value at the lower limit. If the integral $F(x)$ has a particular interpretation, such as for example the distance an object has travelled, then the definite integral has the obvious interpretation as the distance travelled in a specified interval of time. In this example the function $f(x)$ denotes the velocity and the argument x is time, and we know that distance travelled is given by multiplying average velocity by the time interval. If the velocity was actually constant, $f(x)$ would be a horizontal line and the definite integral would be equivalent to the area defined by $f(x)$, the x-axis and the points a and b as shown in figure 11.1(a). To verify this, calculate

$$\int_a^b k\,dx = [kx]_a^b = kb - ka$$

$$= k(b - a).$$ [11.26]

Now consider the function shown in figure 11.1(b). The shaded area may be easily calculated as the area of the trapezium – base × average height. In this case the area will be

$$(b - a) \times \left[\frac{f(a) + f(b)}{2} \right].$$ [11.27]

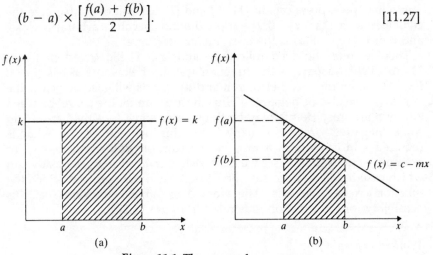

Figure 11.1 *The area under a curve*

With the function $f(x) = c - mx$, [11.27] will become

$$(b - a)\frac{[(c - ma) + (c - mb)]}{2} = c(b - a) - \frac{m}{2}(b^2 - a^2).$$ [11.28]

But performing the integration gives

$$\int_a^b (c - mx)\mathrm{d}x = \left[cx - \frac{mx^2}{2}\right]_a^b$$

$$= c(b - a) - \frac{m}{2}(b^2 - a^2)$$ [11.29]

and we can again identify the definite integral as the shaded area.

We have established that for a simple linear function the definite integral represents the area 'under the curve', but we can generalize this result to all functions. Suppose that we choose a very small interval, Δx. In this case the area under the curve between the points a and $(a + \Delta x)$ is very close to the height of the function at that point, $f(a)$, multiplied by the width of the interval, Δx, since with a small enough interval the value of the function hardly changes – see figure 11.2(a).

$$A_1 \doteqdot \int_a^{a + \Delta x} f(x)\mathrm{d}x = F(a + \Delta x) - F(a).$$ [11.30]

By the same token we can calculate the area between $(a + \Delta x)$ and $(a + 2\Delta x)$:

$$A_2 \doteqdot F(a + 2\Delta x) - F(a + \Delta x).$$ [11.31]

Summing the expressions in [11.30] and [11.31] will of course give the combined area. As $\Delta x \rightarrow 0$, the approximation becomes arbitrarily close, and hence $F(b) - F(a)$ *is* the area 'under the curve'.

There is one slight complication, and that is illustrated in figure 11.2(b). When a part of the function $f(x)$ lies below the x-axis (i.e. if $f(x) < 0$), then the area between it and the x-axis will also lie below the x-axis. (It will also be negative.) Thus the area 'under the curve' between any two arbitrary points may be the sum of some 'positive' areas and some 'negative' areas. In many cases this may be exactly what is required – in economics it may be the sum of profits and losses, for example – but in some cases we may wish to treat all areas as positive, in which case it will be necessary first to establish the points at which the function crosses the axis. The worked example below looks at this possibility for the function illustrated in figure 11.2(b).

Worked example

Q. Calculate the area under the curve $x^2 - 3x + 2$ between the limits 0 and 3. How does this differ from the 'absolute' area so defined?

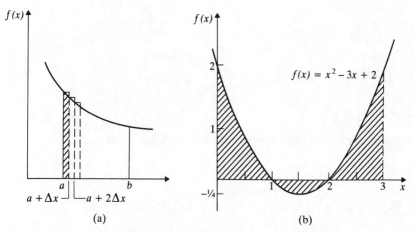

Figure 11.2 'Area under a curve'

A. Area $= \displaystyle\int_0^3 (x^2 - 3x + 2)\mathrm{d}x = \left[\dfrac{x^3}{3} - \dfrac{3x^2}{2} + 2x\right]_0^3 = \dfrac{3}{2}.$

The function crosses the axis when $(x^2 - 3x + 2) = 0$, i.e. when $x = 1$ and $x = 2$. Between those points it is negative and the area of this part is

$$\int_1^2 (x^2 - 3x + 2)\mathrm{d}x = \left[\dfrac{x^3}{3} - \dfrac{3x^2}{2} + 2x\right]_1^2 = \dfrac{2}{3} - \dfrac{5}{6} = \dfrac{-1}{6}.$$

For the absolute area this should have been added rather than subtracted, so the absolute area will be $2 \times (1/6)$ units greater, i.e. 11/6. (Readers may verify for themselves that $\int_0^1 f(x)\mathrm{d}x = \int_2^3 f(x)\mathrm{d}x = \tfrac{5}{6}$.)

11.4 Exercises

Section 11.2 introduction

Integrate the following with respect to x:

(i) 6

(ii) $\dfrac{1}{x}$

(iii) e^x

(vii) $\dfrac{2}{x} - x$

(viii) $\dfrac{1}{1 + x}$

(ix) $-4(1 - 2x)$

(iv) e^{ax}

(x) $\dfrac{2(x + 1)}{(x + 1)^2 - 2}$

(v) $-\frac{1}{2}x^{-3}$

(xi) $4x(x^2 + 1)$

(vi) $x^5 + \sqrt{x}$

(xii) $2x \cdot e^{x^2}$

Section 11.2.1

Integrate the following expressions with respect to x:

(i) $\dfrac{\log_e x}{x}$

(iii) $3x(x + 1)^{(1/2)}$

(ii) $(1 + 2x)e^x$

(iv) $x^2 \log_e x$

Section 11.2.2

Integrate the following expressions with respect to x:

(i) $9x^2(x^3 + 2)^8$

(iii) $2x(x^2 - 2)^{-1}$

(ii) $e^{2x + 1}$

(iv) $-\left(1 - \dfrac{x}{3}\right)^2$

Section 11.3

Evaluate

(i) $\displaystyle\int_1^2 (x^2 - 2)\,dx$

(iv) $\displaystyle\int_0^4 (3x^2 - 4)\,dx$

(ii) $\displaystyle\int_0^1 x^3\,dx$

(v) $\displaystyle\int_{-1}^1 (2x - 1)\,dx$

(iii) $\displaystyle\int_0^1 xe^x\,dx$

(vi) $\displaystyle\int_{-1}^{+2}\left(\dfrac{x}{2} - 1\right)dx$

Further exercises

Find

(i) $\displaystyle\int \log_e x\,dx$

(iii) $\displaystyle\int x\log_e x\,dx$

(ii) $\displaystyle\int \dfrac{x}{x + 2}\,dx$

(iv) $\displaystyle\int \dfrac{2x}{(x^2 + 3)^2}\,dx$

Evaluate

(i) $\displaystyle\int_0^1 \dfrac{6x}{3x^2 + 7}\,dx$

(ii) $\displaystyle\int_1^\infty \dfrac{1}{x^2}\,dx$

(iii) $\int_1^5 \left(\frac{1}{x} + 3x^2\right)dx$ (iv) $\int_0^4 (x^3 - 2x^2 - x + 2)dx$

12 Differential equations

12.1 The general problem

As we have seen in the previous chapter, it is possible to reverse the differentiation procedure so as to determine the nature of $y = f(x)$ given information about $f'(x)$, the derivative. In doing so we had to introduce an arbitrary 'constant of integration'; but, given one additional piece of information, one 'initial condition', this remaining source of ambiguity may be removed. Thus,

$$\frac{dy}{dx} = 2x; \; y(0) = 1 \qquad\qquad [12.1]$$

gives a general solution:

$$y = x^2 + c. \qquad\qquad [12.2]$$

Substituting $x = 0$ into [12.2] and noting from [12.1] the value of the function when $x = 0$, it follows immediately that $c = 1$ and the complete solution is

$$y = x^2 + 1. \qquad\qquad [12.3]$$

We have 'solved' a differential equation. This one was a *first-order equation*, in that it contained only the first derivative. As an example of a simple second-order equation consider

$$\frac{d^2y}{dx^2} = 2 \qquad\qquad [12.4]$$

which we know will produce the solution

$$\frac{dy}{dx} = 2x + c_1$$

$$y = x^2 + c_1 x + c_2. \qquad\qquad [12.5]$$

Notice that this second-order differential equation, since it requires us to integrate twice, has two arbitrary constants, and complete solution therefore requires *two* initial conditions. The obvious question to ask however is, what happens if terms in both d^2y/dx^2 *and* dy/dx appear in the equation? Indeed, what is the effect of including y itself in the equation? It is this combination of terms that distinguishes the differential equation as a problem distinct from straightforward integration.

In many cases this may not actually require any technique beyond integration – for example if

$$\frac{dy}{dx} + ky = 0 \qquad [12.6]$$

we can separate terms in y from terms in x to give

$$\frac{1}{y}dy = -kdx$$

and integrate both sides

$$\int \frac{1}{y}dy = -\int kdx$$

$$\log_e y = -kx + c \qquad [12.7]$$

where c is again the arbitrary constant of integration. Equation [12.7] can be rewritten as

$$y = e^{-kx + c} = e^c e^{-kx}$$

$$\therefore y = c_1 e^{-kx}. \qquad [12.8]$$

This solution to equation [12.6] will prove very useful in what is to follow but before we move on to general linear equations note the technique used in solving it. Any equation where terms in x and y can be separated in this way is said to be *separable* and can, in principle be solved by the simple application of the rules of integration.

Note: Where derivatives are taken with respect to time it is common to use an alternative notation. Instead of dy/dt we use $\dot{y}$. Similarly the second derivative with respect to time is denoted by two dots thus and so on.

$$\frac{d^2y}{dt^2} \equiv \ddot{y}; \frac{d^3y}{dt^3} \equiv \dddot{y}$$

12.2 Solving linear differential equations

The techniques involved are very similar to those used in difference equations (see chapter 6). Although the following discussion does not *require* previous study of that chapter, section 6.2 on solving linear difference equations provides a useful background.

The general linear differential equation may be written as

$$\frac{d^n y}{dt^n} + a_1 \frac{d^{n-1} y}{dt^{n-1}} + \dots + a_{n-1} \frac{dy}{dt} + a_n = f(t). \qquad [12.9]$$

The general solution consists of the complementary solution (y_c), which is the solution to [12.9] when $f(t) = 0$, *plus* the particular solution (y^*), which is any value that solves [12.9]. It is common, if not invariable, practice to refer to y^* as the equilibrium – particularly in economics models.

12.2.1 First-order equations

These may be written in the general form

$$\frac{dy}{dt} + a_1 y = f(t) \qquad [12.10]$$

or, using the notation referred to at the end of section 12.1,

$$\dot{y} + a_1 y = f(t). \qquad [12.11]$$

We have already calculated the solution to the homogeneous equation

$$\dot{y} + a_1 y = 0 \qquad [12.12]$$

(see equations [12.6]–[12.8]) as being $y = ce^{-a_1 t}$. Let us however find the solution in a slightly different way. Assume that $y = ce^{\lambda t}$. Then

$$\dot{y} \equiv \frac{dy}{dt} = \lambda ce^{\lambda t}$$

and [12.12] becomes

$$\lambda ce^{\lambda t} + a_1 ce^{\lambda t} = 0$$

$$ce^{\lambda t}(\lambda + a_1) = 0 \quad \therefore \lambda = -a_1$$

$$y = ce^{-a_1 t}. \qquad [12.13]$$

The *particular* solution will of course depend on $f(t)$. There is in fact a rule deducing y^*, viz.:

$$y^* = e^{-a_1 t} \int e^{a_1 t} f(t) dt. \qquad [12.14]$$

But it is often easier to obtain the solution by trial and error, setting y^* to be a general expression of the same form as $f(t)$; i.e., if $f(t) = 3$ then try $y^* = k$; if $f(t) = e^{3t}$ then try $y^* = e^{kt}$; and so on. This process is best understood by looking at some examples. Before doing so we note that [12.13] still contains one unknown – the arbitrary constant c. To remove this requires an additional piece of information – an initial condition which may be the value of y or $\dot{y}$ for a particular value of t. An example is given below.

Worked examples

Q. Solve $\dot{y} - 3y = -3$.

A. Let $y = k$. Then $\dot{y} \equiv dy/dt = 0$ and we have $0 - 3k = -3$; $\therefore k = 1$. To find the complementary solution we may use [12.13] directly or simply substitute $y = ce^{\lambda t}$ to give $ce^{\lambda t}(\lambda - 3) = 0$; $\lambda = 3$ and $y = ce^{3t}$. Thus the general solution is $y = 1 + ce^{3t}$.

Q. Solve $y - 2\dot{y} + 2t = 6$; $y(0) = 1$.

A. To use the standard solution, rewrite $\dot{y} - \frac{1}{2}y = t - 3$ and the complementary solution is immediately read off as $y = ce^{0.5t}$. To find the particular solution, set $y = k_0 + k_1 t$; thus $\dot{y} = k_1$ and $k_1 - \frac{1}{2}(k_0 + k_1 t) = t - 3$. Rewriting this as

$$-\frac{k_1}{2}t - \left(\frac{k_0}{2} - k_1\right) = t - 3$$

and comparing the coefficients on either side of the equation, it is immediately obvious that

$$\frac{-k_1}{2} = 1 \text{ and } \frac{k_0}{2} - k_1 = 3.$$

Solving these gives $k_1 = -2$, $k_0 = 2$, and thus $y^* = 2 - 2t$. (Notice that 'equilibrium' in this case is dynamic, with the equilibrium itself falling over time.) The general solution is now

$$y = 2 - 2t + ce^{0.5t}.$$

Substituting $t = 0$ gives $y(0) = c + 2 = 1$; $\therefore c = -1$ and the complete solution is

$$y = 2 - 2t - e^{0.5t}.$$

12.2.2 Second-order equations

The second-order equation

$$\frac{d^2y}{dt^2} + a_1\frac{dy}{dt} + a_2y = f(t)$$

or   [12.15]

$$\ddot{y} + a_1\dot{y} + a_2 y = f(t)$$

presents no really new problems. Setting $y = ce^{\lambda t}$ and $f(t) = 0$ enables us to write the auxiliary equation:

$$ce^{\lambda t}(\lambda^2 + a_1\lambda + a_2) = 0 \qquad\qquad [12.16]$$

$$\lambda = \frac{-a_1 \pm \sqrt{(a_1^2 - 4a_2)}}{2}.$$

In general, therefore, there are two values of λ that will solve [12.15]. Since either solution is acceptable, any weighted combination of the two is also acceptable. Adding the particular solution, we have the general solution:

$$y = c_1 e^{\lambda_1 t} + c_2 e^{\lambda_2 t} + y^*.$$

If the roots are repeated (i.e. if $\lambda_1 = \lambda_2$), then it is shown below that the general solution is

$$y = c_1 e^{\lambda t} + c_2 t e^{\lambda t} + y^*.$$

The special case in which $a_1^2 = 4a_2$ gives only one value for λ, which is $(-a_1/2)$. In this case $c_2 t e^{\lambda t}$ will also be a solution since if

$$y = c_2 t e^{\lambda t} \qquad\qquad [12.17]$$

$$\dot{y} \equiv \frac{dy}{dt} = c_2 t\lambda e^{\lambda t} + c_2 e^{\lambda t} = c_2 e^{\lambda t}(\lambda t + 1) \qquad\qquad [12.18]$$

$$\ddot{y} \equiv \frac{d^2 y}{dt^2} = c_2 t\lambda^2 e^{\lambda t} + c_2\lambda e^{\lambda t} + c_2\lambda e^{\lambda t} = c_2 e^{\lambda t}(\lambda^2 t + 2\lambda). \qquad [12.19]$$

Substituting [12.17], [12.18] and [12.19] into [12.15] produces the auxiliary equation:

$$c_2 e^{\lambda t}[(\lambda^2 t + 2\lambda) + a_1(\lambda t + 1) + a_2 t] = c_2 e^{\lambda t}[(\lambda^2 + a_1\lambda + a_2)t + (2\lambda + a_1)] = 0$$

since the first term in the square bracket is zero from [12.16] and the second term is zero if $\lambda = -a_1/2$, which is the condition for repeated roots.

Notice that in each case there are two arbitrary constants c_1 and c_2. To eliminate these will require *two* additional pieces of information and these are usually the values of y for two values of t or, alternatively, the values of both y and $\dot{y}$ for a value of t. An example of the latter is given below.

Worked example

Q. Solve $\ddot{y} - 7\dot{y} + 12y = 12$ where $y(0) = 2$ and $\dot{y}(0) = 0$.

A. For a particular solution try $y = k$. Then $\dot{y} = \ddot{y} = 0$; hence $12k = 12$; $k = 1$. For the complementary solution set $y = ce^{\lambda t}$. Then

$$ce^{\lambda t}(\lambda^2 - 7\lambda + 12) = 0$$

$$\lambda = 4 \text{ or } 3$$

and the general solution is

$$y = c_1 e^{4t} + c_2 e^{3t} + 1.$$

Substituting for $t = 0$ gives

$$y(0) = c_1 e^0 + c_2 e^0 + 1 = 2;$$

i.e., $c_1 + c_2 = 1$. The second initital condition is given in terms of the derivative, so first we must differentiate y to give

$$\dot{y} = 4c_1 e^{4t} + 3c_2 e^{3t}$$

$$\dot{y}(0) = 4c_1 + 3c_2 = 0$$

$$\therefore\ 4c_1 + 3c_2 = 0 \quad c_1 = -\tfrac{3}{4}c_2$$

$$c_1 + c_2 = -\tfrac{3}{4}c_2 + c_2 = \tfrac{1}{4}c_2 = 1$$

$$\therefore\ c_2 = 4;\ c_1 = -3$$

and the complete solution is

$$y = 4e^{3t} - 3e^{4t} + 1.$$

Q. Solve $\ddot{y} - 7\dot{y} = 14$.

A. In this case $y = k$ will not help, since y itself does not appear in the equation. Try instead $y = kt$; then $\dot{y} = k$, $\ddot{y} = 0$ and $-7k = 14$, $k = -2$. The complementary solution is found from

$$ce^{\lambda t}(\lambda^2 - 7\lambda) = 0;\ \lambda = 0 \text{ or } 7.$$

Hence the general solution is

$$y = c_1 e^{7t} + c_2 - 2t.$$

With no initial conditions this is as far as we can go.

*12.2.3 The case of complex roots

When $a_1^2 < 4a_2$ in equation [12.15], the roots of the auxiliary equation will of course be complex. This does not in any way affect the nature of the situation. If we find $\lambda = h \pm iv$ where $h = -a_1/2$ and

$v = \sqrt{(4a_2 - a_1^2)}/2$, then the general solution is still

$$y = c_1 e^{(h + iv)t} + c_2 e^{(h - iv)t} + y^*. \tag{12.20}$$

Notice however that this may be rewritten as

$$y = e^{ht}(c_1 e^{ivt} + c_2 e^{-ivt}). \tag{12.21}$$

It is outside the scope of this book to demonstrate that

$$e^{\pm i\theta t} = \cos \theta t \pm i \sin \theta t \tag{12.22}$$

although the proof may be found in advanced texts (see for example Chiang, pp.523–5). Choosing the arbitrary constants $c_{1,\,2} = m \pm in$, and substituting into [12.21] we have

$$y = e^{ht}(2m \cos vt - 2n \sin vt) \tag{12.23}$$

which demonstrates that the solution for y is in fact real, and that it will be a periodic function.

Figure 12.1 illustrates the possible time-paths resulting from complex roots. These diagrams are drawn on the assumption of a constant equilibrium; shown as the broken line, but they can of course be imposed upon any equilibrium path. Figure 12.2 shows stable cycles on a simple rising trend.

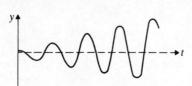

(a)   unstable cycles $(h > 0)$

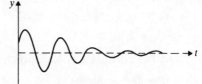

(b)   stable cycles $(h < 0)$

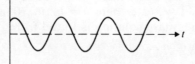

(c)   special case $(h = 0)$

Figure 12.1 'Cyclical time-paths'

12.3 Stability

The general solution to the nth-order differential equation is

$$y = c_1 e^{\lambda_1 t} + c_2 e^{\lambda_2 t} + \dots + y^* \tag{12.24}$$

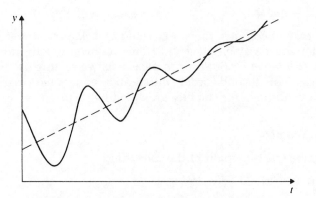

Figure 12.2 Stable cycles about a rising trend

The model is said to be stable (convergent) if

$$\lim_{t \to \infty} (y) = y^*$$

which requires in turn that

$$\lim_{t \to \infty} (e^{\lambda_j t}) = 0 \qquad\qquad \text{for all } j$$

and therefore that

$$\lambda_j < 0 \qquad\qquad \text{for all } j. \qquad\qquad [12.25]$$

The existence of repeated roots will not change this condition, since if $e^{\lambda t}$ tends to zero, so, eventually, must $te^{\lambda t}$. We may well ask, however, whether it is necessary to solve for the λ_j merely to discover whether they will all be negative. Clearly, in the case of the first-order equation [12.11] it is not: $\lambda = -a_1$, so a necessary and sufficient condition is $a_1 > 0$.

Note: Unlike difference equations, first-order differential equations cannot oscillate about equilibrium since the term $e^{\lambda t} > 0$ for all values of λ and t.

The roots of the second-order equation are given by

$$\lambda_{1,2} = \frac{-a_1 \pm \sqrt{(a_1^2 - 4a_2)}}{2}. \qquad\qquad [12.26]$$

For both to be negative, it is immediately obvious that we require $a_1 > 0$. Note however that we also require that (for real solutions)

$$-a_1 + \sqrt{(a_1^2 - 4a_2)} < 0$$

$$a_1 > \sqrt{(a_1^2 - 4a_2)}$$

$$a_1^2 > a_1^2 - 4a_2 \qquad\qquad \text{i.e., } a_2 > 0.$$

In the case of complex roots (i.e. when $a_1^2 < 4a_2$ and therefore $a_2 > 0$) the model will be stable iff $a_1 > 0$. This follows directly from [12.23], noting that $h = -a_1/2$. But for complex roots we require $4a_2 > a_1^2 > 0$ so in the case of second order differential equations necessary and sufficient conditions for stability are $a_1 > 0$, $a_2 > 0$.

Worked examples

Q. Describe the time-path of the following:

(i) $y = b\dot{y} \quad b > 0$

(ii) $\ddot{y} - 6\dot{y} + 7y = 14$

(iii) $t - 1.5y = 3\dot{y} + 2\ddot{y}$

A. (i) Rewriting as $\dot{y} - (1/b)y = 0$, this will be stable if $-(1/b) > 0$, which it cannot be given $b > 0$. First-order equations are necessarily monotonic.

(ii) This equation is already in the desired form. One of the coefficients is negative so the time-path will not converge to its equilibrium of 2. Since $(-6)^2 > 4(7)$, the solutions are real and divergence will be monotonic.

(iii) Rewriting into the standard form, we have $\ddot{y} + 1.5\dot{y} + 0.75y = \frac{1}{2}t$. With all positive coefficients the model is stable, but $(1.5)^2 < 4(0.75)$ so the model cycles about the equilibrium time-path, (But notice that the equilibrium is itself rising over time: $y^* = -(4/3) + (2/3)t$.)

12.4 Exercises

Section 12.2.1

Solve the following if in each case $y(0) = 0$:

(i) $2\dot{y} + 2y - 1 = 0$ (iii) $\dot{y} + by = c$

(ii) $2\dot{y} + 2y - t = 0$

Section 12.2.2

Solve the following (be careful with the initial conditions):

(i) $\ddot{y} - 5\dot{y} + 6y = 2$ where $y(0) = 0$; $\dot{y}(0) = 0$

(ii) $\ddot{y} - 6\dot{y} + 9y = 0$ where $y(0) = 0; y(1) = e^3$

(iii) $2\ddot{y} + y = 3(\dot{y} + 2)$

(iv) $y = 2\dot{y} - \ddot{y}$ where $y(0) = 1; \dot{y}(0) = 2$

Section 12.3

Describe the time-paths of the following:

(i) $\ddot{y} - 4\dot{y} + 8y = 0$ (iv) $y + 2\dot{y} = e^{rt}$

(ii) $\ddot{y} + 3\dot{y} + 4y = 8$ (v) $2\ddot{y} + 18y = 9$

(iii) $y - 2\dot{y} = 4$ (vi) $y = \ddot{y} - 2\dot{y}$

13 Economic applications IV

13.1 Consumer surplus

Faced by a downward-sloping demand function, a firm with the complete monopoly on supply will still be constrained, by the operation of the market, to charge the same price to all. The total revenue the firm receives will still be the price charged multiplied by the quantity sold. A 'discriminating monopoly' is one in which it is possible to identify two or more sectors of the market and to charge different prices to each. If, for example, our firm is the only hairdresser in town, then it may be quite feasible for it to charge different prices to men and women – it is commonly believed that women are more prepared to pay higher prices for such a service than are men, though this is not a universal truth! By exploiting this characteristic of the market our monopolist can increase his or her profits; but that is not our immediate concern. If a market can conceptually be divided into two, it can be divided into many different sectors. Ultimately every individual who wishes to purchase is a separate market, and we define as a 'perfectly discriminating monopoly' one that is able to extract from each purchaser the maximum that he or she is prepared to pay. The total revenue that may be extracted in this way is the area under the demand curve – the sum total of each successive unit multiplied by its price.

In practice such a situation is unlikely ever to occur, but it does allow us to conceptualize the amount that purchasers would be *willing* to pay for a certain quantity of output, Q^*. Mathematically, this may be written as

$$\int_0^{Q^*} g(Q)\mathrm{d}Q \qquad\qquad [13.1]$$

where $P = g(Q)$ is the demand function. The price that would actually be paid for this quantity on the open market would of course be

$$P^* = g(Q^*). \qquad\qquad [13.2]$$

Thus the revenue actually received would be P^*Q^* and the difference between these two amounts, i.e. between what consumers would have been willing to pay and what they actually do pay, is called *consumer* *surplus* (CS). Formally, it is defined as

$$CS = \int_0^{Q^*} g(Q)dQ - P^*Q^* \qquad [13.3]$$

and this is illustrated in figure 13.1. Consumer surplus can be defined for any arbitrary level of output, but Q^* is conventionally that value which clears the market – the equilibrium output.

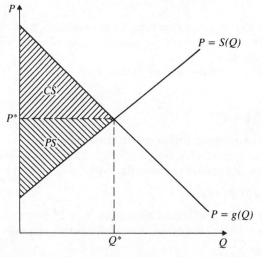

Figure 13.1 Consumer surplus and producer surplus

13.1.1 Producer Surplus

It is worth noting that, corresponding to the concept of consumer surplus there is a concept of producer surplus (PS) which represents the difference between the amount the producer receives from the sale of his output and the amount that would have been required to induce him to produce it. Since the latter is the area under the supply curve $P = S(Q)$, we may define producer surplus as

$$PS = P^*Q^* - \int_0^{Q^*} S(Q)dQ. \qquad [13.4]$$

Both concepts are of considerable use in the study of welfare economics.

13.2 Stabilization policy

In a timeless certain world the problem of ensuring full employment would not be a difficult one. Any government could quickly work out the necessary stimulus to the economy and the vigour with which to pursue fiscal or monetary policy. This sort of economic modelling can be done using the comparative statics models of section 3.2. Such models impose an equilibrium condition that income (Y) is equal to expenditure (E). Let us assume instead that both are continuous variables changing over time. If for any reason the system is not in equilibrium, then this will induce one or both of the variables to change. The most common assumption is that

$$\dot{Y} = \alpha(E - Y) \qquad\qquad \alpha > 0. \qquad\qquad [13.5]$$

In words, income responds directly to excess demand – the greater the excess, the faster income rises; the greater the deficiency of demand, the faster income falls.

Aggregate expenditure is itself defined as

$$E = C + I$$
$$= (a + bY) + I \qquad\qquad 0 < b < 1. \qquad\qquad [13.6]$$

That is, we have a simple linear consumption function ($C = a + bY$) and autonomous investment (I). Substituting [13.6] into [13.5] and collecting terms gives the first-order differential equation:

$$\dot{Y} + \alpha(1 - b)Y = \alpha(a + I). \qquad\qquad [13.7]$$

The particular solution is found by setting $Y = Y^*$ where Y^* is a constant and therefore $\dot{Y} = 0$. This gives an 'equilibrium' income

$$Y^* = \frac{a + I}{1 - b}. \qquad\qquad [13.8]$$

(This is of course the same as the solution to the comparative statics model of section 3.2.) Our knowledge of differential equations tells us that [13.7] is stable (convergent) if and only if $\alpha(1 - b) > 0$, which, given the restrictions on the parameters, is necessarily so. By suitable choice of $(a + I)$ it must always be possible to ensure that this equilibrium value Y^* corresponds to the full-employment level of income Y^F, and we may write, where A denotes all autonomous expenditures,

$$Y^F = \frac{A}{1 - b}. \qquad\qquad [13.9]$$

The problem faced by governments, however, is that there may well be random shocks to the system; for example, overseas events may lead to a fall in exports, or changing expectations to an increase in the propensity to save. Let us represent this fall in aggregate demand by X and any offsetting government expenditure as G, then the equation for aggregate demand may be written as

$$E = A + bY + (G - X) \qquad\qquad [13.10]$$

which will take us back to full-employment equilibrium only if $(G - X)$ is always zero. If in fact X has a once-and-for-all change, it should be possible for the Treasury to estimate the impact in time and compensate for it, but in practice this is highly unlikely. Random shocks occur all the time, and the current level of income will reflect the continued effects of both past shocks and past policy (government expenditures). One possible approach to this problem is to make government expenditure itself a function of the level of income and unemployment. As current income (Y) falls below full employment (Y^F), government expenditure is (automatically) increased and vice versa. This we may represent as

$$G^* = \beta(Y^F - Y) \qquad\qquad \beta > 0. \qquad\qquad [13.11]$$

If the process is automatic, as in the payment of unemployment benefits, then we would call it an *automatic stabilizer*, though as we shall see this may be something of a misnomer. Other expenditures may actually require positive government action. Whatever the mechanism, it is highly unlikely that the amount of government expenditure G^* that is desired will actually take place immediately. In practice, actual government expenditure G will react with a lag to changes in income, the speed of adjustment being a function of the necessary change; thus

$$\dot{G} = \gamma(G^* - G) \qquad\qquad \gamma > 0. \qquad\qquad [13.12]$$

The questions that need to be asked are:

(i)   What level of income represents the equilibrium for this system? Is it full employment income Y^F?
(ii) Is the system stable? Will it converge on its equilibrium?
(iii) Will the time-path exhibit a smooth adjustment process, or will it generate cycles in economic activity?

To answer these questions we consider the effect of disturbing the economy from full employment by an amount X upon the time-path of income. The model is given by equations [13.5], [13.9] – [13.12], and this may be reduced to a second-order linear differential equation in Y as follows. Substitute [13.10] into [13.5] to give

$$\dot{Y} = \alpha[A + bY + (G - X) - Y]$$
$$= \alpha[A - (1 - b)Y + G - X]. \qquad\qquad [13.13]$$

If two expressions represent the same amount then both must change over time in the same way; i.e., we can differentiate both sides of [13.13] with respect to time and preserve the equality thus:

$$\ddot{Y} = \alpha[\dot{G} - (1 - b)\dot{Y}]. \qquad\qquad [13.14]$$

The terms in A and X are constants and their derivatives are therefore zero. $\dot{G}$ may now be removed by substituting from [13.12] to give

$$\ddot{Y} = \alpha[\gamma(G^* - G) - (1 - b)\dot{Y}] \tag{13.15}$$

and G^* may be removed by substituting from [13.11]:

$$\ddot{Y} = \alpha\gamma[\beta(Y^F - Y) - G] - \alpha(1 - b)\dot{Y}. \tag{13.16}$$

To substitute for G we first rewrite [13.13], noting from [13.9] that $A = (1 - b)Y^F$, in the form

$$\begin{aligned} -\alpha G &= \alpha A - \alpha(1 - b)Y - \alpha X - \dot{Y} \\ &= \alpha(1 - b)(Y^F - Y) - \alpha X - \dot{Y}. \end{aligned} \tag{13.17}$$

Then, using [13.17] in [13.16] gives

$$\begin{aligned} \ddot{Y} &= \alpha\gamma\beta(Y^F - Y) + \gamma[\alpha(1 - b)(Y^F - Y) - \alpha X - \dot{Y}] - \alpha(1 - b)\dot{Y} \\ &= \alpha\gamma(\beta + 1 - b)(Y^F - Y) - [\alpha(1 - b) + \gamma]\dot{Y} - \alpha\gamma X. \end{aligned} \tag{13.18}$$

This can be rearranged into the more usual representation:

$$\ddot{Y} + [\alpha(1 - b) + \gamma]\dot{Y} + \alpha\gamma(\beta + 1 - b)Y = \alpha\gamma(\beta + 1 - b)Y^F - \alpha\gamma X. \tag{13.19}$$

Do not be put off by the apparent complexity of either the solution process or the resulting equation. Given that $\alpha, \beta, \gamma > 0$ and $0 < b < 1$, the coefficients of [13.19] are unambiguously positive and the system is necessarily stable. Furthermore, if we solve for the particular solution by setting $Y = \bar{Y}$ (constant), we have simply

$$\alpha\gamma(1 - b + \alpha)\bar{Y} = \alpha\gamma(1 - b + \beta)Y^F - \alpha\gamma X \tag{13.20}$$

$$\bar{Y} - Y^F = -\frac{X}{1 - b + \beta} \neq 0. \tag{13.21}$$

That is, the system converges not to full-employment equilibrium but to some level of income less than that. The size of the unemployment gap will vary with the initial shock (X), the marginal propensity to consume (b) and the size of the 'automatic stabilizer' (β). Note that the more responsive is government expenditure (the higher is β), the smaller the gap will be

Now, if [13.19] is to have real roots and not produce cycles, we require that

$$[\alpha(1 - b) + \gamma]^2 \geqslant 4\alpha\gamma(\beta + 1 - b). \tag{13.22}$$

But that condition is most likely to be met when β is small. Indeed for given values of b, α and γ it is always possible to produce cycles by raising β, so the very policy that might appear to be recommended by consideration of [13.21] would, by [13.22], be inappropriate. Controlling the economy is not the simple process that comparative statics models might lead one to believe.

13.3 Exercises

Section 13.1.1

Calculate consumer and producer surpluses for the following demand and supply model if price and quantity are determined by the market:

$$Q^D = 5 - \frac{P}{3}$$

$$P = (Q^S + 1)^2$$

Part V

Multivariate calculus

In this Part we extend the analysis of Part III to functions of more than one variable. In particular, we are interested in the case where the two or more explanatory variables or 'arguments' are themselves related or constrained in some way. The technique of 'constrained optimization' provides the key to understanding a wide range of economic problems. The applications in chapter 16 are the derivations of two of the most fundamental concepts in economics: the production function and the demand function.

14 Differentiation with more than one variable

14.1 Partial differentiation

When a function has more than one argument, as in equation [14.1], there are two different types of differentiation that we have to consider: total differentiation and partial differentiation. The *total derivative* allows all the variables to be changing at the same time, and we shall look at this possibility in section 14.2. First, however, let us consider the case where only one of the arguments is allowed to change. The *partial derivative* assumes that the arguments of the function are independent of one another, and so, for the purposes of this technique, we may treat all other arguments as if they were constants. Thus, if

$$y = f(u, v) \qquad\qquad [14.1]$$

we may calculate the partial derivative of y with respect to (say) u simply using the technique of differentiation developed in chapter 8 since v is being treated as a constant.

The partial derivative of a function $f(u, v)$ is defined as

$$\frac{\delta y}{\delta u} \equiv \lim_{\Delta u \to 0} \left(\frac{\Delta y}{\Delta u} \right)$$

$$= \lim_{\Delta u \to 0} \left[\frac{f(u + \Delta u, v) - f(u, v)}{\Delta u} \right]. \qquad [14.2]$$

Now, if v is a constant there can be no difference between the derivatives of

(i) $y = 3u^2 + 3$ and (ii) $y = 3u^2 + 3v$

since the constants will disappear under differentiation. In both case we have $dy/du = 6u$ (or rather, in the case of the multivariate function (ii), $\delta y/\delta u = 6u$). Exactly the same conclusion is reached if we have a multiplicative function such as

$$y = 3u^2v. \qquad\qquad\qquad [14.3]$$

Treating v as a constant means that it behaves in exactly the same way as the constant 3. The function is, in effect,

$$y = 3v \cdot u^2$$

and the derivative with respect to u,

$$\frac{\delta y}{\delta u} = 2(3v)u = 6vu. \qquad\qquad\qquad [14.4]$$

Note: To avoid confusion over the type of derivative, it is common to adopt a slightly different notation with respect to partial derivatives than that used for single-variable functions:

Single-variate function	Multivariate function
$y = f(u)$	$y = f(u, v, \dots)$
$\dfrac{dy}{du}$ or $f'(u)$	$\dfrac{\delta y}{\delta u}$ or f_u
$\dfrac{d^2y}{du^2}$ or $f''(u)$	$\dfrac{\delta^2 y}{\delta u^2}$ or f_{uu}

Leaving aside the problem of notation, there is no new technique involved in doing partial differentiation. All variables other than the one under consideration are treated as constants and everything proceeds as for single-variate differentiation. In equation [14.4] we gave the partial derivative of y with respect to one its arguments, u. If we were interested in the effect of changing v instead, we would have to treat u as the constant and hence find

$$\frac{\delta y}{\delta v} = 3(u^2) \cdot 1 = 3u^2. \qquad\qquad\qquad [14.5]$$

In calculating partial derivatives it may actually help to substitute for expressions involving the unchanging variables, since it clarifies the actual expression to be differentiated. An example of this technique is given below. Notice that, in general, there are as many partial derivatives as there are arguments to the function. Thus, if we have a three-variable function there will be three first-order partial derivatives, and so on. Notice also that the expressions for the partial derivatives will in general be functions of *all* the variables. Thus the partial derivative $\delta y / \delta u$ in equation [14.4] was itself a function of both u and v.

Worked examples

Q. Find all the first-order partial derivatives of the following:

(i) $y = (u + 2v + w^2)^2$

(ii) $y = e^{u + v}$

A. (i) There are three arguments to the function so there will be three partial derivatives. If v and w are both constant, then $2v + w^2$ is a constant. The derivative of $y = (u + a)^2$ is $dy/du = 2(u + a)$, so if we think of $2v + w^2$ as being a, then we have

$$\frac{\delta y}{\delta u} = 2(u + 2v + w^2).$$

The same process may be used for the other partial derivatives. Setting $b = u + w^2$ gives $y = (2v + b)^2$, the derivative of which is

$$\frac{dy}{dv} = 2(2v + b)\cdot(2),$$

and thus

$$\frac{\delta y}{\delta v} = 4(u + 2v + w^2).$$

Similarly, setting $c = u + 2v$, we have

$$y = (c + w^2)^2$$

and

$$\frac{dy}{dw} = 2(c + w^2)\cdot 2w:$$

$$\frac{\delta y}{\delta w} = 4w(u + 2v + w^2).$$

(ii) The rule for differentiating $y = e^{f(u)}$ is given in equation [8.29] as

$$\frac{dy}{du} = f'(u)e^{f(u)}$$

and it is equally applicable even if $f(u)$ is actually a multivariate function (though, strictly speaking, one ought to revise the notation; i.e., $y = e^{f(u,\ v)}$ $\delta y/\delta u = f_u e^{f(u,\ v)}$). However you look at it, the answers are

$$\frac{\delta y}{\delta u} = e^{u + v} \text{ and } \frac{\delta y}{\delta v} = e^{u + v}$$

14.1.1 An intuitive interpretation

Defining partial derivatives, then, is easy, but what do they mean? The simple derivative of a univariate function had a ready interpretation as the slope of a graph, and that analogy can be used again in a slightly different form. Suppose that we have an ordnance survey map. The map references are given by specifying one number to be found along the N–S axis and one number to be found along the E–W axis. We could call these u and v, respectively. For every value of u and v – i.e., for every point on the map – we can read off the height above sea level by looking at the contour lines and call this value y. Then in functional notation we have $y = f(u, v)$. In fact, it would be possible to construct from this information a three-dimensional model landscape which would be useful for planners, architects and playing with toy soldiers!.

Actually, the map contains only imperfect information about the height, by means of contours at 50 ft intervals, and so the model-maker may unknowingly smooth out some of the irregular features to be found in the true landscape. From our point of view that is fortunate, for we can now assume all the hills and valleys to be smooth and the function $f(u, v)$ to be continuous in both u and v. What, then, is a partial derivative?

Imagine that we have an initial value of v – a starting-point on the E–W axis at the bottom of the map – and that, without changing the value of v, we progressively increase the value of u. In terms of the map,

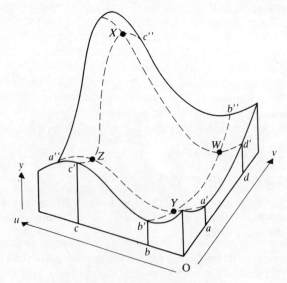

Figure 14.1 Partial derivatives I

we would be moving due north like the proverbial Roman road. Restricted to this one direction, our progress would emulate that of the univariate functions of chapter 8 and might be described in exactly the same way. A positive (partial) derivative would indicate that the road climbs, a negative (partial) derivative that it is going downhill, and a zero value that we have a stationary point. (Furthermore, the second-order partial derivative would tell us about the curvature of the surface in this direction, but more of this later.)

The corresponding partial derivative $\delta y/\delta v$ gives the analogous information when travelling in the E–W direction. Figure 14.1 illustrate this with a three-dimensional representation of a point of the landscape that looks not unlike a 'Dutch girl's hat'. If we start with $v = a$ and then move in the direction of u, the path traced is given by the dotted line $a'a''$ and this is plotted in figure 14.2(a). Note the minimum at $u = b$ and the maximum at $u = c$: we shall have more to say about them later. Similarly, fixing $u = b$ and changing only v moves us along the dotted line $b'b''$, which is plotted in figure 14.2(b); while figure 14.2(c) represents $c'c''$. Calculating partial derivatives means calculating the slope of the curves in figure 14.2 and hence clearly depends not only on the value of the changing variable but also upon the value of the unchanged variable (compare parts (b) and (c) of the figure).

14.1.2 Second-order partial derivatives

If partial derivatives are the slopes of the functions in figure 14.2, it would seem logical that second-order partial derivatives may be defined as the curvature of these functions, as in the univariate case. Thus, $\delta^2 y/\delta u^2$ gives the curvature of figure 14.2(a) and $\delta^2 y/\delta v^2$ the curvature of figures 14.2(b) and 14.2(c). Again, we note that these second-order derivatives will in general be functions of all the variables.

Consider the example of equation [14.3]. We found the first-order partial $\delta y/\delta u$ in equation [14.4], so differentiating again with respect to u and still treating v as a constant, we have

$$y = 3u^2v; \quad \frac{\delta y}{\delta u} = 6uv; \quad \frac{\delta^2 y}{\delta u^2} = 6v \qquad [14.6]$$

and differentiating with respect to v gives

$$y = 3u^2v; \quad \frac{\delta y}{\delta v} = 3u^2; \quad \frac{\delta^2 y}{\delta v^2} = 0. \qquad [14.7]$$

There is, however, one other possibility. We saw in figures 14.2(b) and (c) that not only will the value of y change when u is different but also, the slope of the function – the partial derivative – will be different for

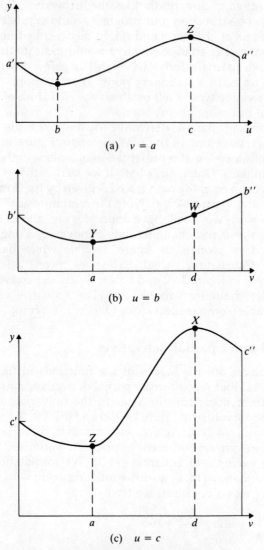

Figure 14.2 Partial derivatives II

different values of u. If $\delta y/\delta v$ can be written as a function of u, then it can be differentiated with respect to u and we can define a *cross-partial derivative*:

$$\frac{\delta}{\delta u}\left(\frac{\delta y}{\delta v}\right) \equiv \frac{\delta^2 y}{\delta u \delta v} \text{ or } f_{vu}. \hspace{2cm} [14.8]$$

Similarly, there exists a corresponding cross-partial obtained by partially differentiating $\delta y/\delta u$ with respect to v; i.e.,

$$\frac{\delta}{\delta v}\left(\frac{\delta y}{\delta u}\right) \equiv \frac{\delta^2 y}{\delta v \delta u} \text{ or } f_{uv}.$$ [14.9]

The usage of these cross-partials will be made clear in the following chapter.

Note: For any function $f(u, v, ...)$ for which f_u and f_v are continuous,

$$f_{uv} = f_{vu}$$ [14.10]

This is actually an important point, for it tells us that if we need to differentiate any function with respect to two of its arguments, then the order in which we perform the differentiations is unimportant. For the example of equations [14.6] and [14.7], we have

$$f_{uv} = f_{vu} = 6u.$$

An example is given below of a three-variable function. Notice that in this case we can calculate third-order cross-partials, and again we find the order of differentiation to be unimportant.

Worked example

Q. Find the second-order partial derivatives of the following function and demonstrate that the third-order cross-partial is independent of the order of differentiation:

$$y = uvw^2 + uv + u.$$

A. We start by finding the three first-order derivatives:

$$f_w = 2uvw; f_v = uw^2 + u; f_u = vw^2 + v + 1.$$

Differentiate each in turn with respect to each variable to give

$$f_{ww} = 2uv; f_{vw} = 2uw; f_{uw} = 2vw$$

$$f_{wv} = 2uw; f_{vv} = 0; f_{uv} = w^2 + 1$$

$$f_{wu} = 2uw; f_{vu} = w^2 + 1; f_{uu} = 0$$

and we see at once that there is a symmetry about these results $f_{wv} = f_{vw}$; $f_{uv} = f_{vu}$ and so on. It follows immediately that $f_{wvu} = f_{vwu} = 2w$. Similarly, $f_{uvw} = f_{vuw} = 2w$ and $f_{wuv} = f_{uwv} = 2w$.

14.2 Total differentials and total derivatives

Before proceeding to look at maxima and mimima, it will be useful to consider the concept of a total differential. In equation [8.5] we defined the differential as a very small change in the function caused by a small change in its argument, so if we have a small change in the value of u, which we denote as du, then the consequent change in the value of y is given by

$$dy = \left(\frac{\delta y}{\delta u}\right)du.$$

[14.11]

When, as in chapter 8, there is only one argument to the function, the process stops there and we stated that the derivative was indeed the ratio of the differentials, but this is no longer true. In addition to the effect that the small change in u will have, we should consider any change in v. Denoting this as dv, we shall have to multiply this change by the partial derivative $(\delta y/\delta v)$ to see what effect this has on the value of the function and then add it to the effect of the change in u.

The total differential of a function $f(u, v, ...)$ is defined as the sum of the marginal changes in the arguments of the function multiplied by the corresponding partial derivatives:

$$dy \equiv \left(\frac{\delta y}{\delta u}\right)du + \left(\frac{\delta y}{\delta v}\right)dv + ...$$

$$\equiv f_u du + f_v dv + ...$$

[14.12]

14.2.1 Total differentiation

Let us now suppose that the arguments of this multivariate function are themselves functions of another variable, time (t). The way in which y will vary with t is described by the derivative dy/dt and, given all the requisite information, we could perform the substitutions and do the differentiation. There is however an easier and a conceptually useful alternative. We know from [14.12] that, if $y = f(u, v)$, then

$$dy = \left(\frac{\delta y}{\delta u}\right)du + \left(\frac{\delta y}{\delta v}\right)dv.$$

[14.13]

But we also know that the derivative (dy/dt) can be expressed as the ratio of two differentials dy and dt. Dividing [14.13] by dt gives

$$\frac{dy}{dt} = \left(\frac{\delta y}{\delta u}\right)\frac{du}{dt} + \left(\frac{\delta y}{\delta v}\right)\frac{dv}{dt}$$

[14.14]

which is known as the *total derivative* of y with respect to t. Not only have we divided the operation into a number of simpler parts, but we no longer actually need to know the form of $u = g(t)$, etc., since knowledge of du/dt is seen to be sufficient. We have also established an important principle. To illustrate, let $t = u$. Then [14.14] becomes

$$\frac{dy}{du} = \left(\frac{\delta y}{\delta u}\right)\frac{du}{du} + \left(\frac{\delta y}{\delta v}\right)\frac{dv}{du}$$

$$= \frac{\delta y}{\delta u} + \left(\frac{\delta y}{\delta v}\right)\frac{dv}{du} \qquad [14.15]$$

and we can see clearly the difference between the partial derivative $\delta y/\delta u$ and the total derivative dy/du. The latter allows for any indirect influence that a change in u makes upon the other variables in the function and hence upon the value of the function.

The total derivative of a multivariate function $f(u, v, w,...)$ with respect to one of its variables u is defined as

$$\frac{dy}{du} \equiv \frac{\delta y}{\delta u} + \left(\frac{\delta y}{\delta v}\right)\frac{dv}{du} + \left(\frac{\delta y}{\delta w}\right)\frac{dw}{du} + ...$$

$$\equiv f_u + f_v\frac{dv}{du} + f_w\frac{dw}{du} + ... \qquad [14.16]$$

14.2.2 An intuitive explanation

To return briefly to the model landscape of section 14.1, the differential dy measures the change in height (above sea level) as a result of moving one pace in any direction. We are no longer constrained to move N–S or E–W but, for example, may choose to change both u and v by the same amount and thus move NE or SW. It is this information that will be of most use in determining maxima and minima in chapter 15.

14.3 Implicit differentiation

The concept of total differentiation can be used to differentiate univariate functions which would be rather difficult to handle in the usual way. For example, the implicit function

$$3y^2 + 4x = 0 \qquad [14.17]$$

can be solved by writing

$$x = -\tfrac{3}{4}y^2 \qquad [14.18]$$

and then we can calculate dy/dx from [14.18] by use of the inverse rule (see equation [8.27]). It can also be solved by thinking of it as a function of two variables x and y, thus:

$$f = f(x, y) = 0$$

$f = 3y^2 + 4x = 0$.

But, by definition,

$$df = \frac{\delta f}{\delta x}dx + \frac{\delta f}{\delta y}dy = 0 \qquad\qquad [14.19]$$

since, if the function is always equal to zero, then it cannot change and df must equal zero. Performing the partial differentiations, [14.19] becomes

$$df = 4dx + 6ydy = 0$$

$$\frac{dy}{dx} = \frac{-4}{6y} = -\tfrac{2}{3}y^{-1}. \qquad\qquad [14.20]$$

Readers should check that this is in fact the same answer as may be deduced from [14.18].

14.4 Exercises

Section 14.1 introduction

Find all the first-order partial derivatives of the following:

(i) $y = u^3 + u^2v + uv^2 + v^3$ (v) $y = (u^2 + v^2)^2$

(ii) $y = (u - v)(u - w)$ (vi) $y = e^{u + 2v}$

(iii) $y = \log(u + v)$ (vii) $y = u^2 + 2uv + uvw + \log_e w^2$

(iv) $y = (u + v)^2$

Section 14.1.2

Calculate second-order partial derivatives of the following functions:

(i) $y = u^3 + u^2v + uv^2 + v^3$ (iv) $y = e^{u - v}$

(ii) $y = \log(u + v)$ (v) $y = \dfrac{1}{2u + v}$

(iii) $y = (u + v)^2$

Section 14.2.2

Find the total derivative with respect to t of the following where $u = g(t)$ but v is *not* a function of t:

(i) $y = 3t^2$

(ii) $y = 3t^2 + 2u$

(iii) $y = 3ut^2$

(iv) $y = 3t^2 + uv$

(v) $y = 3t^2 + uvt$

Section 14.3

Find dy/dx where

(i) $x^2 - y^2 = 6$

(ii) $xy^2 - 6 = 0$

(iii) $x^3 + 2y^2 = -3$

(iv) $xy + y^2 - x = 0$

Further exercises

In each case find the total derivative dy/dt:

(i) $y = \log_e(x)$; $x = t^2$

(ii) $y = 3u^2 + 2v$; $u = \log_e t$, $\dfrac{dv}{dt} = \dfrac{1}{t}$

(iii) $y^2 = 2t$

(iv) $y = 2ut + vt^2 + w$ where u, v and w are functions of t

(v) $y = 2t + \log_e v^2$ where v is a function of t

(vi) $t = y^2 + 2y + 4$

15 Optimization

15.1 Maxima and minima again

In chapter 9 we looked at the nature of stationary points – situations in which the first-order derivative is equal to zero – and in this section we shall extend the analysis to the multivariate case.

The most obvious way to proceed would be to look at the first- and second-order partial derivatives, but we shall find that the problem is a little more complicated than that. To illustrate why, consider again figures 14.1 and 14.2(c). Looking at the latter, it would appear that there is a maximum at X ($u = c$, $v = d$), but by referring to figure 14.1 it is clear that the point X is not a true maximum, if by that we mean a point that is greater in value than all those points in its immediate neighbourhood. The line $c'c''$ is like a path across the side of a hill; when one has reached the highest point on the path, it does not mean that you are at the top of the hill. By contrast, the point $Y(b,a)$ does appear to be a true minimum, and if we look at the figures 14.2(a) and (b) we do indeed see that they both indicate a minimum at this point. The point $Z(a, c)$, on the other hand, would appear from 14.2(a) to be a maximum, but from figure 14.2(c) it would appear to be a minimum! It is clear from figure 14.1 that it is in fact neither.

Thus, while consideration of the first- and second-order partial derivatives has been of some help, it has not given us a clear rule to apply. It is to find this rule that we know turn our attention.

15.1.1 Using the differential

In section 14.2 we defined the total differential

$$dy = f_u du + f_v dv \qquad [15.1]$$

as being the total change in the value of the function when all the variables are permitted to change simultaneously. If we are seeking a true maximum or minimum that is exactly what we must do – allow all the variables to change simultaneously. In terms of the landscape analogy of section 14.1.1, we must be allowed to walk NE or SSW or in any other direction. If the differential is zero, then the ratio of dy to any small change in any of the variables must be zero and we have a true stationary point.

Rule: The first-order condition for a relative extremum (maximum or minimum) for a multivariate function $y = f(u, v, ...)$ is

$$dy = f_u du + f_v dv + ...$$

$$= \left(\frac{\delta y}{\delta u}\right) du + \left(\frac{\delta v}{\delta v}\right) dv + ... = 0.$$

This has to be true whatever the values of du, dv, ..., so the only way it can be assured is if *all* the partial derivatives are zero; i.e., if

$$\frac{\delta y}{\delta u} = \frac{\delta y}{\delta v} = ... = 0. \tag{15.2}$$

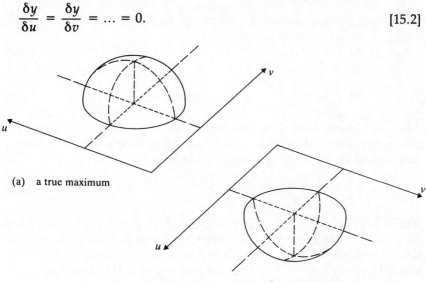

(a)   a true maximum

(b)   a true minimum

Figure 15.1 Maxima and minima

15.1.2 Second-order conditions

Consider figure 15.1(a). This is a diagram of a true maximum, and it is clear that to be so it must be a maximum in both N–S and E–W directions; that is to say, both second-order partials must be negative:

$$\frac{\delta^2 y}{\delta u^2} < 0; \frac{\delta^2 y}{\delta v^2} < 0$$

are *necessary* conditions. Similarly, in figure 15.1(b) the two second-order partial derivatives are positive; i.e.,

$$\frac{\delta^2 y}{\delta u^2} > 0; \frac{\delta^2 y}{\delta v^2} > 0.$$

If one of the second-order partials is positive and the other is negative, then we have what is known as a 'saddle point'. In one direction of travel it would appear to be a minimum but in the other a maximum (as was the case with point Z in figure 14.1). A physical analogy of such a surface is a pass or col between two hills or a 'saddle'; hence the term 'saddle point'.

This concentration on partial derivatives can, however, still lead us into trouble. Consider the following example:

$$y = u^2 + 2v^2 + 4uv. \tag{15.3}$$

The first-order conditions for a stationary point are

$$\frac{\delta y}{\delta u} = 2u + 4v = 0 \tag{15.4}$$

$$\frac{\delta y}{\delta v} = 4v + 4u = 0 \tag{15.5}$$

which are simultaneously satisfied when $u = v = 0$. Is this point a maximum, a minimum or a saddle point? Evaluating the second-order partial derivatives at the point $(0, 0)$, we have

$$\frac{\delta^2 y}{\delta u^2} = 2 > \text{ and } \frac{\delta^2 y}{\delta v^2} = 4 > 0 \tag{15.6}$$

which implies a minimum at $(0, 0)$, at which point the value of the function is itself zero. Yet this *cannot* be a true minimum, as may be simply demonstrated by substituting some values for u and v. If for example $u = 0.1$, $v = -0.1$, then substituting into [15.3] we have

$$y = (0.1)^2 + 2(-0.1)^2 + 4(0.1)(-0.1) = -0.01.$$

That is, the value of the function has *decreased* and $(0, 0)$ was not a minimum. The values chosen for this demonstration were *both* different from those at the stationary point; thus the direction of travel does not correspond to that of either partial derivative. How then do we allow for this possibility? The formal derivation is given in section 15.1.3, but in order to have *either* a maximum *or* a minimum it is necessary that

$$\left(\frac{\delta^2 y}{\delta u^2}\right)\left(\frac{\delta^2 y}{\delta v^2}\right) > \left(\frac{\delta^2 y}{\delta u \delta v}\right)^2 \tag{15.7}$$

at the stationary point in question. The same condition may be written rather more concisely as

$$f_{uu} \cdot f_{vv} > (f_{uv})^2. \qquad [15.8]$$

Returning to the example used above, differentiating [15.4] gives

$$\frac{\delta^2 y}{\delta u \delta v} = 4 \qquad [15.9]$$

and substituting from [15.6] and [15.9] into [15.8], we see that this additional criterion is not satisfied; i.e., $(2)(4) \not> (4)^2$.

Once there are more than two arguments to the function this additional restriction becomes rather more complex, and a proper treatment requires a knowledge of matrix algebra (see section 18.2).

Worked example

Q. Find any relative extrema of the function $u = 4xy - x^2 - 2y^4$.

A. Note first that the variables used here are different from those in the text, so be careful in stating the necessary conditions. First we require that

$$f_x = 4y - 2x = 0 \quad \therefore x = 2y$$
$$f_y = 4x - 8y^3 = 0 \quad \therefore 4(2y) - 8y^3 = 0 \quad \therefore 8y(1 - y^2) = 0$$

and there are three stationary points when $y = 0$ $(x = 0)$, $y = 1$ $(x = 2)$ and $y = -1$ $(x = -2)$. The second-order partials are

$$f_{xx} = -2; \quad f_{yy} = -24y^2; \quad f_{xy} = 4.$$

Taking each point in turn, at the point $(2, 1)$, when $x = 2$ and $y = 1$,

$$f_{yy} = -24(1)^2 = -24 < 0; \quad (-2)(-24) > (4)^2$$

and we have a true minimum. At the point $(-2, -1)$ the sign of f_{yy} is reversed but the others are unchanged. Clearly, the conditions cannot be satisfied. At the point $(0, 0)$ $f_{yy} = 0$ and again the condition $f_{xx} \cdot f_{yy} > (f_{xy})^2$ cannot be satisfied. •

*15.1.3 Deriving the second-order condition

The first-order condition for stationarity of the function $f(u, v)$ is given by

$$dy = f_u du + f_v dv. \qquad [15.10]$$

For this to represent a maximum the second-order *total differential* $d^2 y$ must be negative. Similarly, a minimum requires that $d^2 y > 0$; i.e., it is the rate at which the total differential is changing that matters.

Let $g = dy$; then we may write

$$\frac{\delta g}{\delta u} = \frac{\delta}{\delta u}(f_u du + f_v dv)$$

$$= f_{uu} du + f_{vu} dv. \tag{15.11}$$

Similarly, noting that $f_{uv} = f_{vu}$, we have

$$\frac{\delta g}{\delta v} = f_{vu} du + f_{vv} dv. \tag{15.12}$$

By definition, the change in $g(dg)$ is also the change in dy (i.e. d^2y); therefore

$$d^2y = dg = \frac{\delta g}{\delta u} du + \frac{\delta g}{\delta v} dv. \tag{15.13}$$

So, substituting [15.11] and [15.12] into [15.13],

$$d^2y = (f_{uu} du + f_{uv} dv)du + (f_{uv} du + f_{vv} dv)dv$$

$$= f_{uu}(du)^2 + 2f_{uv}(du)(dv) + f_{vv}(dv)^2 \tag{15.14}$$

and the sign of [15.14] clearly depends upon the sign of all three second-order partials *including* the cross-partial derivative. If the sign of [15.14] is to be the same for all possible combinations of du and dv (i.e. for all possible du/dv), d^2y can never equal zero. Now for non-zero dv we may write [15.14] as

$$d^2y = \left[f_{uu}\left(\frac{du}{dv}\right)^2 + 2f_{uv}\left(\frac{du}{dv}\right) + f_{vv}\right](dv)^2 \tag{15.15}$$

which is a quadratic equation in (du/dv). To say that it can never take the value zero is to say that the quadratic has no real roots. The condition for there to be no real roots to the equation $ax^2 + bx + c = 0$ is that $b^2 < 4ac$ (see section 2.2.1), and applying this to [15.15] gives us

$$(2f_{uv})^2 < 4f_{uu} \cdot f_{vv}$$

$$f_{uu} \cdot f_{vv} > (f_{uv})^2$$

which is the additional restriction given in [15.8]. Note that it requires that f_{uu} and f_{vv} have the same sign, so if [15.8] is satisfied then we only need to look at the sign of one of these to establish whether we have a maximum or a minimum.

15.2 Constrained optimization

In practice, it often occurs that the ability to maximize or minimize some particular function is constrained by some other factor. Distance travelled may be constrained by time available, the amount of profit by the size of the market or the need to earn a minimum profit rate per unit of output, and so on. When the function to be optimized is univariate the problem is relatively simple. Suppose that $y = f(x)$ and $x \leq x_{max}$. The optimum (maximum or minimum) value(s) of $f(x)$ can be calculated without reference to the constraint and then these can be compared to the value of $f(x_{max})$. Thus, in figure 15.2 constraining the value of x to be less than $\bar{x}$ where $(8 < \bar{x} < 11)$ will actually lead to the constraint being effective in that the best we can now do is $\bar{y} = f(\bar{x})$, which is less than the global maximum $y^{**} = f(11)$.

Restricting the value of x to be less than 8 would have moved us to the local maximum $y^* = f(3)$, while choosing any $x_{max} > 11$ would have no effect at all. In no case is any new technique required, since it is merely a matter of locating and evaluating the three points y^{**}, y^* and $\bar{y}$.

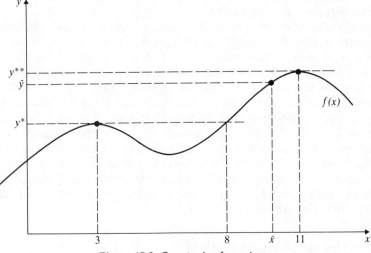

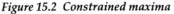

Figure 15.2 Constrained maxima

Now let us consider a slightly more interesting type of constraint in which both x and y occur. For example, we might wish to maximize $y = f(x)$ subject to $y \leq ax$. This is illustrated in figure 15.3. Again, the constraint may result in a shift to a local maximum (if $y \leq a_1x$), a constrained maximum defined by the intersection of function and constraint ($y \leq a_2x$), or it may have no effect at all (if $y \leq a_3x$); and, again, the techniques required are simple. We still calculate relative

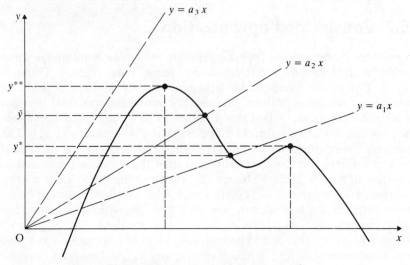

Figure 15.3 Constrained maxima again

optima as before, but we also evaluate the function at the point(s) of intersection with the constraint.

When we have a multivariate function to cope with, both of the types of constraint already considered may occur. There may be a constraint on one or more of the arguments of the function or upon the value of the function itself. In either case the solution procedure is exactly the same as it was for the univariate function. There is, however, an additional possibility, and that possibility is the subject of the rest of this chapter. With a multivariate function it is possible for two or more of the arguments to be jointly constrained. Thus, in the analogy of the landscape that was presented in section 14.1.1, we might be searching for the highest point in the domain yet be constrained not to be out of radio contact with base. If the base is at the origin and the radio has a range of x miles, then by Pythagoras we require $u^2 + v^2 \leq x^2$. It is to the solution of such problems we now turn.

15.2.1 The substitution method

Suppose that we wish to minimize the function $y = f(u, v)$ subject to some joint constraint on the variables such as

$$y = u^2 + v^2 \quad \text{subject to } u + v = 4. \tag{15.16}$$

The obvious method of solution is to rewrite the constraint as $v = 4 - u$ and substitute into the *objective function* $(u^2 + v^2)$ to give

$$y = u^2 + (4 - u)^2 = 2u^2 - 8u + 16$$

$$\frac{dy}{du} = 4u - 8 = 0 \qquad\qquad \therefore\ u = 2,\ v = 2$$

$$\frac{d^2y}{du^2} = 4 > 0.$$

So we have a minimum at (2, 2) at which point $y = 8$.

Notice that, if the constraint had been $u + v \le 4$, we should compare the constrained minimum with the unconstrained. Thus, in the case of $y = u^2 + v^2$ we find an unconstrained minimum where

$$\frac{\delta y}{\delta u} = 2u = 0; \quad \frac{\delta y}{\delta v} = 2v = 0 \quad u = 0,\ v = 0.$$

The value of the function at this point is zero, which is less than it is at (2, 2). The constraint $u + v \le 4$ is not an effective one, whereas $u + v = 4$ is.

In principle, all constrained optima problems can be dealt with in this way, but the substitutions are not always easy. The sort of problem suggested above might be a case in point. For example, maximizing

$$y = 3u + 4v \text{ subject to } (u^2 + v^2)^{(1/2)} \le 4$$

might be better tackled by the alternative method given in the next section. First, however, another example of the substitution method.

Worked example

Q. Minimize $y = 2u + 4v$ subject to $uv^2 = 64$.

A. Rewriting the constraint as $u = 64v^{-2}$ and substituting, we have

$$y = 128v^{-2} + 4v$$

$$\frac{dy}{dv} = -256v^{-3} + 4 = 0$$

$$\therefore\ v = 4 \text{ and } u = 4.$$

The second-order condition is

$$\frac{d^2y}{dv^2} = 768v^{-4} > 0 \text{ when } v = 4$$

so there is a minimum at $u = 4$, $v = 4$.

15.2.2 The Lagrange method

Consider the following problem. Maximize

$$y = 3u + 4v \text{ subject to } uv = 3. \qquad [15.17]$$

Although this can be solved by substitution (the actual solution being left to the reader as an exercise), let us adopt an alternative procedure. The Lagrange method is to replace the existing objective function (in this case, $3u + 4v$) by one that actually incorporates the constraint explicitly. So as not to alter the value of the function itself, we must first transform the constraint in such a way that it equals zero. Thus, instead of $uv = 3$ we would write $uv - 3 = 0$ and so on. Now, adding or subtracting any multiple of it to the objective function will not alter the value of the function. We write this new function, the *Lagrangean*, as

$$L = 3u + 4v - \lambda(uv - 3). \qquad [15.18]$$

The new variable λ is known as the *Lagrange multiplier*.

Now to find a stationary point of a three-variable function requires that all three first-order partial derivatives be equal to zero.

$$L_u \equiv \frac{\delta L}{\delta u} = 3 - \lambda v = 0 \qquad [15.19]$$

$$L_v \equiv \frac{\delta L}{\delta v} = 4 - \lambda u = 0 \qquad [15.20]$$

$$L_\lambda \equiv \frac{\delta L}{\delta \lambda} = -uv + 3 = 0. \qquad [15.21]$$

Solving [15.19] for λ and substituting into [15.20] gives

$$4 - \left(\frac{3}{v}\right)u = 0$$

solving which for v and substituting into [15.21] gives

$$u\left(\frac{3}{4}u\right) - 3 = 0.$$

And there are two possible solutions:

$$u = 2 \quad \therefore v = \tfrac{3}{2}, \lambda = 2$$

$$u = -2 \quad \therefore v = \tfrac{-3}{2}, \lambda = -2.$$

The diligent reader will notice that these are the same solutions as are obtained by the substitution method (see exercise (ii) for section 15.2.1 at the end of the chapter). The proof that these two methods will always give the same solution is given in section 15.2.3, but we must first establish that one of these solutions does indeed give a maximum. Unfortunately, the second-order conditions for these problems are not easy to demonstrate. The complete set of conditions is given in section 18.2, but for most purposes in economics the two-variable case is quite sufficient and the rules applying here may be stated quite simply.

Rules: The conditions for a maximum (minimum) to the function $f(u, v)$ subject to $g(u, v) = 0$ and represented by the Lagrangean $L = f(u, v) - \lambda g(u, v)$ are that

(i) $L_u = L_v = L_\lambda = 0$

and for a maximum

(ii) $2(L_{uv} \cdot g_u \cdot g_v) > L_{uu}(g_v)^2 + L_{vv}(g_u)^2$

or for a minimum

(ii)' $2(L_{uv} \cdot g_u \cdot g_v) < L_{uu}(g_v)^2 + L_{vv}(g_u)^2.$ [15.22]

These conditions are quite easy to manipulate in practice, as is illustrated by the example above. Differentiation of [15.19] and [15.20] gives

$$L_{uu} = L_{vv} = 0; \quad L_{uv} = -\lambda.$$

By construction, $-L_\lambda = g(u, v)$; hence, differentiating [15.21],

$$-L_{\lambda u} = g_u = v; \quad -L_{\lambda v} = g_v = u$$

and the second-order condition simplifies to

$$-2\lambda uv > 0 \text{ for a maximum}$$

$$< 0 \text{ for a minimum}.$$

Thus there is a maximum at $(-2, -\tfrac{3}{2})$ and a minimum at $(2, \tfrac{3}{2})$.

Worked example

Q. Minimize $y = 2u + 4v$ subject to $\dfrac{u^2}{4} + v^2 = 2$

A. The Lagrangean is

$$L = 2u + 4v - \lambda\left(\frac{u^2}{4} + v^2 - 2\right)$$

$$L_u = 2 - \frac{\lambda u}{2} = 0 \qquad \qquad \therefore \lambda = \frac{4}{u}$$

$$L_v = 4 - 2\lambda v = 0 \qquad\qquad \therefore 4 - 2\left(\frac{4}{u}\right)v = 0;\ u = 2v$$

$$L_\lambda = \frac{u^2}{4} + v^2 - 2 = 0 \qquad\qquad \therefore \frac{(2v)^2}{4} + v^2 = 2;\ v^2 = 1$$

and there are two solutions: $v = 1$, $u = 2$, $\lambda = 2$ and $v = -1$, $u = -2$, $\lambda = -2$. The second-order partials are

$$L_{uu} = \frac{-\lambda}{2};\ L_{vv} = -2\lambda;\ L_{uv} = 0;\ g_u = \frac{u}{2};\ g_v = 2v$$

and, substituting these into the condition for a minimum, we require that

$$2(L_{uv} \cdot g_u \cdot g_v) < L_{uu}(g_v)^2 + L_{vv}(g_u)^2$$
$$0 < -\frac{\lambda}{2}(2v)^2 - 2\lambda\left(\frac{u}{2}\right)^2$$

which will be true if and only if $\lambda < 0$. Therefore there is a constrained minimum at $(-2, -1)$, at which point $\lambda = -2$.

*15.2.3 Proof of the Lagrange method

The first-order condition for a stationary point of $y = f(u, v)$ is

$$dy = f_u du + f_v dv = 0. \qquad\qquad [15.23]$$

It must also be true by definition that, if $g(u, v) = 0$,

$$dg = g_u du + g_v dv = 0. \qquad\qquad [15.24]$$

Solving [15.24] for dv, we have

$$dv = -\frac{g_u}{g_v}du$$

which can be substituted into [15.23] to give

$$f_u du - f_v \cdot \frac{g_u}{g_v}du = 0 \qquad\qquad [15.25]$$

$$\frac{f_u}{g_u} = \frac{f_v}{g_v} = \lambda. \qquad\qquad [15.26]$$

Equation [15.26] follows directly from [15.25], since $du \lfloor 0$ and g_u cannot be zero if the constraint is really a function of u. The common ratio is arbitrarily given the symbol λ, and it is what we have called the Lagrange multiplier. From [15.26] we may derive two equations which are the exact equivalent of those derived from the Lagrangean function $L = f(u, v) - \lambda g(u, v)$:

$$L_u = f_u - \lambda g_u = 0$$
$$L_v = f_v - \lambda g_v = 0$$

and, as we have already seen, the third condition is the constraint itself:

$$L_\lambda = g(u, v) = 0.$$

15.3 Exercises

Section 15.1.2

Find any relative extrema of the following, stating in each case whether they are maxima or minima:

(i) $F = 4xy - x^2 - 5y^2$

(ii) $y = 4uv - u^2 - 2v^2$

(iii) $u = -\frac{8}{3}x^3 + 4xy - 2x^2 + 2y^2$

(iv) $y = (u - 2)^2 + (v - 3)^2 + 4uv$

(v) $F = x^2 + xy + 2y^2 - 2x - y$

(vi) $y = 3x_1 + 6x_2 + 3x_1x_2 - 3x_1^2 - x_2^2$

Section 15.2.1

Maximize the following subject to the specified constraints:

(i) $F = 6x + 3xy$ s.t. $x + y = 10$

(ii) $y = 3u + 4v$ s.t. $uv = 3$

(iii) $u = x_1^{(1/2)}x_2$ s.t. $x_1 + 4x_2 = 48$

(iv) $y = 2u + 4v$ s.t. $\dfrac{u^2}{4} + v^2 = 2$

Section 15.2.2

Maximize the following subject to the specified constraints:

(i) $u = 2x^2 + 3y^2 + 3xy$ s.t. $2x + 3y = 8$

(ii) $F = 3u + 4v$ s.t. $u^2 + v^2 = 1$

Further exercises

Find the maxima or minima (if any) of the following:

(i) $F = x^3 + y(1 + x + 2y)$

(ii) $y = (120 - 2u)u + (320 - 4v)v - (u + v)^2$ s.t. $u + v \leqslant 55$

(iii) $w = x^2 + xy + 2y^2 - 2x - y$

16 Economic applications V

16.1 Production functions

In section 10.2 we introduced the concept of a production function – a technical relationship between the input of a resource and the resultant level of output. At that time we were constrained to consider only one variable input (labour), but in reality most production processes involve more than one factor input. Armed with the techniques of multivariate calculus, we can now consider the case where output is the result of combining inputs (factors of production) in a wide variety of different ways. While the forms such a function could take are numerous, most practical work has centred on one special function – the Cobb–Douglas. This postulates two factor inputs – capital (K) and labour (L) – which are combined to produce output (Q) according to the relationship

$$Q = AK^{\beta}L^{\alpha} \qquad\qquad A > 0, \; 0 < \alpha, \beta < 1. \qquad [16.1]$$

The constant (A) subsumes all the other possible influences on output such as entrepreneurial ability, technical progress and so on. In more sophisticated treatments A itself may be a function of other variables (e.g. time), but for the purpose of exposition we shall treat it as a constant. To find the effect upon output of changing labour while leaving the level of capital unchanged, we find the partial derivative

$$\frac{\delta Q}{\delta L} = \alpha AK^{\beta}L^{\alpha-1} = \frac{\alpha}{L} \cdot AK^{\beta}L^{\alpha} = \frac{\alpha Q}{L}. \qquad [16.2]$$

As in section 10.2, we define this as the marginal product of labour (MP_L), but notice that in this expanded model we can also define a marginal product of capital (MP_K):

$$\frac{\delta Q}{\delta K} = \beta AK^{\beta-1}L^{\alpha} = \frac{\beta Q}{K}. \qquad [16.3]$$

Both factors exhibit diminishing marginal returns; i.e., both marginal products decline as the amount of the factor is increased relative to the fixed factor. Formally,

$$\frac{\delta^2 Q}{\delta L^2} = \alpha(\alpha - 1)AK^\beta L^{\alpha - 2} = \alpha(\alpha - 1)\frac{Q}{L^2} < 0 \qquad [16.4]$$

$$\frac{\delta^2 Q}{\delta K^2} = \beta(\beta - 1)AK^{\beta - 2}L^\alpha = \beta(\beta - 1)\frac{Q}{K^2} < 0. \qquad [16.5]$$

Indeed, the restrictions on the parameters α and β are chosen so as to ensure these properties. Notice also that the *partial elasticities* are both constants:

$$\frac{\delta Q}{\delta L} \cdot \frac{L}{Q} = \frac{\alpha Q}{L} \cdot \frac{L}{Q} = \alpha$$

$$\frac{\delta Q}{\delta K} \cdot \frac{K}{Q} = \frac{\beta Q}{K} \cdot \frac{K}{Q} = \beta.$$

Much of the appeal of the Cobb–Douglas production function lies in its mathematical tractability and the simple, testable predictions that it implies. Its conception was due to the desire to explain, with the use of conventional economic theory, the apparent stability of the share of wages in national income. (Although much of the criticism of the function likewise stems from the fact that this share no longer appears to be constant, if it ever was.) Before we can establish this result, however, we need to make a small digression.

16.1.1 Profit maximization again

In a perfectly competitive market (see section 10.3 for a discussion of this terminology) a firm is faced by fixed prices for both its output and its inputs. Let the prices of output, labour and capital be P, W and H respectively; then its profits are given by the formula

$$\Pi = P \cdot Q - W \cdot L - H \cdot K \qquad [16.6]$$

where output is itself a function of K and L. The decision facing the firm is to choose the levels of K and L so as to maximize its profit. The first-order conditions for such a maximum are

$$\frac{\delta \Pi}{\delta L} = P \cdot \frac{\delta Q}{\delta L} - W = 0 \qquad \text{i.e.,} \quad \frac{\delta Q}{\delta L} = \frac{W}{P} \qquad [16.7]$$

$$\frac{\delta \Pi}{\delta K} = P \cdot \frac{\delta Q}{\delta K} - H = 0 \qquad \text{i.e.,} \quad \frac{\delta Q}{\delta K} = \frac{H}{P}. \qquad [16.8]$$

That is to say, the wage paid to labour, expressed in real terms (i.e. in terms of the amount of output it will buy), will be equal to the marginal product of labour. If marginal product is falling, as was the case in

[16.4], then employing any more labour will lead to an increase in output that is less than the wage that will have to be paid to produce it, which would of course reduce profit. Similarly, capital must also receive its marginal product. Again, the second-order conditions for a maximum, viz.

$$\frac{\delta^2\Pi}{\delta L^2}, \frac{\delta^2\Pi}{\delta K^2} < 0; \quad \left(\frac{\delta^2\Pi}{\delta L^2}\right)\left(\frac{\delta^2\Pi}{\delta K^2}\right) > \left(\frac{\delta^2\Pi}{\delta L \delta K}\right)^2$$

require diminishing returns to capital. Adopting the notation that

$$w = \frac{W}{P} \text{ and } h = \frac{H}{P}$$

we now return to the main theme.

16.1.2 Distribution of the product

Under the assumption of perfect competition, then, we may expect $w = MP_L$, and substituting this result into [16.2],

$$\frac{\delta Q}{\delta L} = \frac{\alpha Q}{L} = w$$

which may be alternatively expressed as

$$\frac{wL}{Q} = \alpha.$$

This tells us that the share of the product that goes to wages is constant – indeed, it is equal to the partial elasticity of output with respect to labour. Similarly, it can be shown that the share going to capital is

$$\frac{hK}{Q} = \beta.$$

Notice that, if all the product is to be shared between the two factors then $\alpha + \beta = 1$. In this case it is trivial to solve for $\beta = 1 - \alpha$, and imposing this condition upon [16.1] gives the original form of the Cobb–Douglas production function:

$$Q = AK^{1-\alpha}L^{\alpha}. \tag{16.9}$$

If we are seeking to apply this function to the economy as a whole then [16.9] may well be the appropriate formulation, but for any one firm or industry [16.1] would seem adequate. Notice that the total increase in product is given by the total differential

$$dQ = \left(\frac{\delta Q}{\delta L}\right)dL + \left(\frac{\delta Q}{\delta K}\right)dK.$$

In the case of the Cobb–Douglas function this becomes, substituting from [16.2] and [16.3],

$$dQ = \frac{\alpha Q}{L}dL + \frac{\beta Q}{K}dK.$$

Dividing both sides by Q and noting that dx/x represents a proportional rate of increase, we have

$$\frac{dQ}{Q} = \alpha\frac{dL}{L} + \beta\frac{dK}{K}$$

and the rate of growth of output is seen to be a weighted average of the rates of growth of factor inputs. If both inputs grow at the same rate g, then

$$\frac{dQ}{Q} = (\alpha + \beta)g.$$

If $\alpha + \beta = 1$, as was suggested above, then we have *constant returns to scale*. If on the other hand $\alpha + \beta < 1$, there are *decreasing returns*, and if $\alpha + \beta > 1$ there are *increasing returns*. Thus the Cobb–Douglas function is more flexible than it might appear at first sight.

16.2 Deriving demand curves

In the same way that we may conceive of combining different inputs to produce output, we may also postulate that the consumption of one or more commodities produces satisfaction. How much satisfaction it will be difficult to say, since, unlike physical output, satisfaction is not an easy concept to measure. Economists talk of deriving 'utility' from goods, but defining a new terminology does not alter the measurement problem. Fortunately, it does not always prove to be necessary to measure something in order for the concept to be useful. It is possible to derive implications about the shape of demand curves directly from the form of the utility function or vice versa. First, however, we need to introduce the *indifference curve*.

16.2.1 Indifference curves

In the previous section we considered a production function in which output could be produced in a wide variety of ways. The firm might

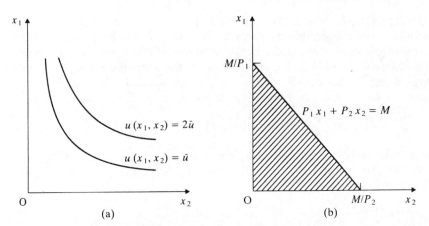

Figure 16.1 Indifference curve and budget constraint

have chosen to use a lot of labour and not much capital, or vice versa. The actual decision was found to depend upon the real costs of the two factors of production. In the same way, we might expect the individual consumer to combine goods in varying proportions depending upon the prices of the various goods. The total utility derived may be expressed as

$$U = U(x_1, x_2, x_3, \ldots) \qquad\qquad x_1, x_2, \ldots \geqslant 0 \qquad\qquad [16.10]$$

where x_1, etc., are the quantities of the various goods, and we assume that all goods are consumed in positive amounts (strictly speaking, in non-negative amounts). Although we cannot measure U, we can argue that there are any number of different combinations of the goods that will produce the same level of satisfaction. If the total amount of utility is unchanged when the actual quantities of the goods are changed, we may write

$$dU = \left(\frac{\delta U}{\delta x_1}\right)dx_1 + \left(\frac{\delta U}{\delta x_2}\right)dx_2 + \left(\frac{\delta U}{\delta x_3}\right)dx_3 + \ldots = 0. \qquad [16.11]$$

Equation [16.11] defines an *indifference curve*. In the case of only two goods this simplifies to

$$dU = \left(\frac{\delta U}{\delta x_1}\right)dx_1 + \left(\frac{\delta U}{\delta x_2}\right)dx_2 = 0$$

and we can quickly establish the relationship between the two goods as

$$\frac{dx_1}{dx_2} = -\left(\frac{\delta U}{\delta x_2}\right)\Bigg/\left(\frac{\delta U}{\delta x_1}\right) \equiv -U_2/U_1. \qquad [16.12]$$

The partial derivatives U_1, U_2 represent the *marginal utilities* of the different goods, and we see that the slope of the indifference curve, as given by [16.12], is in fact the (negative) ratio of the marginal utilities. It would seem reasonable to suppose that, as there is an increase in the consumption of any good, marginal utility will fall; i.e., we postulate that there is *diminishing marginal utility*. At the same time marginal utility will never be negative; i.e., no amount of a good will actually make anyone feel worse off. Formally, we have

$$\frac{\delta U}{\delta x_i} \equiv U_i > 0; \quad \frac{\delta^2 U}{\delta x_i^2} \equiv U_i < 0 \text{ for all } i.$$

An indifference curve depicting these assumptions is shown in figure 16.1(a). An example of such a function is given by $u = x_1 x_2$. Setting the level of utility at $\bar{U}$,

$$x_1 x_2 = \bar{U}$$

$$x_1 = \bar{U} x_2^{-1}$$

$$\frac{dx_1}{dx_2} = -\bar{U} x_2^{-2} = -\frac{x_1 x_2}{x_2^2} = -\frac{x_1}{x_2} < 0$$

$$\frac{d^2 x_1}{dx_2^2} = 2\bar{U} x_2^{-3} = \frac{2 x_1 x_2}{x_2^3} = \frac{2 x_1}{x_2^2} > 0.$$

So the indifference curve is convex to the origin.

16.2.2 The budget constraint

An individual with a fixed income (M) may choose to spend it all on one good or to divide it beteen two or more goods. Whichever he does, the sum of the expenditures upon each of the goods cannot exceed his total income. If we represent the price of good x_i by P_i, then this constraint may be written as

$$\sum_i P_i x_i \leq M.$$

In the case of the two-goods model this simplifies to

$$P_1 x_1 + P_2 x_2 \leq M \tag{16.13}$$

and this case is depicted in figure 16.1(b). The shaded area represents all the possible combinations of purchases, the equation of the constraint itself being

$$x_1 = \frac{M - P_2 x_2}{P_1}.$$

From this we may calculate the slope of the constraint as

$$\frac{dx_1}{dx_2} = -\frac{P_2}{P_1}. \qquad\qquad [16.14]$$

16.2.3 Derivation of the demand curves

The problem now faced by the consumer is to maximize utility (satisfaction) subject to the constraint on expenditure, i.e. to maximize

$U(x_1, x_2, ...)$ subject to $\sum_i P_i x_i \leqslant M.$

The principles are the same irrespective of the number of goods to be considered, but it is convenient to concentrate on the two-goods case, for which the Lagrangean is, assuming all income is spent,

$L = U(x_1, x_2) - \lambda(P_1 x_1 + P_1 x_1 - M).$

The first-order conditions for a maximum are

$$L_1 = U_1 - \lambda P_1 = 0 \qquad\qquad [16.15]$$

$$L_2 = U_2 - \lambda P_2 = 0 \qquad\qquad [16.16]$$

$$L_\lambda = P_1 x_1 + P_2 x_2 - M = 0 \qquad\qquad [16.17]$$

where L_1 refers to $\delta L/\delta x_1$, U_1 refers to $\delta U/\delta x_1$, and so on. From [16.15] and [16.12], we have

$$\frac{U_2}{U_1} = \frac{P_2}{P_1}. \qquad\qquad [16.18]$$

Substituting [16.18] into [16.12], the condition is seen to be

$$\frac{dx_1}{dx_2} = -\frac{P_2}{P_1}$$

which is, from [16.14], the slope of the budget constraint. The final first-order condition, [16.17], is the constraint itself, so the optimum must lie on the constraint where the slopes of the indifference curve and that of the budget constraint are equal, i.e. at the point of tangency. This is shown graphically in figure 16.2.

The solution for x_1^* and x_2^* are in general functions of both prices and income level – they are what we refer to as *demand functions*. It is possible to establish many general properties about these derived demand functions but this must be left to the economics texts. Instead, let us look at a particular example.

Suppose that the utility function is again $U = x_1 x_2$; then

$U_1 = x_2, U_2 = x_1$

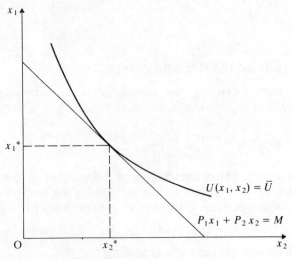

Figure 16.2   Utility maximization

and [16.18] becomes

$$\frac{x_1}{x_2} = \frac{P_2}{P_1} \text{ or } P_1 x_1 = P_2 x_2. \tag{16.19}$$

Substituting into [16.17], we can solve for the two demand functions:

$$x_1 = \frac{M}{2P_1} \text{ and } x_2 = \frac{M}{2P_2}.$$

To ensure that these solutions do in fact represent the true maximum, we require that (see equation [15.22])

$$2L_{12} \cdot g_1 \cdot g_2 > L_{11}(g_2)^2 + L_{22}(g_1)^2$$

where

$$L_{11} = L_{22} = 0, L_{12} = 1, g_1 = P_1 \text{ and } g_2 = P_2$$

which is seen to be true. The demand functions for this particular utility function are symmetric and are functions only of their own price level of income. The shape of the demand curves is given by

$$\frac{\delta x_i}{\delta P_i} = -\frac{M}{2P_i^2} < 0; \frac{\delta^2 x_i}{\delta P_i^2} = \frac{M}{P_i^3} > 0$$

which conforms to standard assumptions. Note also that they are homogeneous of degree zero in prices and income, i.e., that doubling both prices and income leaves the quantities demanded unchanged.

16.3 Exercises

1. A monopolist's demand function is $P = 4Q^{-(1/2)}$, while his production function is $Q = 36K^{(1/2)}L^{(1/2)}$. If the fixed wage rate is 12 and the cost of capital given at $\frac{3}{4}$, find the profit-maximizing levels of the inputs K and L.

2. A consumer has a utility function defined on two goods (x_1 and x_2) given by $u = x_1^{(1/2)} + x_2^{(1/2)}$. Calculate her demand curve for the good x_1 if the prices of the two goods are P_1 and P_2 respectively and she has an available income of M.

Part VI

Matrix algebra

This final part is rather different from the others. Matrix algebra is a powerful tool for the mathematical economist and for the statistician, but its use in basic economic analysis has always been rather limited. This may be due both to its preoccupation with linear relationships – indeed, it is often called 'linear algebra' – and to the effort required to master the mathematics. Certainly it is true that it would take a complete book to do justice to the subject rather than the two chapters devoted to it here, but the essential principles are not difficult to grasp and it is with these that we shall concern ourselves. The notation of matrix algebra is particularly concise and increasingly being used in economics texts and articles. Furthermore, the limitations of linearity may not be so important as appear at first sight. Very often linear approximations are sufficiently good over a small range of values for the technique to be applicable. A good example of this is given in chapter 18. What makes this Part different is that, unlike the others, it is concerned not with introducing new techniques to solve new problems, but rather with expressing and solving old problems in a new way.

17 Vectors and matrices

The concept of algebra was introduced in chapter 1, where we argued that it was a sort of code – a set of rules for manipulating numbers which would preserve the message intact yet allow us to read the message and work out its implications more readily. Matrix algebra is exactly that. Unlike ordinary algebra, however, each symbol refers not to one number but to a whole array of information. It is this conciseness of notation that provides much of its appeal, and it is on this aspect that we shall concentrate in this chapter.

17.1 Basic definitions and operations

As already indicated, matrix algebra deals with more than one number at a time. Any collection of numbers is known as a *set*. Thus, the numbers of the houses in a particular road form a set. In this case each of the numbers is likely to be unique, but that is not necessary. If we asked at each house how many children lived there the answers would be a set of numbers most of which would be repeated many times. If we arranged these numbers in a particular order, say by the number of the house itself, then it becomes a *vector*. Thus, if there are x_1 children in house number 1, x_2 in house number 2 and so on, then we can write the vector of children in the road as

$$\mathbf{x}' = [x_1 \quad x_2 \quad x_3 \quad ... \quad x_n]$$ [17.1]

where there are n houses in the road.

Notice the notation in [17.1]. Vectors are usually denoted by underscoring or by use of bold-face type. (By convention, the prime sign indicates that the vector is written as a *row* of elements, as in [17.1]. Without the prime sign the elements would be written in a column. We shall return to this soon, but unless otherwise specified all statements refer to both row and column vectors.)

The information contained in [17.1] is very specific. It assigns to each house the number of children in that house. Change the order of any of the elements (x_i) in this vector and you change the information. It follows that two vectors **x** and **y** are equal to each other only if every piece of information contained in them is identical.

Rule: Two vectors **x** and **y** will be equal if and only if they have the same number of elements (dimension) and iff

$$x_i = y_i \qquad\qquad i = 1, \ldots, n. \qquad [17.2]$$

Now suppose that we also know the number of adults living in each house. We could present this information in the form of a *matrix*:

$$x_1 \; x_2 \ldots x_n$$
$$y_1 \; y_2 \ldots y_n .$$

This matrix contains two rows since there are now two pieces of information for each house. We say that it has the dimension $(2 \times n)$. If we were to include further information on (say) the number of cats in the house we would have a $(3 \times n)$ matrix and so on. As we add information it becomes less and less convenient to use different letters for each row and we adopt instead a notation using two subscripts:

$$\mathbf{A} = \begin{bmatrix} a_{11} & a_{12} & a_{13} & \ldots a_{1n} \\ a_{21} & a_{22} & a_{23} & \ldots a_{2n} \\ \cdot & \cdot & \cdot & \cdot \\ \cdot & \cdot & \cdot & \cdot \\ \cdot & \cdot & \cdot & \cdot \\ a_{m1} & a_{m2} & a_{m3} \ldots & a_{mn} \end{bmatrix}.$$

Convention has it that the first of the subscripts always refers to the row and the second to the column; thus, the element a_{ij} refers to the *j*th element in the *i*th row. It remains true that each row is itself a vector of dimension *n*, and we may write

$$\mathbf{a}'_i = [a_{i1} \quad a_{i2} \; \ldots \; a_{in}]. \qquad [17.3]$$

At the same time we may conceive of a row vector as being a matrix with only one row, a $(1 \times n)$ matrix.

So far we have read the information from the matrix *across* each row of the matrix, but we could have read down each column. If for example we were interested in the family at number *j*, we could extract the information on this house writing it as

$$\mathbf{a}_j = \begin{bmatrix} a_{1j} \\ a_{2j} \\ \cdot \\ \cdot \\ \cdot \\ a_{mj} \end{bmatrix}. \qquad [17.4]$$

Since this is still an ordered set of numbers we would still wish to call it a vector, but we add that it is a *column* vector so as to distinguish it from the *row* vectors we have met hithereto. Just as a row vector can be thought of as a special matrix with only one row, so a column vector is a matrix with only one column – an $(m \times 1)$ matrix.

Note: Any $(m \times n)$ matrix $\mathbf{A}$ normally written as

$$\mathbf{A} = \begin{bmatrix} a_{11} & \cdots & a_{1n} \\ & & \\ & & \\ a_{m1} & \cdots & a_{mn} \end{bmatrix} \text{ or } [a_{ij}]$$

can alternatively be expressed as a row of column vectors:

$$\mathbf{A} = [\mathbf{a}_1 \quad \mathbf{a}_2 \quad \cdots \quad \mathbf{a}_n]$$

or as a column of row vectors:

$$\mathbf{A} = \begin{bmatrix} \mathbf{a}_1' \\ \mathbf{a}_2' \\ \vdots \\ \mathbf{a}_m' \end{bmatrix} \tag{17.5}$$

It follows immediately from the definition of equality of vectors in [17.2] that two matrices will be equal if and only if all the elements are identical.

Rule: Two $(m \times n)$ matrices $\mathbf{A}$ and $\mathbf{B}$ are said to be equal iff

$$a_{ij} = b_{ij} \text{ all } i, j \tag{17.6}$$

17.1.1 Partitioning a matrix

There are occasions upon which it is convenient to isolate or draw attention to particular parts of a matrix. This is particularly true when the complete matrix is actually a composite of two or more sub-matrices. Such partitioning is denoted by broken lines, and sub-matrices so constructed are sometimes referred to by adding subscripts to the letter denoting the matrix. Various alternative notations do occur depending upon the context and some of these are illustrated below.

$$\begin{bmatrix} a_{11} & a_{12} & a_{13} & a_{14} \\ a_{21} & a_{22} & a_{23} & a_{24} \\ a_{31} & a_{32} & a_{33} & a_{34} \end{bmatrix} \qquad \begin{bmatrix} \mathbf{A}_{11} & \mathbf{A}_{12} \\ \mathbf{A}_{21} & \mathbf{A}_{22} \end{bmatrix}$$

$$\begin{bmatrix} a_{11} & \vdots & a_{12} & a_{13} \\ a_{21} & \vdots & a_{22} & a_{23} \end{bmatrix} \qquad [\mathbf{a}_1 \vdots \ \mathbf{a}_2 \ \ \mathbf{a}_3] \qquad [\mathbf{a}_1 \vdots \ \mathbf{A}_2]$$

$$\begin{bmatrix} a_{11} & a_{12} & \vdots & 1 & 0 \\ a_{21} & a_{22} & \vdots & 0 & 1 \end{bmatrix} \qquad [\mathbf{A} \vdots \ \mathbf{I}]$$

$$\begin{bmatrix} 1 & \vdots & a_{11} & a_{12} & \vdots & b_1 \\ 1 & \vdots & a_{21} & a_{22} & \vdots & b_2 \end{bmatrix} \qquad [1 \vdots \ \mathbf{A} \vdots \ \mathbf{b}]$$

17.1.2 Transposing a matrix

Having written an ordered set of numbers as a column vector $\mathbf{x}$, it may become necessary to express it instead as a row vector. We use a dash or prime sign to denote the transpose operation.

Rule: If $\mathbf{x}$ is the vector $\begin{bmatrix} x_1 \\ x_2 \\ \cdot \\ \cdot \\ \cdot \\ x_n \end{bmatrix}$ then its transpose is given by

$$\mathbf{x}' = (x_1, x_2, \ldots, x_n)$$

The transpose of the row vector $\mathbf{x}'$ is the column vector $\mathbf{x}$; thus,

$$(\mathbf{x}')' = \mathbf{x} \qquad\qquad [17.7]$$

From [17.5], an $(m \times n)$ matrix may be written as a column of row vectors. Transposing each of these in turn gives a row of column vectors that is said to be the transpose of $\mathbf{A}$. The element in the ith row and jth column of the original matrix will now be in the ith column and jth row of the transposed matrix. Notice that transposition, by reversing rows and columns, will also reverse the dimension of the matrix.

Rule: The transpose of an $(m \times n)$ matrix

$$\mathbf{A} = \begin{bmatrix} a_{11} & \cdots & a_{1n} \\ \cdot & & \cdot \\ \cdot & & \cdot \\ \cdot & & \cdot \\ a_{m1} & \cdots & a_{mn} \end{bmatrix}$$

is an $(n \times m)$ matrix:

$$\mathbf{A'} = \begin{bmatrix} a_{11} & \cdots & a_{m1} \\ \cdot & & \cdot \\ \cdot & & \cdot \\ \cdot & & \cdot \\ a_{1n} & \cdots & a_{mn} \end{bmatrix}$$ [17.8]

Worked example

Q. Transpose the following matrices:

(i) $\begin{bmatrix} 2 & 4 & 3 \\ -1 & 0 & 1 \end{bmatrix}$ (ii) $\begin{bmatrix} 2 & 1 \\ 1 & 0 \end{bmatrix}$

A. (i) $\begin{bmatrix} 2 & -1 \\ 4 & 0 \\ 3 & 1 \end{bmatrix}$ (ii) $\begin{bmatrix} 2 & 1 \\ 1 & 0 \end{bmatrix}$

17.1.3 Special matrices

When a matrix is transposed its dimensions are reversed. In the special case of a *square* matrix, i.e. an $(n \times n)$ matrix, this will not change the dimension of the matrix. If the transpose of a matrix is actually equal to the original matrix then it is said to *symmetric*. (A symmetric matrix must, of course, be square.) A special case of the symmetric matrix is when all elements not on the main diagonal are zero and the matrix is said, not surprisingly, to be diagonal. An example is given below, as is a formal definition. If in turn the elements on the diagonal are all equal to 1 (unity) then it is called the *identity* matrix.

Rule: An $(n \times n)$ matrix **A** is diagonal if and only if

$\mathbf{a}_{ij} = 0 \quad i \neq j$ e.g., $\mathbf{A} = \begin{bmatrix} 2 & 0 & 0 \\ 0 & -1 & 0 \\ 0 & 0 & 3 \end{bmatrix}$

For all diagonal matrices $\mathbf{A} = \mathbf{A'}$.   [17.9]

Rule: The identity matrix is an $(n \times n)$ matrix in which

$a_{ii} = 1 \quad i = 1,\dots, n$

$a_{ij} = 0 \quad i \neq j.$ [17.10]

It is commonly written as $\mathbf{I}$ or $\mathbf{I}_n$.

The identity matrix is in fact a very useful concept. It is to matrix algebra what the number 1 is to ordinary algebra, as will be seen in section 17.2. Corresponding to the concept of zero in ordinary algebra there is the *null* matrix, which may be of any dimension but all of whose elements are zero. Just as a matrix may be refered to as $[a_{ij}]$, so the null matrix is often written as $[0]$. Other possibilities are $\mathbf{0}$ or $\emptyset$.

17.1.4 Basic operations

The first thing that we may wish to do with matrices, and we use the term 'matrix' to include the special case of vectors, is to add them up. Thus, if we have two $(m \times n)$ matrices which contain information on (**A**), the number of boys and men in each house, and (**B**), the number of girls and women in each house, we could add the two together to give (**C**), the numbers of children and adults in each house. As we have stated before, such operations make sense only if both matrices have the same dimensions. Given that, then the addition procedure is simply a matter of adding corresponding elements in the two matrices. Subtraction is carried out in an analogous fashion. This can be stated formally as follows.

Rule: If **A** and **B** are two $(m \times n)$ matrices, then

$$\mathbf{C} = \mathbf{A} + \mathbf{B} \text{ iff } c_{ij} = a_{ij} + b_{ij} \qquad [17.11]$$

and

$$\mathbf{C} = \mathbf{A} - \mathbf{B} \text{ iff } c_{ij} = a_{ij} - b_{ij} \qquad [17.12]$$

for all i and j. In each case **C** will be $(m \times n)$.

Sometimes it may be necessary to scale a set of numbers, i.e. to multiply each element of a matrix by the same constant or *scalar*. In matrix algebra the term 'scalar' is used to refer to a single number. It is, in a sense, a special case of a matrix in that it is a matrix of dimension (1×1), but to treat it as such would contravene the rules of matrix multiplication discussed in the next section. It is to avoid possible confusion that we define the term *scalar multiplication*.

Rule: If **A** is an $(m \times n)$ matrix and λ is a scalar, then

$$\mathbf{B} = \lambda\mathbf{A} = \mathbf{A}\lambda \text{ iff } b_{ij} = \lambda a_{ij} \text{ for all } i, j.$$

Worked example

Q. Calculate $2(\mathbf{A} + \mathbf{B}) - \mathbf{C}$ where
$$\mathbf{A} = \begin{bmatrix} 1 & 2 & 0 \\ 0 & 1 & 0 \end{bmatrix}; \mathbf{B} = \begin{bmatrix} -1 & -1 & 1 \\ 1 & 0 & 1 \end{bmatrix}; \mathbf{C} = \begin{bmatrix} 2 & 0 & 1 \\ 1 & 0 & 0 \end{bmatrix}.$$

A. The order of addition and subtraction is not important, but, as in ordinary algebra, multiplication must precede both (in the absence of brackets indicating to the contrary), so we have

$$A + B = \begin{bmatrix} 0 & 1 & 1 \\ 1 & 1 & 1 \end{bmatrix}; \; 2(A + B) = \begin{bmatrix} 0 & 2 & 2 \\ 2 & 2 & 2 \end{bmatrix};$$

$$2(A + B) - C = \begin{bmatrix} -2 & 2 & 1 \\ 1 & 2 & 2 \end{bmatrix}.$$

Alternatively, each element of the solution matrix X may be calculated separately; e.g. $x_{11} = 2(a_{11} + b_{11}) - c_{11} = 2[(1 + (-1)] - 2$; and so on.

17.2 Matrix multiplication

Before proceeding to multiply two matrices together, let us first consider the problem of multiplying two vectors, or, to be more precise, of calculating their *inner product*. In this operation we multiply the corresponding elements of the two vectors and then add all the results together. If for example x' contained information on the quantities of each of n goods purchased by an individual and p contained the prices of each good, then

$$r_1 = x' \cdot p \qquad\qquad [17.14]$$

would denote the total expenditure of this individual.

Rule: The inner product of two vectors x and p of equal dimension n is defined as

$$x'p = x_1 p_1 + x_2 p_2 + \ldots + x_n p_n \qquad\qquad [17.15]$$
$$= \sum_{j=1}^{n} x_j p_j.$$

Since the result r_1 is a scalar, this operation is also known as a scalar product or, as a result of the notation commonly used, as a dot product. It may be of some help to visualize x' as a row vector and p as a column vector, thus writing the operation as

$$r_1 = [x_1 \;\; x_2 \; \ldots \; x_n] \begin{bmatrix} p_1 \\ p_2 \\ \cdot \\ \cdot \\ \cdot \\ p_n \end{bmatrix} = \sum_{j=1}^{n} x_j p_j. \qquad\qquad [17.16]$$

Now, suppose that we actually have information on two individuals.

This is contained in the $(2 \times n)$ matrix $\mathbf{A}$. It is now possible to calculate the expenditure of both individuals and display the results as a (2×1) column vector $\mathbf{r}$. This double operation may be written as in [17.17]. Note that the first row of the $\mathbf{A}$ matrix corresponds to the first individual whose purchases we previously referred to as $\mathbf{x}$:

$$\mathbf{r} \equiv \begin{bmatrix} r_1 \\ r_2 \end{bmatrix} = \begin{bmatrix} a_{11} & a_{12} & \cdots & a_{1n} \\ a_{21} & a_{22} & \cdots & a_{2n} \end{bmatrix} \begin{bmatrix} p_1 \\ p_2 \\ \cdot \\ \cdot \\ \cdot \\ p_n \end{bmatrix} \text{where } a_{1j} = x_j \text{ for } j = 1, \dots, n.$$

[17.17]

The answer that we get from multiplying the matrix $\mathbf{A}$ by the vector $\mathbf{p}$ must be the same as when we take the individuals one at a time; thus,

$$r_1 = \sum_{j=1}^{n} x_j p_j = \sum_{j=1}^{n} a_{1j} p_j.$$

Similarly,

$$r_2 = \sum_{j=1}^{n} a_{2j} p_j.$$

Let us now suppose that there are two different shops in which we can make the purchases and that each charges a different set of prices. This means that each individual could have two different expenditures depending upon which shop he went to. We represent this multiple operation as follows where the first column of the $(n \times 2)$ matrix of prices $\mathbf{B}$ refers to the first shop and the first column of the results matrix $\mathbf{C}$ corresponds to our previous results, vector $\mathbf{r}$:

$$\mathbf{C} \equiv \begin{bmatrix} c_{11} & c_{12} \\ c_{21} & c_{22} \end{bmatrix} = \begin{bmatrix} a_{11} & a_{12} & \cdots & a_{1n} \\ a_{21} & a_{22} & \cdots & a_{2n} \end{bmatrix} \begin{bmatrix} b_{11} & b_{12} \\ b_{21} & b_{22} \\ b_{31} & b_{32} \\ \cdot & \cdot \\ b_{n1} & b_{n2} \end{bmatrix}$$

[17.18]

where $a_{1j} = x_j$ for $j = 1, \dots, n$ and $b_{i1} = p_i$ for $i = 1, \dots, n$.

Again, we note that the results obtained in this matrix mutiplication must be the same as those obtained when we treated each shop and individual separately; thus,

$$c_{21} \equiv r_2 = \sum_{j=1}^{n} a_{2j} p_j = \sum_{j=1}^{n} a_{2j} b_{j1}.$$

Similarly,

$$c_{22} = \sum_{j=1}^{n} a_{2j}b_{j2}$$

$$c_{12} = \sum_{j=1}^{n} a_{1j}b_{j2}; \ ...; \ \text{etc.}$$

These results can be generalized to include any number of consumers m and any number of shops q. The result will be a $(m \times q)$ matrix of possible expenditures. Thus matrix multiplication is really a matter of calculating a series of inner products – the element c_{ij} is the inner product of row i of matrix **A** and column j of matrix **B**.

Rule: The product of two matrices can be defined only if there are the same number of elements in each row of **A** as there are in each column of **B**. They are then said to be *conformable*, and each element of the matrix **C** is given by

$$c_{ij} = \sum_{k=1}^{n} a_{ik}b_{kj} \ \text{all } i, j. \qquad\qquad [17.19]$$

A simple check for conformability is to write the dimensions of each matrix underneath the matrix; thus,

$$\begin{array}{ccc} \mathbf{A} & \mathbf{B} & = & \mathbf{C}. \\ (m \times n) & (n \times q) & & (m \times q) \end{array} \qquad\qquad [17.20]$$

For conformability the two 'middle numbers' must be the same. If we cross out these two numbers, the remaining two 'outside numbers' give the dimensions of the product matrix.

17.2.1 Pre-multiplying and post-multiplying

We have defined the element c_{ij} as the product of the ith row of matrix **A** and the jth column of matrix **B**. In our example it was the ith individual's expenditure if he shopped in the jth shop. With 2 consumers and 2 shops we had a (2×2) product matrix **C**. Notice, however, that there is no mathematical reason why we could not calculate the $(n \times n)$ matrix $\mathbf{C}^*$ where

$$\begin{array}{ccc} \mathbf{C}^* & = & \mathbf{B} & \mathbf{A} \\ (n \times n) & & (n \times 2) & (2 \times n) \end{array} \qquad\qquad [17.21]$$

even though the results would have no obvious economic interpretation.

Note: Unlike ordinary algebra, the *order* of the matrix multiplication *is* important. In general,

AB ≠ BA.   [17.22]

In order to specify the order of multiplication it is convenient to use the terms 'pre-multiply' and 'post-multiply'. In equation (17.20) matrix **B** is *pre-multiplied* by **A** whereas in [17.21] **B** is *post-multiplied* by **A**. There are occasions where the order does not matter, of which the most common is the identity matrix **I**; i.e., **IA = AI**. Similarly, the order does not matter when a matrix is raised to a power. By convention, **AA = A²**; **AA² = A²A = A³**; and so on.

Worked example

Let $\mathbf{A} = \begin{bmatrix} 1 & 2 \\ 0 & 1 \end{bmatrix}$ and $\mathbf{B} = \begin{bmatrix} 2 & 3 \\ 1 & 4 \end{bmatrix}$. Find **AB**, **BA** and **A²**.

$$\mathbf{AB} = \begin{bmatrix} 1 & 2 \\ 0 & 1 \end{bmatrix}\begin{bmatrix} 2 & 3 \\ 1 & 4 \end{bmatrix} = \begin{bmatrix} (1 \times 2) + (2 \times 1) & (1 \times 3) + (2 \times 4) \\ (0 \times 2) + (1 \times 1) & (0 \times 3) + (1 \times 4) \end{bmatrix}$$

$$= \begin{bmatrix} 4 & 11 \\ 1 & 4 \end{bmatrix}$$

$$\mathbf{BA} = \begin{bmatrix} 2 & 3 \\ 1 & 4 \end{bmatrix}\begin{bmatrix} 1 & 2 \\ 0 & 1 \end{bmatrix} = \begin{bmatrix} (2 \times 1) + (3 \times 0) & (2 \times 2) + (3 \times 1) \\ (1 \times 1) + (4 \times 0) & (1 \times 2) + (4 \times 1) \end{bmatrix}$$

$$= \begin{bmatrix} 2 & 7 \\ 1 & 6 \end{bmatrix}$$

$$\mathbf{A}^2 = \begin{bmatrix} 1 & 2 \\ 0 & 1 \end{bmatrix}\begin{bmatrix} 1 & 2 \\ 0 & 1 \end{bmatrix} = \begin{bmatrix} (1 \times 1) + (2 \times 0) & (1 \times 2) + (2 \times 1) \\ (0 \times 1) + (1 \times 0) & (0 \times 2) + (1 \times 1) \end{bmatrix}$$

$$= \begin{bmatrix} 1 & 4 \\ 0 & 1 \end{bmatrix}$$

17.3 Matrix inversion

We have seen that it is possible to multiply matrices provided only that they are conformable, but is it possible to divide them? In a sense, yes. In chapter 1 we considered the reciprocal of a number. The reciprocal of 2 is $\frac{1}{2}$; the reciprocal of x is $1/x$ or x^{-1}. We know that a number multiplied by its reciprocal is by definition equal to unity; i.e. that

$$x \cdot \frac{1}{x} \equiv xx^{-1} \equiv 1.$$

In matrix algebra we use an exactly analogous procedure, defining the reciprocal or *inverse* of a matrix **A** with reference to the identity matrix (**I**).

The inverse of the matrix **A** is defined as $\mathbf{A}^{-1}$ where

$$\mathbf{A}\mathbf{A}^{-1} = \mathbf{A}^{-1}\mathbf{A} = \mathbf{I}. \qquad\qquad [17.23]$$

Notice that, to ensure a unique answer, we require that the order of the multiplication be irrelevant and therefore that **A** must be square. Only square matrices can be inverted. Indeed, not all square matrices can necessarily be inverted and we shall return to this point shortly. For the moment let us demonstrate that matrix inverses can exist. There are in practice many methods of finding the inverse of a matrix, some more efficient and/or more complicated than others. For large problems it is common to use one of the purpose-written computer packages, but for small problems the method outlined below is fairly common and easy to follow.

17.3.1 Inversion by row operations

In ordinary algebra the operation that enables us to transform the expression x into 1 (i.e. division by x) is the same as that which transforms 1 into $1/x$. Given the analogous definition of the matrix inverse, it would seem logical to employ the same sort of procedure in our search for the inverse. Specifically, we are looking for a sequence of operations that will transform the matrix **A** into the matrix **I**. The same sequence of operations applied to the matrix **I** should then produce the matrix inverse $\mathbf{A}^{-1}$. In practice, the procedure can be simplified by performing both transformations simultaneously.

Define a matrix $\mathbf{B} = [\mathbf{A} \vdots \mathbf{I}]$ and call the first row of this matrix $\mathbf{r}_1$, the second row $\mathbf{r}_2$ and so on. We can now define a new row $\mathbf{r}_1^*$ as a weighted combination of any other rows in the matrix. For simplicity of calculation it is convenient to limit these to one or two rows at a time. By successive manipulations, the matrix **B** can be transformed into the new matrix $\mathbf{C} = [\mathbf{I} \vdots \mathbf{A}^{-1}]$. This may sound a little complicated but in practice it is relatively simple, as the worked example below demonstrates.

One is less likely to make mistakes if each 'operation' is as simple as possible and to that end we may reduce all to two simple rules:

1. Multiply any row by a constant.
2. Add/subtract any row or multiple thereof to/from another.

Facility with the technique requires practice, but the steps are straightforward. The first task is to obtain a 1 on the main diagonal. The second is to get 0 for each of the other elements in that column. We then choose another element on the main diagonal and repeat. Although the experienced mathematician will spot short-cuts, the above procedure will always work and is that employed in the worked example.

Worked example

Q. Calculate the inverse of $\mathbf{A} = \begin{bmatrix} 2 & 1 \\ 3 & 2 \end{bmatrix}$

A. Define $\mathbf{B} = \begin{bmatrix} 2 & 1 & 1 & 0 \\ 3 & 2 & 0 & 1 \end{bmatrix}$

Step (i): $\mathbf{r}_1^{(i)} = \frac{1}{2}\mathbf{r}_1$ transforms $\mathbf{B}$ to $\mathbf{B}^{(i)} = \begin{bmatrix} 1 & \frac{1}{2} & \frac{1}{2} & 0 \\ 3 & 2 & 0 & 1 \end{bmatrix}$

Step (ii): $\mathbf{r}_2^{(ii)} = \mathbf{r}_2^{(i)} - 3\mathbf{r}_1^{(i)}$; hence $\mathbf{B}^{(ii)} = \begin{bmatrix} 1 & \frac{1}{2} & \frac{1}{2} & 0 \\ 0 & \frac{1}{2} & -\frac{3}{2} & 1 \end{bmatrix}$

Step (iii): $\mathbf{r}_2^{(iii)} = 2\mathbf{r}_2^{(ii)}$; hence $\mathbf{B}^{(iii)} = \begin{bmatrix} 1 & \frac{1}{2} & \frac{1}{2} & 0 \\ 0 & 1 & -3 & 2 \end{bmatrix}$

Step (iv): $\mathbf{r}_1^{(iv)} = \mathbf{r}_1^{(iii)} - \frac{1}{2}\mathbf{r}_2^{(iii)}$; hence $\mathbf{C} = \begin{bmatrix} 1 & 0 & 2 & -1 \\ 0 & 1 & -3 & 2 \end{bmatrix}$

(Check for yourself that $\mathbf{A}^{-1} = \begin{bmatrix} 2 & -1 \\ -3 & 2 \end{bmatrix}$ satisfies the definition.)

17.3.2 Inversion of $(\mathbf{I} - \mathbf{A})$

A particular matrix much used in economics is the so-called Leontief matrix $(\mathbf{I} - \mathbf{A})$. Its inverse $(\mathbf{I} - \mathbf{A})^{-1}$ can be calculated by the procedure outlined above, but there is an alternative approximation that is frequently used. In section 5.1 we calculated the sum of a geometric progression. Provided that $-1 < c < 1$, we showed that

$$1 + c + c^2 + c^3 + \ldots = \frac{1}{1 - c}.$$

One of the more useful results of matrix algebra is that, provided all the elements of a square matrix $\mathbf{A}$ are similarly constrained, i.e., $-1 < a_{ij} < 1$, then

$$\mathbf{I} + \mathbf{A} + \mathbf{A}^2 + \mathbf{A}^3 + \ldots = (\mathbf{I} - \mathbf{A})^{-1}. \qquad [17.24]$$

With a large matrix the inversion procedure is tedious, and if the elements are themselves of small orders of magnitude calculation errors may be a serious problem. In this case, however, the higher-order matrices tend to zero quickly and good approximations may be achieved with very few terms.

17.3.3 Solving systems of equations

So far we have assumed that the benefits of matrix algebra are largely to be found in the conciseness of its notation, but there are more immediate applications. In chapter 2 we considered methods for solving systems of equations. For example, we wished to know what values of x_1 and x_2 would simultaneously satisfy the two equations

$$4x_1 + 2x_2 = 60; \; x_1 - 2x_2 = 5$$

and discovered that the only solution was $x_1 = 13$, $x_2 = 4$. Graphically, this could be portrayed as the intersection of two straight lines defined by the two equations. In the notation of matrix algebra this problem would be written as

$$\begin{bmatrix} 4 & 2 \\ 1 & -2 \end{bmatrix} \begin{bmatrix} x_1 \\ x_2 \end{bmatrix} = \begin{bmatrix} 60 \\ 5 \end{bmatrix} \text{ or } \mathbf{Ax} = \mathbf{b}. \qquad [17.25]$$

Solving the system meant finding the values of x_1 and x_2 that satisfied the two equations, i.e. finding the elements of the vector $\mathbf{x}$. Now, if we were to pre-multiply both sides of [17.25] by $\mathbf{A}^{-1}$, we have

$$\mathbf{A}^{-1}\mathbf{Ax} = \mathbf{A}^{-1}\mathbf{b} \qquad [17.26]$$

but by definition $\mathbf{A}^{-1}\mathbf{A} = \mathbf{I}$, and multiplying anything by the identity matrix leaves it unchanged, so [17.16] becomes

$$\mathbf{x} = \mathbf{A}^{-1}\mathbf{b} \qquad [17.27]$$

and we have solved the system. The reader is invited to verify that inverting the matrix $\mathbf{A}$ and post-mutiplying by $\mathbf{b}$ does in fact give the correct answer. The computational advantages of this approach for large systems of linear equations are obvious. Other advantages are less obvious but no less real, as we shall see in the following sections.

17.3.4 Linear dependence

Consider the solution of the following pair of simultaneous equations:

$$4x_1 + 2x_2 = 60; \qquad\qquad 2x_1 + x_2 = 40. \qquad [17.28]$$

Or, to be more accurate, consider the absence of a solution. There is in fact no pair of values that will simultaneously satisfy the two conditions, and if you draw the two functions on a graph you will see why: they are in fact two parallel lines that will never intersect. Written in matrix form, we have

$$\begin{bmatrix} 4 & 2 \\ 2 & 1 \end{bmatrix} \begin{bmatrix} x_1 \\ x_2 \end{bmatrix} = \begin{bmatrix} 60 \\ 40 \end{bmatrix}. \qquad [17.29]$$

If you try to invert this matrix using row operations as shown above, you will immediately run into difficulty. Subtract twice the second row from the first (i.e. $r_1^* = r_1 - 2r_2$) and it becomes apparent that no amount of manipulation will enable us to solve the problem. We have

$$\mathbf{B}^* = \begin{bmatrix} 0 & 0 & \vdots & 1 & -2 \\ 2 & 1 & \vdots & 0 & 1 \end{bmatrix}$$

and can go no further.

Rule: If it is possible by row operations to produce a complete row (or column) of zeroes, then the matrix *cannot* be inverted.

This result can be generalized to systems of more than two equations and two unknowns. This is exceedingly useful since it is not possible to represent graphically *n*-dimensional equations and hence to determine graphically whether a solution exists.

Formally, we call this concept linear dependence. If any row (column) may be written as a linear combination of the other rows (columns) of the matrix, they are said to be *linearly dependent*. The information contained in this row (column) simply duplicates information contained in the other rows (columns). If we look back to [17.29], we see that the information on row 1 of the matrix duplicates row 2. The latter tells us what $2x_1 + x_2$ is (in this case $2x_1 + x_2 = 40$). Dividing row 1 by 2 also gives us information about the value of $2x_1 + x_2$ (in this case the information is contradictory since $2x_1 + x_2 = 30$, but that is unimportant). Either the information must be contradictory and there is no solution, or the information is identical and there is an infinite number of solutions. With two unknowns a unique solution is possible only if there are two independent pieces of information.

We have seen that for an inverse to exist the matrix must be square. We now see that this is not enough. If the rows of the matrix are not independent of each other, then at least one equation is redundant. Omitting this equation would not change anything, yet the implied matrix is no longer square and cannot therefore be inverted. For an inverse to exist, not only must the matrix be square, but all its rows must be linearly independent.

17.3.5 Rank

If a matrix has more rows than columns it must necessarily have linear dependence in the rows. Conversely, if it has more columns than rows there will be linear dependence in the columns. We define the *rank* of a matrix, $r(\mathbf{A})$, as the maximum number of independent rows (and therefore columns) that can be found in the matrix. It is formally written as follows.

Rule: If we have a set of m equations in n unknowns written as

$\mathbf{Ax = b}$

there will be a unique solution if and only if $r(\mathbf{A}) = n$.

Another rule then follows.

Rule: A square matrix $(\mathbf{A})$ of dimension n will have an inverse if and only if $r(\mathbf{A}) = n$.

Worked example

Q. Solve the following simultaneous equation system by the use of matrix inversion:

$$x_1 + 2x_2 + 2x_3 = 7$$

$$x_1 + x_3 = 4 - x_2$$

$$x_1 + 3x_3 - x_2 - 6 = 0.$$

A. First rewrite in standard matrix form $\mathbf{Ax = b}$:

$$\begin{bmatrix} 1 & 2 & 2 \\ 1 & 1 & 1 \\ 1 & -1 & 3 \end{bmatrix} \begin{bmatrix} x_1 \\ x_2 \\ x_3 \end{bmatrix} = \begin{bmatrix} 7 \\ 4 \\ 6 \end{bmatrix}.$$

Now invert the $\mathbf{A}$ matrix by row operations (follow this through carefully, noting how we proceed one stage at a time):

$$\mathbf{B} = \left[\begin{array}{ccc:ccc} 1 & 2 & 2 & 1 & 0 & 0 \\ 1 & 1 & 1 & 0 & 1 & 0 \\ 1 & -1 & 3 & 0 & 0 & 1 \end{array} \right]$$

(i) $r_2^{(i)} = r_2 - r_1$
$r_3^{(i)} = r_3 - r_1$

$$\mathbf{B}^{(i)} = \left[\begin{array}{ccc:ccc} 1 & 2 & 2 & 1 & 0 & 0 \\ 0 & -1 & -1 & -1 & 1 & 0 \\ 0 & -3 & 1 & -1 & 0 & 1 \end{array} \right]$$

(ii) $r_1^{(ii)} = r_1^{(i)} - 2r_3^{(i)}$
$r_2^{(ii)} = r_2^{(i)} + r_3^{(i)}$

$$\mathbf{B}^{(ii)} = \left[\begin{array}{ccc:ccc} 1 & 8 & 0 & 3 & 0 & -2 \\ 0 & -4 & 0 & -2 & 1 & 1 \\ 0 & -3 & 1 & -1 & 0 & 1 \end{array} \right]$$

(iii) $r_2^{(iii)} = -\frac{1}{4}r_2^{(ii)}$

$$\mathbf{B}^{(iii)} = \left[\begin{array}{ccc:ccc} 1 & 8 & 0 & 3 & 0 & -2 \\ 0 & 1 & 0 & \frac{1}{2} & -\frac{1}{4} & -\frac{1}{4} \\ 0 & -3 & 1 & 1 & 0 & 1 \end{array} \right]$$

(iv) $r_1^{(iv)} = r_1^{(iii)} - 8r_2^{(iii)}$
$r_3^{(iv)} = r_3^{(iii)} + 3r_2^{(iii)}$

$$\mathbf{C} = \left[\begin{array}{ccc:ccc} 1 & 0 & 0 & -1 & 2 & 0 \\ 0 & 1 & 0 & \frac{1}{2} & -\frac{1}{4} & -\frac{1}{4} \\ 0 & 0 & 1 & \frac{1}{2} & -\frac{3}{4} & \frac{1}{4} \end{array} \right]$$

Having found $\mathbf{A}^{-1}$, calculate $\mathbf{x = A^{-1}b}$:

$$\begin{bmatrix} -1 & 2 & 0 \\ \frac{1}{2} & -\frac{1}{4} & -\frac{1}{4} \\ \frac{1}{2} & -\frac{3}{4} & \frac{1}{4} \end{bmatrix} \begin{bmatrix} 7 \\ 4 \\ 6 \end{bmatrix} = \begin{bmatrix} 1 \\ 1 \\ 2 \end{bmatrix}$$

and check that $x_1 = 1$, $x_2 = 1$, $x_3 = 2$ does in fact solve the system by substituting back into the original equations.

17.4 Determinants

Let us consider again the solution of a pair of simultaneous equations. The general case may be written

$$a_{11}x_1 + a_{12}x_2 = b_1; \quad a_{21}x_1 + a_{22}x_2 = b_2 \qquad [17.30]$$

which can be solved as follows:

$$x_1 = \frac{b_1 - a_{12}x_2}{a_{11}}$$

$$a_{21}\frac{(b_1 - a_{12}x_2)}{a_{11}} + a_{22}x_2 = b_2$$

$$x_2 = \frac{b_2 a_{11} - a_{21}b_1}{a_{11}a_{22} - a_{21}a_{12}}$$

$$\therefore x_1 = \frac{b_1 a_{22} - b_2 a_{12}}{a_{11}a_{22} - a_{21}a_{12}}.$$

There will therefore be a solution to the general problem if and only if

$$a_{11}a_{22} - a_{21}a_{12} \neq 0. \qquad [17.31]$$

This condition depends upon each and every one of the a_{ij} coefficients. In our matrix algebra terminology it is a property of the matrix **A**.

This particular function of the elements is known as the *determinant* of the matrix and is denoted by the symbol $|\mathbf{A}|$. Equation [17.32] shows how it may be thought of in terms of the diagonals of the matrix. (The solid line traces out the positive diagonal, the broken line indicates the negative diagonal).

$$A = \begin{bmatrix} a_{11} & a_{12} \\ a_{2i} & a_{22} \end{bmatrix} \qquad |\mathbf{A}| = a_{11}a_{22} - a_{12}a_{21}. \qquad [17.32]$$

In the example in section 17.3.4, the determinant would be calculated as

$$|\mathbf{A}| = \begin{vmatrix} 4 & 2 \\ 2 & 1 \end{vmatrix} = 4 \cdot 1 - 2 \cdot 2 = 0.$$

By contrast, the example in section 17.3.2 produces the following:

$$\begin{vmatrix} 4 & 2 \\ 1 & -2 \end{vmatrix} = 4 \cdot (-2) - 1 \cdot 2 = -11.$$

These two examples are both of (2×2) matrices but it is possible to define, for any square matrix, a function of the elements of that matrix called the determinant such that the following rule applies.

Rule: The matrix **A** will have an inverse if and only if its determinant is non-zero; i.e., iff $|\mathbf{A}| \neq 0$.

The proof of this assertion takes us beyond the scope of this book.

There are almost as many different definitions of determinants as there are authors, for although the concept is not a particularly difficult one the actual process of calculation for large matrices can be rather complex. In practice there is little reason to perform the calculations for large matrices. While determinants provide an alternative method for inverting matrices, we have already devised a simple method by which to undertake that task (see section 17.3.1). Determinants also provide an alternative method for solving systems of equations (known as Cramer's rule), which may be of use in handling large analytic problems. These and other properties of determinants are to be found in specialist texts but need not concern us here. It is however of some interest to note that there is a relatively straightforward way of evaluating the determinant of a (3×3) matrix and this is illustrated below. (Note that the same procedure does *not* work for larger matrices.)

The (3×3) matrix **A** may be 'enhanced' by the repetition of each of the four 'corner' elements as shown in [17.33]. Note carefully the positioning of these. Each appears to be at the 'wrong' end of its row:

$$\begin{matrix} a_{13} \\ \\ a_{33} \end{matrix} \begin{bmatrix} a_{11} & a_{12} & a_{13} \\ a_{21} & a_{22} & a_{23} \\ a_{31} & a_{32} & a_{33} \end{bmatrix} \begin{matrix} a_{11} \\ \\ a_{31} \end{matrix} \qquad\qquad [17.33]$$

From the enhanced matrix we can now define three positive diagonals, shown below by solid lines, and three negative diagonals, shown below by broken lines:

Multiplying along the diagonals, we can calculate the determinant as the sum of the three positive diagonals less the three negative diagonals. The complete expression is then

$$a_{13}a_{21}a_{32} + a_{11}a_{22}a_{33} + a_{12}a_{23}a_{31} - a_{33}a_{21}a_{12} - a_{31}a_{22}a_{13} - a_{32}a_{23}a_{11}. \quad [17.34]$$

Worked example

Calculate the determinant of the matrix $\begin{bmatrix} 1 & 2 & 2 \\ 1 & 1 & 1 \\ 1 & -1 & 3 \end{bmatrix}$.

The enhanced matrix becomes

$$\begin{array}{ccccc} 2 & 1 & 2 & 2 & 1 \\ & 1 & 1 & 1 & \\ 3 & 1 & -1 & 3 & 1 \end{array}$$

and the determinant

$$\begin{aligned} & 2\cdot1\cdot(-1) + 1\cdot1\cdot3 + 2\cdot1\cdot1 - 3\cdot1\cdot2 - 1\cdot1\cdot2 - (-1)\cdot1\cdot1 \\ = & -2 + 3 + 2 - 6 - 2 + 1 \\ = & -4 \end{aligned}$$

Since it is non-zero it must be invertible, and indeed it is (see section 17.3.5).

17.5 More definitions and some properties

In this section are set out briefly some more definitions and concepts which you may come across together with a few of the properties thereof. The section should be treated as a checklist or *aide memoire*, as no attempt will be made to prove this material. For the economist a working knowledge of the terminology and the rules is quite sufficient.

17.5.1 Minors

A *minor* of a matrix is formed by deleting certain rows and columns from the full matrix, usually one row and one column. Let us denote by $\mathbf{M}_{ij}$ the minor formed by deleting the ith row and jth column. The *principal minors* are those obtained by deleting the *last* k rows and columns; hence an $(n \times n)$ matrix has n principal minors. For reasons that will become obvious later, let us denote by $\mathbf{H}_m$ the principal minor formed by deleting the last $(n - m)$ rows and columns; thus,

$$\mathbf{H}_1 = [a_{11}] \quad \mathbf{H}_2 = \begin{bmatrix} a_{11} & a_{12} \\ a_{21} & a_{22} \end{bmatrix} \quad \mathbf{H}_3 = \begin{bmatrix} a_{11} & a_{12} & a_{13} \\ a_{21} & a_{22} & a_{23} \\ a_{31} & a_{32} & a_{33} \end{bmatrix}$$

and so on up to $\mathbf{H}_n = \mathbf{A}$.

17.5.2 Cofactors

The *cofactor* of any element a_{ij} of a matrix is the signed determinant of its minor; i.e.,

$$a_{ij}^+ = (-1)^{i+j} |\mathbf{M}_{ij}| \qquad [17.35]$$

It can be shown that the determinant of any $(n \times n)$ matrix $\mathbf{A}$ can be expressed in terms of the cofactors of any row or column of the matrix; i.e.,

$$|\mathbf{A}| = \sum_{j=1}^{n} a_{kj} a_{kj}^+ = \sum_{i=1}^{n} a_{ik} a_{ik}^+ \text{ for all } k. \qquad [17.36]$$

This is a particularly useful property since we are at liberty to choose that row or column that contains the greatest number of zeroes, thus reducing the required computation. It also means that calculating the determinant of (say) a (4×4) matrix can be reduced to calculating a series of determinants of (3×3) matrices – a process which we have already seen to be relatively easy. (Indeed, it is possible to express each (3×3) determinant as a series of (2×2) determinants if so desired.) It also implies that consistency requires that we define $|a_{11}| = a_{11}$.

17.5.3 Adjoint

The *adjoint* of a matrix $(\mathbf{A}^+)$ is the matrix of cofactors; i.e.,

$$\mathbf{A}^+ = [a_{ij}^+]. \qquad [17.37]$$

The principal use of this concept is as an alternative method of inverting a matrix since it can be shown that

$$\mathbf{A}^{-1} = \frac{\mathbf{A}^+}{|\mathbf{A}|}. \qquad [17.38]$$

17.5.4 Summary of the properties of matrices

(i) $\mathbf{A} + \mathbf{B} = \mathbf{B} + \mathbf{A}$
(ii) $\mathbf{A} + (\mathbf{B} + \mathbf{C}) = (\mathbf{A} + \mathbf{B}) + \mathbf{C}$
(iii) $\mathbf{AB} \neq \mathbf{BA}$
(iv) $(\mathbf{AB})\mathbf{C} = \mathbf{A}(\mathbf{BC})$
(v) $\mathbf{A}(\mathbf{B} + \mathbf{C}) = \mathbf{AB} + \mathbf{AC}$
(vi) $(\mathbf{B} + \mathbf{C})\mathbf{A} = \mathbf{BA} + \mathbf{CA}$
(vii) $\mathbf{AI} = \mathbf{IA} = \mathbf{A}$
(viii) $(\mathbf{A}')' = \mathbf{A}$
(ix) $(\mathbf{A} + \mathbf{B})' = \mathbf{A}' + \mathbf{B}'$

(x) $(AB)' = B'A'$
(xi) $A^{-1}A = AA^{-1} = I$
(xii) $(A^{-1})^{-1} = A$
(xiii) $(AB)^{-1} = B^{-1}A^{-1}$
(xiv) $(A')^{-1} = (A^{-1})'$

where it is assumed throughout that the matrices are conformable. Note that two assumptions of ordinary algebra cannot be made in matrix algebra, viz.:

(xv) $AB = 0$ does not imply that either A or B equals 0.
(xvi) $AB = AC$ does not imply that $B = C$.

17.5.5 Quadratic forms

A quadratic form in the variables $x_1, x_2, ..., x_n$ is a quantity that can be written in the form

$$q = c_{11}x_1^2 + c_{22}x_2^2 + ... + c_{nn}x_n^2 + c_{12}x_1x_2 + c_{13}x_1x_3 + ... + c_{n-1,n}x_{n-1}x_n$$
$$[17.39]$$

where the c_{ij} $(i \le j \le n)$ are constants. It contains only terms that are squares or simple cross-products of the variables. If we write the x_i variables in the form of a column vector x, then the expression $x'Ax$ is a scalar quantity q given by

$$q = [x_1 \; x_2 \; ... \; x_n]\begin{bmatrix} a_{11} & a_{12} & ...a_{1n} \\ a_{21} & a_{22} & ...a_{2n} \\ . & . & . \\ . & . & . \\ . & . & . \\ a_{n1} & a_{n2}... & a_{nn} \end{bmatrix}\begin{bmatrix} x_1 \\ x_2 \\ . \\ . \\ . \\ x_n \end{bmatrix} \qquad [17.40]$$

and the matrix A has dimension $(n \times n)$. Expanding this multiplication gives

$$q = a_{11}x_1^2 + a_{22}x_2^2 + ... + a_{nn}x_n^2 + (a_{12} + a_{21})x_1x_2 + ... + (a_{nn-1} + a_{n-1,n})x_nx_{n-1}$$

$$[17.41]$$

and we see that equations [17.39] and [17.40] are in fact the same. We merely require that

$$a_{ii} = c_{ii} \; i = 1, ..., n \text{ and } a_{ij} + a_{ji} = c_{ij} \text{ all } i \ne j. \qquad [17.42]$$

If we impose the restriction that the matrix A is symmetric, then it follows that

$$a_{ij} = a_{ji} \quad \therefore \quad a_{ij} = c_{ij}/2 \text{ all } i \ne j \qquad [17.43]$$

and the matrix **A** is uniquely defined.

It can be very useful to know whether the sign of q depends upon the values of the x_i, as we shall see in section 18.2. Formally, we can make the following definition.

Rule: The quadratic form $q = $ **x'Ax** is said to be

positive definite	if q is positive (> 0)	
positive semi-definite	if q is non-negative (≥ 0)	[17.44]
negative semi-definite	if q is non-negative (≤ 0)	
negative definite	if q is negative (< 0)	

for all values of **x** $\neq 0$ (i.e., there is at least one non-zero variable).

There are a number of ways of establishing whether a quadratic form falls into one of these categories, the simplest being through the principal minors of the **A** matrix. If it is positive definite the determinants of all principal minors will be positive, whereas for it to be negative definite the determinants will alternate in sign. These are the two results that will be of most use to us and they are expressed formally as follows.

Rule: The quadratic form **x'Ax** will be

positive definite if $|\mathbf{H}_1| > 0$, $|\mathbf{H}_2| > 0$, ..., $|\mathbf{H}_n| > 0$
negative definite if $|\mathbf{H}_1| < 0$, $|\mathbf{H}_2| > 0$, $|\mathbf{H}_3| < 0$, ...   [17.45]

where $\mathbf{H}_1$, ..., $\mathbf{H}_n$ are the principal minors of the matrix.

Note: The determinant of the (1×1) matrix $\mathbf{H}_1 = [a_{11}]$ is simply a_{11}.

17.5.6 Matrix differentiation

In principle, there is no difference between the differentiation of vectors and matrices and that of simple algebraic functions, with most of the rules translating directly into matrix terms. Some of these are of particular use in section 18.3 and are therefore detailed below.

If **A** is an ($n \times n$) matrix and **x** and **b** are ($n \times 1$) column vectors, then the vector partial derivatives are given by

(i) $\dfrac{\delta}{\delta \mathbf{x'}}(\mathbf{x'b}) = \mathbf{b}$ $\dfrac{\delta}{\delta \mathbf{x}}(\mathbf{b'x}) = \mathbf{b'}$ [17.46]

(ii) $\dfrac{\delta}{\delta \mathbf{x'}}(\mathbf{x'A} + \mathbf{b'}) = \mathbf{A}$ $\dfrac{\delta}{\delta \mathbf{x}}(\mathbf{Ax} + \mathbf{b}) = \mathbf{A}$ [17.47]

(iii) $\dfrac{\delta}{\delta \mathbf{x'}}(\mathbf{x'Ax}) = (\mathbf{A} + \mathbf{A'})\mathbf{x}$ $\dfrac{\delta}{\delta \mathbf{x}}(\mathbf{x'Ax}) = \mathbf{x'}(\mathbf{A} + \mathbf{A'})$ [17.48]

If **A** is symmetric, then $\mathbf{A'} = \mathbf{A}$ and we have (iii)' $\dfrac{\delta}{\delta x'}(x'Ax) = 2Ax$ $\qquad\qquad \dfrac{\delta}{\delta x}(x'Ax) = 2x'A$ $\qquad$ [17.28']

which looks not unlike the familiar $(d(ax^2)/dx) = 2ax$.

17.6 Exercises

Section 17.1.2

Transpose the following:

(i) $\begin{bmatrix} 1 & 0 & 3 \\ 0 & 1 & 0 \\ 2 & -1 & 1 \end{bmatrix}$ $\qquad$ (ii) $\begin{bmatrix} 2 & 0 & 1 & -1 \\ -1 & 1 & 0 & 2 \end{bmatrix}$

Section 17.1.4

Given the definitions of the matrices in the worked example on p.000 calculate, where possible, the following (if the calculation cannot be performed state why not):

(i) $A - B$ $\qquad$ (v) $A + I$

(ii) A' $\qquad$ (vi) $A + A'$

(iii) B' $\qquad$ (vii) $A + B + C$

(iv) $A' + B'$ $\qquad$ (viii) $A + 2B + 3C$

Section 17.2.1

In the following exercises the matrices A, B and C are defined as

$$A = \begin{bmatrix} 2 & 0 \\ 0 & 3 \end{bmatrix} \quad B = \begin{bmatrix} 1 & 1 \\ 2 & 1 \\ 0 & 1 \end{bmatrix} \quad C = \begin{bmatrix} 1 & 0 & 0 \\ 2 & 1 & 0 \\ 0 & 3 & 1 \end{bmatrix}$$

1. Which of the matrices are square?

2. Which of the matrices is diagonal?

3. Calculate, if possible,

(i) $A + B$ $\qquad$ (iv) ABC

(ii) AB $\qquad$ (v) AI

(iii) BA $\qquad$ (vi) CBA

(vii) **BC**   (ix) **I − A**

(viii) **CB**

4. Find the transposes of each matrix and hence

　(i) **AB′**   (iv) **AA′**

　(ii) **B′B**   (v) **A²**

　(iii) **BB′**

Section 17.3.1

Find the inverses, if they exist, of the following matrices:

(i) $\begin{bmatrix} -1 & 2 \\ 0 & 2 \end{bmatrix}$ (iv) $\begin{bmatrix} 2 & 1 & 3 \\ -1 & 1 & 1 \\ 0 & 3 & 3 \end{bmatrix}$

(ii) $\begin{bmatrix} 1 & 3 \\ 2 & 4 \end{bmatrix}$ (v) $\begin{bmatrix} 1 & 2 & 3 \\ 2 & 1 & 0 \end{bmatrix}$

(iii) $\begin{bmatrix} 0 & -1 \\ 2 & 3 \end{bmatrix}$

Section 17.3.5

Solve the following simultaneous equations, where possible:

　(i) $x_1 + x_2 = 7; 2x_1 - x_2 = 2$

　(ii) $x_1 + x_2 - x_3 = 0; x_1 - 2x_2 + x_3 = 0; 2x_1 + x_2 - x_3 = 1$

　(iii) $2x_1 + 3x_2 + 4x_3 = 16; x_2 = 8 - 3x_3 - x_1; x_1 + x_3 = 8 - 2x_2$

Section 17.4

Calculate the determinants of the following matrices:

(i) $\begin{bmatrix} 2 & -1 \\ -1 & -1 \end{bmatrix}$ (iii) $\begin{bmatrix} 1 & 1 & 0 \\ 2 & 0 & 2 \\ 3 & 1 & 2 \end{bmatrix}$

(ii) $\begin{bmatrix} 3 & -1 & 2 \\ 0 & 0 & 1 \\ 1 & 1 & 0 \end{bmatrix}$

Further exercises

1. Demonstrate the truth of each of rules (i)–(xiv) in section 17.5.4 for

$$\mathbf{A} = \begin{bmatrix} 2 & 0 \\ 1 & 1 \end{bmatrix} \quad \mathbf{B} = \begin{bmatrix} 0 & -1 \\ 1 & 2 \end{bmatrix} \quad \mathbf{C} = \begin{bmatrix} -1 & 1 \\ 1 & -1 \end{bmatrix}.$$

2. Invent matrices **A**, **B** and **C** that prove rules (xv) and (xvi) in section 17.5.4.

3. Are the quadratic forms of the following matrices positive definite, negative definite or neither?

$$\mathbf{A} = \begin{bmatrix} 2 & -1 & 2 \\ 3 & 1 & -1 \\ 1 & 3 & 2 \end{bmatrix} \quad \mathbf{B} = \begin{bmatrix} 2 & 1 & 1 \\ 4 & 2 & 3 \\ 0 & 0 & 1 \end{bmatrix} \quad \mathbf{C} = \begin{bmatrix} -1 & -1 \\ 3 & 2 \end{bmatrix}$$

18 Applications of matrix algebra

18.1 Input–output analysis

In a modern economy it is the exception rather than the rule that goods pass directly from producer to consumer. In practice, most final purchases will have passed through the hands of many different productive enterprises engaged upon a variety of activities before they arrive in the shops. Thus, while it is possible to obtain some vegetables direct from the farmer, it is more common to find them sold to manufacturers for processing. They are then sold in cans bought in from another manufacturer, which in turn obtained the sheet metal from another, which may or may not have mined the ore. All of these processes require the output of the energy industry.

This interrelation of production processes is an essential feature of any developed economy, yet it is one that makes planning extremely difficult. It may be clear that the economy needs to produce more cars, but what are the implications for the steel producers, the chemical industry, transport, farming and so on? The government would obviously like to identify the likely bottlenecks, the necessary increases in raw materials and the effect on the balance of payments. The role of input–output analysis is to provide a framework for answering these and other related questions.

In order to demonstrate the principles involved it is sufficient to look at just three sectors. (In reality, the economy could be divided into any number of arbitrarily defined industries and the choice of definitions will reflect the availability of data, industrial structure, international trade patterns, historical accident, etc.) In what follows we assume that the economy consists of agriculture, manufacturing and service sectors. Each sector will sell a part of its output directly to the public – this is the final demand. A part of its output will be sold to the other two sectors as inputs to their production processes. Thus, the manufacturing sector sells office equipment, computers, etc., to the service sector and fertilizers and machinery to the agricultural sector. The service sector meanwhile sells its insurance and banking services to the other two, and so on. Finally, we must recognize that each sector will actually use up a portion of its own output. Farmers produce much of their own feedstuff, manufacturing produces its own machine tools, and even hairdressers need lawyers and accountants.

We can characterize each sector by the inflows of goods and services from the other sectors and by the outflows of its own output. Let us ignore, for the moment, extraneous requirements such as capital and labour inputs and imported inputs, and consider the intersectoral flows. For a hypothetical economy they might be as shown in table 18.1 (all figures are given in value terms so that they may be added together).

Table 18.1 INTERSECTORAL FLOWS

| | Input to | | | | |
| | Intermediate outputs | | | Final | Total |
Output from	Agriculture	Manufacturing	Services	demand	output
Agriculture	4	10	6	10	30
Manufacturing	1	2	5	32	40
Services	1	4	1	34	40

Reading across the first row shows us what happens to the output of the first sector: 4 units are used up within the sector itself, 10 are sold to manufacturing and 6 to the service sector; a further 10 are sold direct to the public making a total output of 30. Similarly, we can see the destination of the 40-unit ouput of the manufacturing sector by reading across the second row; and so on. Reading down the columns identifies the sources of the inputs to each sector. In the first column we see that 4 units of agricultural output are used up in that sector together with 1 unit from each of the other sectors. Note that the total inputs must be less than the total output of the sector if there is to be anything left with which to pay wages, profit, etc.

Let us define the following vectors and matrices:

$$\mathbf{f} = \begin{bmatrix} 10 \\ 32 \\ 34 \end{bmatrix} \text{ is the vector of final demand.}$$

$$\mathbf{x} = \begin{bmatrix} 30 \\ 40 \\ 40 \end{bmatrix} \text{ is the vector of total outputs.}$$

$$\mathbf{S} = \begin{bmatrix} 4 & 10 & 6 \\ 1 & 2 & 5 \\ 1 & 4 & 1 \end{bmatrix} \text{ is the matrix of intersectoral flows.}$$

It is immediately apparent that total outputs are the sum of final demands (**f**) and intermediate demands (**g**); i.e.,

$$\mathbf{x} = \mathbf{g} + \mathbf{f}. \tag{18.1}$$

If we wish to increase the output of the agriculture sector by one unit, how much input would it require from each of the sectors? If there is a linear technology then the answer is straightforward. If 30 units of output require inputs of 4, 1 and 1 respectively, then 1 unit requires inputs of 4/30, 1/30 and 1/30. The assumption that the ratios of inputs to outputs are fixed is crucial to the technique. (It is an assumption that is plausible for small changes in the pattern of production and over fairly short intervals of time; one should be careful to avoid claiming too much for the technique in other circumstances.) Maintaining this assumption enables us to produce a new matrix in which each element of the intersectoral flow matrix is divided by the appropriate total output; i.e.,

$$\mathbf{A} = \begin{bmatrix} \frac{4}{30} & \frac{10}{40} & \frac{6}{40} \\ \frac{1}{30} & \frac{2}{40} & \frac{5}{40} \\ \frac{1}{30} & \frac{4}{40} & \frac{1}{40} \end{bmatrix} \text{ or } a_{ij} = \frac{s_{ij}}{x_i}. \tag{18.2}$$

This new matrix is the input–output matrix and its elements are the *input–output* or *technical coefficients*. It follows from its definition that

$$\mathbf{A}\mathbf{x} = \mathbf{g}. \tag{18.3}$$

Putting equations [18.1] and [18.3] together, we have

$$\mathbf{x} = \mathbf{A}\mathbf{x} + \mathbf{f} \tag{18.4}$$

which may be rewritten as

$$\mathbf{I}\mathbf{x} = \mathbf{A}\mathbf{x} + \mathbf{f}$$

$$(\mathbf{I} - \mathbf{A})\mathbf{x} = \mathbf{f} \tag{18.5}$$

$$\mathbf{x} = (\mathbf{I} - \mathbf{A})^{-1}\mathbf{f}. \tag{18.6}$$

In this form we see that total outputs may be readily deduced from the vector of final outputs. If the government wishes to estimate the impact upon each industry/sector of any particular pattern of final demand it can readily do so. In particular, it can calculate the required changes in the output of each consequent upon changes in one or more of the final demands.

At this point we might reintroduce labour and capital inputs or balance of payments effects. Each change in total output implies a change in, for example, labour inputs, so summing these employment effects allows us to see whether the proposed change will lead to labour shortages or unemployment. The possibilities for this sort of analysis are enormous provided only that we bear in mind the limiting assumption of linear technology. (There are in fact ways of incorporating changing technology into the analysis, but this would take us beyond the scope of this text.)

By way of an example, consider the impact of a 10 per cent increase in the final demand for manufactures, such that the final demand vector becomes

$$\mathbf{f}^* = \begin{bmatrix} 10 \\ 35.2 \\ 34 \end{bmatrix}.$$

we could of course calculate both $\mathbf{x}$ and $\mathbf{x}^*$ and hence the difference, but it is simpler to note that

$$\Delta\mathbf{x} \equiv \mathbf{x}^* - \mathbf{x} = (\mathbf{I} - \mathbf{A})^{-1}\mathbf{f}^* - (\mathbf{I} - \mathbf{A})^{-1}\mathbf{f} = (\mathbf{I} - \mathbf{A})^{-1}\Delta\mathbf{f}. \qquad [18.7]$$

In order to calculate $(\mathbf{I} - \mathbf{A})^{-1}$ we shall make use of the result of section 17.3.2 that

$$(\mathbf{I} - \mathbf{A})^{-1} = \mathbf{I} + \mathbf{A} + \mathbf{A}^2 + \dots \qquad |a_{ij}| < 1 \qquad [18.8]$$

In this example

$$\mathbf{A} = \begin{bmatrix} 0.1333 & 0.2500 & 0.1500 \\ 0.0333 & 0.0500 & 0.1250 \\ 0.0333 & 0.1000 & 0.0250 \end{bmatrix} \quad \mathbf{A}^2 = \begin{bmatrix} 0.0311 & 0.0608 & 0.0550 \\ 0.0103 & 0.0233 & 0.0144 \\ 0.0086 & 0.0158 & 0.0181 \end{bmatrix}.$$

To be certain that we have a good approximation, we could include

$$\mathbf{A}^3 = \begin{bmatrix} 0.0080 & 0.0163 & 0.0136 \\ 0.0028 & 0.0056 & 0.0071 \\ 0.0023 & 0.0047 & 0.0037 \end{bmatrix}$$

but $\mathbf{A}^4$ will have no impact upon the first three places of decimals; hence

$$(\mathbf{I} - \mathbf{A})^{-1} \doteq \begin{bmatrix} 1.172 & 0.327 & 0.219 \\ 0.046 & 1.079 & 0.147 \\ 0.044 & 0.121 & 1.047 \end{bmatrix}$$

$$\Delta\mathbf{x} = (\mathbf{I} - \mathbf{A})^{-1} \begin{bmatrix} 0 \\ 3.2 \\ 0 \end{bmatrix} = \begin{bmatrix} 1.046 \\ 3.453 \\ 0.387 \end{bmatrix}.$$

The solution tells us that the policy would raise total output of the manufacturing sector by a little less that 10 per cent ($3.453 \div 40 = 8.63$ per cent) but that it would also require a $3\frac{1}{2}$ per cent increase in output from the agricultural sector. If the intention had been to raise manufacturing output alone the correct policy can be deduced from equation [18.5]. A 10 per cent increase in total manufacturing output is 4 units; hence the required changes in final demand would be given by

$$\Delta f = \begin{bmatrix} 0.8667 & -0.2500 & -0.1500 \\ -0.0333 & 0.9500 & -0.1250 \\ -0.0333 & -0.1000 & 0.9750 \end{bmatrix} \begin{bmatrix} 0 \\ 4 \\ 0 \end{bmatrix} = \begin{bmatrix} -1.0 \\ 3.8 \\ -0.4 \end{bmatrix}.$$

That is to say, there would actually have to be a switch in expenditure patterns by consumers.

If the results of a simple 3×3 input–output table can be surprising, those of more complex models can be even more so, and it is not without good reason that economic forecasters, policy-makers and statisticians have invested effort in developing and refining the technique since its introduction by Leontieff in the 1940s.

*18.2 Maxima and minima yet again

In chapter 15 we discussed the optimization of functions of two or more variables. The first-order conditions turned out to be very easy to establish, but the second-order conditions did not prove to be quite so straightforward. Section 15.1.3 derived the conditions for the two-variable case from the fundamental proposition that the nature of the stationary point depends upon the behaviour of the second-order total differential. We are now in a position to extend the analysis to the n-variable case by utilizing the concept of a quadratic form introduced in section 17.5.5.

Consider a function of n choice variables

$$y = f(x_1, x_2, \ldots, x_n), \text{ i.e., } y = f(\mathbf{x}). \tag{18.9}$$

for there to be a maximum or minimum we require that the first-order differential be zero; i.e.,

$$dy = \frac{\delta f}{\delta x_1}dx_1 + \frac{\delta f}{\delta x_2}dx_2 + \ldots + \frac{\delta f}{\delta x_n}dx_n = 0 \tag{18.10}$$

Writing $\dfrac{\delta f}{\delta x_i} = f_i$, we can define

$$\mathbf{f} = \begin{bmatrix} f_1 \\ f_2 \\ \cdot \\ \cdot \\ \cdot \\ f_n \end{bmatrix} \text{ and } \mathbf{dx} = \begin{bmatrix} dx_1 \\ dx_2 \\ \cdot \\ \cdot \\ \cdot \\ dx_n \end{bmatrix} \tag{18.11}$$

and [18.10] is expressed as

f'dx = 0. [18.12]

Since the differentials dx_i are arbitrary changes in the independent variables, not all of which can be zero, it follows immediately that the partial derivatives must be zero; i.e.,

$f_1 = f_2 = \ldots = f_n = 0$ or **f** = **O**. [18.13]

The solution of [18.13] defines a stationary point or points. For such a point to be a maximum we require that the second-order differential evaluated at the point be negative whatever the values of the dx_i. Writing this expression out we have

$$d^2y = \frac{\delta}{\delta x_1}(f_1 dx_1 + \ldots + f_n dx_n)dx_1 + \frac{\delta}{\delta x_2}(f_1 dx_1 + \ldots + f_n dx_n)dx_2$$

$$+ \ldots + \frac{\delta}{\delta x_n}(f_1 dx_1 + \ldots + f_n dx_n)dx_n \qquad [18.14]$$

which we can now see to be a quadratic form alternatively written as

$$d^2y = f_{11}(dx_1)^2 + f_{12}dx_1 dx_2 + \ldots + f_{1n}dx_1 dx_n + f_{21}dx_2 dx_1 + f_{22}(dx_2)^2$$
$$+ f_{23}dx_2 dx_3 + \ldots + f_{nn}(dx_n)^2 \qquad [18.15]$$

where $f_{ij} \equiv \delta^2 f/\delta x_i \delta x_j$. In matrix form this becomes the quadratic form

$$dy = [dx_1 \quad dx_2 \quad \ldots \quad dx_n] \begin{bmatrix} f_{11} & f_{12} & \ldots f_{1n} \\ f_{21} & f_{22} & \ldots f_{2n} \\ \cdot & \cdot & \cdot \\ \cdot & \cdot & \cdot \\ f_{n1} & f_{n2} \ldots & f_{nn} \end{bmatrix} \begin{bmatrix} dx_1 \\ dx_2 \\ \cdot \\ \cdot \\ dx_n \end{bmatrix} = \mathbf{dx'Hdx} \quad [18.16]$$

Since $f_{ij} = f_{ji}$, the matrix of second-order partials **H** is symmetric and **H** is known as the *Hessian*. If we are to have a maximum, the value of the quadratic form has to be negative whatever the values of **dx**. The condition for this to be true was given in section 17.5.5, where it was shown that negative definiteness could be expressed in terms of the determinants of the principal minors. The nature of a stationary point can therefore be established by reference to the Hessian matrix. Since the f_{ij} are in general functions of **x**, the Hessian must be evaluated for each stationary point defined by [18.13]. This can be stated formally as follows.

Rule: If **H** is the matrix of second-order partial derivatives evaluated at a stationary point **x***, then **x*** will be a

maximum if and only if $|\mathbf{H}_1| < 0, |\mathbf{H}_2| > 0, |\mathbf{H}_3| < 0$ and so on
minimum if and only if $|\mathbf{H}_1| > 0, |\mathbf{H}_2| > 0, |\mathbf{H}_3| > 0 \ldots |\mathbf{H}_n| > 0.$ [18.17]

It may be of help to note that in the two-dimensional case we have

$$\mathbf{H} = \begin{bmatrix} f_{11} & f_{21} \\ f_{12} & f_{22} \end{bmatrix}; \ |\mathbf{H}_1| = f_{11}; \ |\mathbf{H}_2| = f_{11}f_{22} - f_{12}f_{21} \qquad [18.18]$$

and the conditions are seen to resolve to those given in section 15.1 (equation [15.8]).

18.2.1 Constrained optima

In section 15.2 we developed the concept of optimization to include the case of constrained optima. While it is possible to solve such cases by substituting the constraints into the objective function, we found that an alternative procedure was often more helpful. This 'Lagrange method' was the subject matter of section 15.2.2. The general case of the problem considered there is to optimize (find maxima or minima for) the function

$$y = f(x_1, x_2, \ldots, x_n) \quad \text{subject to } g(x_1, x_2, \ldots, x_n) = 0. \qquad [18.19]$$

The method of solution of this problem is to construct the Lagrangean

$$L = f(x_1, x_2, \ldots, x_n) - \lambda g(x_1, x_2, \ldots, x_n) \qquad [18.20]$$

where λ is called the Lagrange multiplier. The first-order conditions for a stationary point are simply the now familiar

$$\frac{\delta L}{\delta x_i} \equiv \frac{\delta f}{\delta x_i} - \frac{\lambda \delta g}{\delta x_i} = 0 \text{ or } \frac{\delta L}{\delta x'} \equiv \mathbf{f} - \lambda \mathbf{g} = \mathbf{0}. \qquad [18.21]$$

The second-order conditions are rather more complex, but although the proof is outside the scope of this text our knowledge of matrix algebra does allow us to define and evaluate the conditions.

In the previous section we defined the Hessian matrix of second-order partial derivatives. We now introduce the concept of a 'bordered Hessian'. If we differentiate the Lagrangean with respect to λ, the Lagrange multiplier, we obtain the original constraint $\mathbf{g}$. Differentiating this a second time with respect to the Lagrange multiplier gives an answer of zero, while differentiating with respect to any other variable simply produces the partial derivative of the constraint with respect to that variable; i.e.,

$$\frac{\delta^2 L}{\delta \lambda^2} = 0; \ \frac{\delta^2 L}{\delta \lambda \delta x_i} = \frac{\delta g}{\delta x_i} \equiv (\text{say}) \ g_i \qquad [18.22]$$

It proves to be convenient to write the full matrix of second-order partials in a particular form, writing the first row and column corresponding to the Lagrange multiplier. This produces a matrix that looks like this:

$$\bar{H} = \begin{bmatrix} 0 & g_1 & g_2 & \cdots & g_n \\ g_1 & L_{11} & L_{12} & \cdots L_{1n} \\ \cdot & \cdot & \cdot & & \cdot \\ \cdot & \cdot & \cdot & & \cdot \\ \cdot & \cdot & \cdot & & \cdot \\ g_n & L_{n1} & L_{n2} \cdots & & L_{nn} \end{bmatrix} \qquad \text{where } L_{ij} \equiv \frac{\delta^2 L}{\delta x_i \delta x_j} \qquad [18.23]$$

and is known as a bordered Hessian. The second-order conditions for a maximum or minimum can still be thought of in terms of a quadratic form and thus in terms of non-negative (positive) definiteness, but the conditions must now be expressed in terms of the *bordered* principal minors:

$$\bar{H}_2 = \begin{bmatrix} 0 & g_1 & g_2 \\ g_1 & L_{11} & L_{12} \\ g_2 & L_{21} & L_{22} \end{bmatrix} \qquad \bar{H}_3 = \begin{bmatrix} 0 & g_1 & g_2 & g_3 \\ g_1 & L_{11} & L_{12} & L_{13} \\ g_2 & L_{21} & L_{22} & L_{23} \\ g_3 & L_{31} & L_{32} & L_{33} \end{bmatrix}$$

and so on. This can be stated specifically as follows.

Rule: If H is the bordered matrix of second-order partial derivatives evaluated at a constrained optima x^*, then x^* will truly be a

maximum if and only if	$|\bar{H}_2| > 0, |\bar{H}_3| < 0, |\bar{H}_4| > 0, \ldots$	
minimum if and only if	$|\bar{H}_2| < 0, |\bar{H}_3| < 0, |\bar{H}_4| < 0, \ldots$	[18.24]

N.B. The conditions are *not* the same as for the unconstrained case given in [18.17].

Readers should verify for themselves that these conditions when applied to the two-variable case do in fact resolve to those of equation [15.22].

*18.3 Linear regression

The final application of matrix algebra that we shall consider is that of linear regression. Even those who have not progressed very far in the realms of statistics are likely to have come across the concepts of correlation and regression. These concepts are easy enough to demonstrate in terms of two variables, but little work of practical importance can be achieved with only two variables. As we increase the number of variables, the algebraic manipulation required becomes daunting. Armed with some basic knowledge of matrix algebra the task becomes much easier, and anyone who has read and understood chapter 17 need have no fear of tackling courses in econometrics. In this section we reformulate the basic linear regression model in matrix algebra terms by way of illustration.

We postulate that there is a true functional relationship between the variable y and the variables $x_1, x_2, ..., x_k$ which may be written as the linear equation

$$y = \beta_1 x_1 + \beta_2 x_2 + ... + \beta_k x_k + u. \qquad [18.25]$$

The final variable in the function, u, is an unknown quantity about which we have certain beliefs. If we were actually to observe what happens in the 'real world', we could collect information about the values of y that correspond to observed values of the x_j, ... From these we wish to deduce what the true values of β_j are. Suppose that we have some estimates of the unknowns $\beta_1, \beta_2, ..., \beta_k$ which we denote $b_1, b_2, ..., b_k$. We can now estimate what value of y we expect and compare it with that which was actually observed. In most cases there will be an error or discrepancy which can be written as, for the ith observation,

$$e_i = y_i - (b_1 x_{i1} + b_2 x_{i2} + ... + b_k x_{ik}). \qquad [18.26]$$

Assuming the same underlying model for all n observations, we can write, in vector notation,

$$\mathbf{e} = \mathbf{y} - (b_1 \mathbf{x}_1 + b_2 \mathbf{x}_2 + ... + b_k \mathbf{x}_k) \qquad [18.27]$$

where $\mathbf{e}, \mathbf{y}, \mathbf{x}_1, ..., \mathbf{x}_k$ are $(n \times 1)$ column vectors.

Better still, we can define a matrix $\mathbf{X}$ whose columns are the k column vectors $\mathbf{x}_1, ..., \mathbf{x}_k$. Thus, the element x_{ij} represents the ith observation on the jth variable. If $\mathbf{b}$ is the $(k \times 1)$ column vector

$$\begin{bmatrix} b_1 \\ \cdot \\ \cdot \\ \cdot \\ b_k \end{bmatrix}$$

then [18.27] becomes

$$\mathbf{e} = \mathbf{y} - \mathbf{Xb}. \qquad [18.28]$$

(Note that $\mathbf{e}$ does *not* represent the same quantity as u. The former is the error associated with this particular set of estimates $\mathbf{b}$, while the latter is the true, unknowable random component of the model.)

The problem that faces the econometrician is that of choosing the estimates. The principle of least squares states that they should be chosen so as to minimize the sum of the squared errors (SSE); i.e.,

$$\text{SSE} = \sum_{i=1}^{n} e_i^2 \qquad [18.29]$$

or in matrix notation

SSE = e'e.   [18.30]

We shall consider not whether or under what circumstances this is an appropriate criterion, but rather how it may be effected. Substituting [18.28] into [18.30],

$$e'e = (y - Xb)'(y - Xb)$$
$$= (y' - b'X')(y - Xb)$$
$$= y'y - b'X'y - y'Xb + b'X'Xb. \qquad [18.31]$$

Now, b'X'y is a scalar and must therefore be equal to its transpose y'Xb. Equation [18.31] is therefore

$$e'e = y'y - 2b'X'y + b'X'Xb. \qquad [18.32]$$

To minimize this quantity by choosing b, we use differential calculus. Using the rules in section 17.5.6 and noting that X'X is symmetric,

$$\frac{d(e'e)}{db'} = -2X'y + 2X'Xb. \qquad [18.33]$$

For there to be a stationary point this must be zero; i.e.,

$$X'Xb = X'y$$
$$b = (X'X)^{-1}X'y. \qquad [18.34]$$

Provided that (X'X) is invertible, we can solve the system of equations for $b_1, ..., b_k$ uniquely. These estimates are known as *ordinary least squares* (OLS) estimates. The properties of this technique, its advantages and its drawbacks form the major part of most elementary econometrics texts.

Answers to selected exercises

Chapter 1

1.2.2 (iii) x^4 (vi) $x^{(1/3)}$ (vii) $x^3 + x$
1.2.4 (ii) $(x + 1)(x + 1)(x - 1)$ (iv) $(x - 3)(2 - x)$
1.3.3 (iii) $(1 - x)^2$ (iv) $1 - x^2$
1.3.5 (ii) degree 2 (v) degree 1
Further 1. (iv) $0.8\dot{3}$
exercises 2. (iv), (v), (vii) and (viii) are true
3. $(x + 1)$ is not a factor of (iii) or (iv)

Chapter 2

2.2.1 (iii) $x = 3$ or $x = \frac{1}{2}$ (v) $x = 1$ or $x = 2$
2.3 (i) $x < -2$; $x > 2$ (iii) $x < 2$ (vi) $x \neq 2$
2.4 (ii) $x = 2$, $y = 3$ or $x = -1$, $y = 0$

Chapter 3

3.1.2 2. $P_1 = 4$, $P_2 = 7$, $Q_1^D = Q_1^S = 7$, $Q_2^D = Q_2^S = 13$
3. (ii) $P = 2$, $Q^D = Q^S = 1$

Chapter 4

4.1.1 (iii) (a) 0 (b) $-\infty$ (v) (a) $\frac{1}{2}$ (b) ∞

Chapter 5

5.1.3 (i) ∞ (iii) $r/(r - 1)$
5.2 (i) Ayton (ii) Beeham (iii) Beeham and Ceaford identical
Further 2. 5.98% 4. 6.93%
exercises

Chapter 6

6.2.2   (ii) $-5 + 7t + t^2$ (iii) $x_t = 3 - 2(-\frac{1}{2})^t$

Further   1. (ii) $y_t = 1 + (-2)^t$; unstable

exercises   2. (ii) $y* = 500$; stable

           3. (i) and (ii) generate cycles

           4. (i) $1 - \frac{3}{2}(\frac{1}{2})^t + \frac{1}{2}(-\frac{1}{2})^t$

Chapter 7

7.1.2   16.75%

Chapter 8

8.2.1   (ii) $x^{-(1/2)}$ (iv) $6x^2$ (vi) $-x^{-2}$

8.2.3   (ii) $dy/dx = 2x + 1 - x^{-2}$ (v) $\dfrac{dy}{dx} = \dfrac{4x}{(1 - x^2)^2}$

8.2.4   (ii) $dy/dx = 34(1 + 2x)^{16}$ (iv) $dy/dx = x(2 + 5x)(1 + x)^2$

8.3.1   (ii) $\dfrac{d^2y}{dx^2} = 8$ (v) $\dfrac{d^2y}{dx^2} = e^x$

Further   1. (ii) $\dfrac{dy}{dx} = 3e^{3x}$ (v) $\dfrac{dy}{dx} = e^x\left(\dfrac{1}{x} + \log_e x\right)$

exercises   2. (i) $\dfrac{d^2y}{dx^2} = a^2e^{ax}$ (iii) $\dfrac{d^2y}{dx^2} = 2a$

Chapter 9

9.1   (ii) $d^2y/dx^2 = -e^{-2y}$

9.2   (i) minimum at $x = -\frac{3}{2}$

(v) minimum at $x = 4$; maximum at $x = -4$

Chapter 11

11.2   (iii) $e^x + c$ (vi) $\frac{1}{6}x^6 + \frac{2}{3}x^{(3/2)} + c$ (ix) $-4x + 4x^2 + c$

           (x) $\log_e[(x + 1)^2 - 2] + c$ (xii) $e^{x^2} + c$

11.2.1   (i) $\dfrac{(\log_e x)^2}{2} + c$ (iv) $\dfrac{x^3}{3}\left[\log_e x - \dfrac{1}{3}\right] + c$

11.2.2   (i) $\frac{1}{3}(x^3 + 2)^9 + c$ (iv) $\left(1 - \dfrac{x}{3}\right)^3 + c$

11.3   (ii) $\frac{1}{4}$ (iv) 48   (vi) $-\frac{9}{4}$

Chapter 12

12.2.1   (i) $y = \frac{1}{2} - \frac{1}{2}e^{-t}$

12.2.2   (iii) $y = c_1 e^{(1/2)t} + c_2 e^t$ (iv) $y = e^t(1 + t)$

12.3   (i) unstable cycles   (iii) explosive.

Chapter 14

14.1   (iv) $\dfrac{\delta y}{\delta u} = 2(u + v); \dfrac{\delta y}{\delta v} = 2(u + v)$

(v) $\dfrac{\delta y}{\delta u} = 4u(u^3 + v^2); \dfrac{\delta y}{\delta v} = 4v(u^2 + v^2)$

(vii) $\dfrac{\delta y}{\delta u} = 2u + 2v + vw; \dfrac{\delta y}{\delta v} = 2u + uw; \dfrac{\delta y}{\delta w} = uv + \dfrac{2}{w}$

14.1.2   (ii) $\dfrac{\delta y}{\delta u} = \dfrac{\delta y}{\delta v} = \dfrac{1}{u + v}; \dfrac{\delta^2 y}{\delta v^2} = \dfrac{\delta^2 y}{\delta u^2} = \dfrac{\delta^2 y}{\delta u \delta v} = \dfrac{-1}{(u + v)^2}$

(iv) $\dfrac{\delta y}{\delta u} = \dfrac{\delta^2 y}{\delta u^2} = \dfrac{\delta^2 y}{\delta v^2} = e^{u - v}; \dfrac{\delta y}{\delta v} = \dfrac{\delta^2 y}{\delta u \delta v} = -e^{u - v}$

14.2.2   (ii) $6t + 2\dfrac{du}{dt}$ (iv) $6t + v\dfrac{du}{dt}$

Further exercises   (ii) $\dfrac{\delta y}{\delta t} = \dfrac{2}{t}(3\log_e t + 1)$ (v) $\dfrac{\delta y}{\delta t} = 2 + \dfrac{2}{v}\dfrac{dv}{dt}$

Chapter 15

15.1.2   (ii) no extrema (point of inflexion at (0, 0))
(v) minimum at (1, 0)

15.2.1   (ii) maximum at $v = -\frac{3}{2}$, $u = -2$

15.2.2   (ii) $v = 0.8$, $u = 0.6$

Chapter 17

17.1.4   (iv) $\begin{bmatrix} 0 & 1 \\ 1 & 1 \\ 1 & 1 \end{bmatrix}$ (v) not possible since **A** is not a square matrix but **I** is.

17.2.1   3. (ii) not conformable (iii) $\begin{bmatrix} 2 & 3 \\ 4 & 3 \\ 0 & 3 \end{bmatrix}$ (ix) $\begin{bmatrix} -1 & 0 \\ 0 & -2 \end{bmatrix}$

         4. (iv) $\begin{bmatrix} 4 & 0 \\ 0 & 9 \end{bmatrix}$ (v) $\begin{bmatrix} 4 & 0 \\ 0 & 9 \end{bmatrix}$

17.3.1   (i) $\begin{bmatrix} -1 & 1 \\ 0 & \frac{1}{2} \end{bmatrix}$ (v) cannot invert a non-square matrix

17.4   (i) -3 (iii) 0

Index